TeX

BY

EXAMPLE

A Beginner's Guide

ARVIND BORDE

TeX: A Reference Chart

Topic	Commands	Examples and Comments	Defaults
Typefaces	`\it` `\sl` `\bf` `\tt` `\rm`	Typing {\it italic} gives *italic*, {\sl slanted} gives *slanted*, {\bf bold} gives **bold** and {\tt typewriter} gives `typewriter` type; \rm restores the default roman typeface of TeX.	Ten-point roman (`\rm`)
Centering	`\centerline`	\centerline{stuff} centers `stuff` on a line. NOTE: To use this in mid-paragraph, you must break the preceding line (see 'line breaks').	
Line spacing	`\baselineskip`	\baselineskip 9 pt gives an interline spacing of 9 points (an inch equals 72.27 points).	12 pt
Line breaks	`\hfil\break`	Ends the current line.	
Other spacing	`\smallskip` `\medskip` `\bigskip` `\quad` , `\qquad`	Gives a 'small' extra vertical space. Gives a 'medium' extra vertical space. Gives a 'big' extra vertical space. Give horizontal spaces.	
Paragraphs	`\parindent` `\parskip` `\noindent`	\parindent 1 in resets indentation to 1 inch. \parskip 1 cm sets 1-cm inter-paragraph gaps. \noindent suppresses indentation locally.	20 pt 0 pt* *Can stretch.
Mathematics	`$ formula $` `$$ formula $$`	Formulas in text are typed between $ signs. Displays the formula on a new line.	
Magnifying a document	`\magnification` `\magstep...`	\magnification 1200 gives a 20% enlargement. \magnification=\magstep1 also enlarges 20%. NOTE: You can use these *only at the start*.	1000
Page size	`\hsize` `\vsize`	\hsize 3 true cm gives a 3-cm horizontal size. \vsize 8 true in gives an 8-inch vertical size. \vsize 8 in gives an 8-inch size, *magnified by whatever magnification is being used.*	6.5 true in 8.9 true in
Page position	`\hoffset` `\voffset`	\hoffset 1 true in shifts pages right 1 inch. \hoffset -1 true in shifts pages left 1 inch. \voffset 1 true in shifts pages down 1 inch. \voffset -1 true in shifts pages up 1 inch.	0 in 0 in
Page numbering	`\pageno` `\nopagenumbers`	\pageno=9 starts numbering at 9; \pageno=-9 also starts at 9, but with roman numerals. Switches off TeX's automatic page-numbering.	\pageno=1
Ending	`\end (or \bye)`	This is *required* at the end of your file.	

This chart summarizes some of the basic conventions of Plain TeX; other packages may use slightly different conventions. Commands that produce special characters, or complicated formats like tables, are systematically listed in the Appendix.

'TeX by Example' by Arvind Borde; published by Academic Press, 1992.

TEX by Example

A Beginner's Guide

T_EX by Example
A Beginner's Guide

Arvind Borde

ACADEMIC PRESS, INC.
Harcourt Brace Jovanovich, Publishers

Boston   San Diego   New York
London   Sydney   Tokyo   Toronto

This book is printed on acid-free paper. ∞

ACADEMIC PRESS, INC.
1250 Sixth Avenue, San Diego, CA 92101

United Kingdom Edition published by
ACADEMIC PRESS LIMITED
24–28 Oval Road, London NW1 7DX

Library of Congress Cataloging-in-Publication Data

Borde, Arvind, date.
    TEX by example : a beginner's guide / Arvind Borde.
        p.   cm.
    Includes bibliographical references and index.
    ISBN 0-12-117650-9
    1. TeX (Computer system)   2. Computerized typesetting.
    3. Mathematics printing—Data processing.   I. Title.
    Z253.4.T47B67   1992
    686.2'2544—dc20   91-30114
                                                 CIP

Printed in the United States of America
91 92 93 94   9 8 7 6 5 4 3 2 1

This book is a significantly expanded version of the author's earlier introduction to
TEX, *An Absolute Beginner's Guide to Using TEX* (© Arvind Borde, 1987).

Apart from its covers, the book was typeset entirely in Plain TEX by the author,
with assistance from the production department of Academic Press, Boston. The
covers were done partially in TEX. The final copy was produced by the American
Mathematical Society on an Autologic APS Micro-5 phototypesetter.

'TEX' is a trademark of the American Mathematical Society.

To my parents

```
 1  \hrule
 2  \vfil
 3  \centerline{\vrule height .06 in width 5 in}
 4  \bigskip
 5  \centerline{\bf HOW TO USE THIS BOOK}
 6  \bigskip
 7  {\narrower\narrower\narrower\narrower
 8  \noindent The bulk of this guide has two interwoven parts. Pages on the right,
 9  called {\it output} pages, explain the basic features of \TeX; more
10  important, they illustrate some of the things that it can do. Pages on the left
11  contain boxes that show what was typed to produce the output. By glancing at
12  these {\it input} boxes you can see quickly how an effect is obtained, e.g.,
13  {\bf bold} type, or an $\int$, or a $\heartsuit$, without having to read
14  long explanations. The input lines are numbered for convenience and a few notes
15  are added where explanations seem necessary.
16
17  The examples in this book cover many of the standard features of \TeX. You can
18  use the book visually by flipping through pages till you spot what you want, and
19  then reading the matching input. If you have trouble finding something (since
20  it is impossible to illustrate everything, this {\it will} happen), you can look
21  it up in the Appendix. There you will find an alphabetical listing of many
22  features of \TeX\ and all its commonly used commands.
23  \bigskip}
24  \centerline{\vrule height .06 in width 5 in}
25  \vfil\vfil
26  \hrule
27  \pageno=-7
28  \eject
29  \end
```

NOTES

IF YOU ARE NEW TO TₑX

Read the facing page first. The text printed there was produced by the instructions listed in the box above. The contents of this box are both 'ordinary text' as well as commands. Commands usually begin with a \.

The facing page exhibits the preset page size of TₑX, some standard typefaces and the results of some standard commands. The preset page size is 6.5 inches by 8.9 inches, positioned to give 1-inch top and left margins. The page size and position are indicated by thin horizontal lines across the top and bottom of the facing page. The default typeface is the one used for the bulk of that page.

1, 26: \hrule draws a horizontal line across the page.

2, 25: \vfil fills the page vertically with white space. The commands on these lines balance the block of text between them, with twice as much space at the bottom (two \vfil commands) as at the top.

3, 5, 24: \centerline{*stuff*} centers *stuff*. On lines 3 and 24, the material centered is a \vrule, a vertical line of the stated height and width (**in** means *inch*). This gives the thick lines above and below the text.

4, 6, 23: \bigskip leaves extra vertical space.

5, 13: \bf gives boldface type. The text to appear in this style must be enclosed within { and }, as shown (unless you want the entire rest of the document to appear in the new style).

7: Each \narrower moves text in by an amount equal

to the paragraph indentation. The command applies to lines 7–23: grouping braces, { and }, are used to control which portions of text are to be set this way.

8: \noindent suppresses paragraph indentation.

9, 12, 20: \it gives italic type.

9, 17, 22: \TeX produces the logo 'TₑX'. On line 22 the second \ ensures that a space is left after the logo. Compare this with lines 9 and 17.

13: Certain symbols are available only in the 'mathematics mode'. $ signs switch this mode on (first appearance) and off (second).

16: A blank line is one way of commanding TₑX to start a new paragraph. The new paragraph is automatically indented. The indentation can be suppressed (line 8) or changed (page *viii*).

27: The starting page number is usually 1. It is reset here to 7; the minus is just an indicator to TₑX to use roman numerals.

28: \eject ejects the page, honoring vertical spacing instructions you may have issued.

29: \end ends the TₑX session. It may be placed anywhere in your file: TₑX will not look beyond it. The command is powerful and it pushes everything on the page up toward the top (which is how you normally want last pages to look). If you have used \vfil commands, you must use \eject (as on line 28) to prevent \end from overriding them.

If TₑX doesn't find an \end in your file, it will flash an * at you, and you must then type it in.

HOW TO USE THIS BOOK

The bulk of this guide has two interwoven parts. Pages on the right, called *output* pages, explain the basic features of TeX; more important, they illustrate some of the things that it can do. Pages on the left contain boxes that show what was typed to produce the output. By glancing at these *input* boxes you can see quickly how an effect is obtained, e.g., **bold** type, or an $\int$, or a $\heartsuit$, without having to read long explanations. The input lines are numbered for convenience and a few notes are added where explanations seem necessary.

The examples in this book cover many of the standard features of TeX. You can use the book visually by flipping through pages till you spot what you want, and then reading the matching input. If you have trouble finding something (since it is impossible to illustrate everything, this *will* happen), you can look it up in the Appendix. There you will find an alphabetical listing of many features of TeX and all its commonly used commands.

```
1  \font\title=cmssdc10 at 27.27pt  % NOTE: A NEW INPUT FILE BEGINS HERE.
2  \pageno=-9
3  \magnification=\magstephalf
4  \hsize 5.5 true in \hoffset .125 true in
5  \vsize 8.5 true in \voffset .1 true in
6  \parindent 35pt \parskip 1pt
7
8  \rightline{\title Prologue} % USE \title ONLY WITH THE DEFINITION ON LINE 1.
9  \vskip 2.5 true in
10 \noindent The core of this book was written in the summer of 1987. I was a
11 postdoctoral fellow at Syracuse University and just beginning to learn \TeX.
12 As a way of better understanding the program, I put together some
13 examples of its uses. The examples seemed to interest my colleagues, so I added
14 some notes and an appendix, called the collection {\sl An Absolute Beginner's
15 Guide to Using \TeX}, and gave away a few copies. That, I thought, was that.
16
17 But my colleagues showed the guide to their colleagues, who in turn showed it
18 to theirs. The learn-by-example approach that it adopted was apparently
19 appealing. In the four years between then and now, the guide has informally
20 circulated among \TeX\ users at several institutions, and requests for copies
21 have regularly come in. It is partly in response to such requests that the
22 guide, now considerably expanded, is being published.\par
23 This book is not a systematic exposition of the workings of \TeX. It has
24 illustrations of what can be done with \TeX, but few explanations of how the
25 program works; it has recipes that create formats of various kinds, but little
26 analysis of their ingredients. It is all practice and no theory. This approach
27 has some obvious drawbacks, but it has one significant advantage: it allows even
28 the complete beginner to start using \TeX\ right away, essentially by copying.
29
30 I have tried to make sure that the examples cover a wide range of features and
31 that the Appendix includes descriptions of all common commands.  Users who have
32 no interest in the inner workings of \TeX, and no desire to achieve unusual or
33 extravagant typesetting effects, should find everything here that they need. But
34 those who want more information on how the program works will have to consult
35 other sources. The best of these is Donald Knuth's book on \TeX, {\sl The
36 \TeX book}. \bigskip\bigskip
37 \line{\it Long Island, New York \hfil \sl Arvind Borde}
38 \line{\it August 1991 \hfil}
39 \vfil\eject
```

NOTES

1: \font allows you to define names for typefaces. The name \title is chosen here for the large typeface for section titles. *It is not a standard TEX command, so you cannot use it without the definition on this line.* See Example X for more information on using non-standard typefaces. The % indicates a comment: something for your eyes only, not TEX's.

2: \pageno has been explained on page *vi*. By default, page numbers are centered at the bottom of the page (page 2 shows how this may be changed). The notes for the next page tell you more about page numbering.

3: \magnification magnifies the entire document. \magstephalf gives an enlargement of about 10%.

4: \hsize allows you to specify the horizontal size; true means 'actual size', ignoring magnification; in stands for inches. \hoffset shifts the page away from the default 1-inch left margin; a positive number gives a shift to the right, a negative number to the left.

5: \vsize and \voffset are the vertical analogues of the horizontal commands of the previous line. The default top margin is also 1 inch. A positive offset shifts the page down; negative, up.

6: The unit pt stands for *point*. One inch equals 72.27 points. \parindent sets the indentation; the default value is 20pt. \parskip sets the gap between paragraphs; the default is 0pt. (However, as discussed in the Appendix, the space can stretch if needed.)

8: \rightline sets text flush right.

9: \vskip gives vertical white space, as specified.

14, 35, 37: \sl gives slanted type.

22: \par is another way to end a paragraph.

36: \bigskip (see page *vi*) does not need its own line.

37, 38: \line{ } puts the stuff within { } on one line. \hfil is the horizontal analogue of \vfil: it fills a line with white space. \it gives italics.

39: \eject ejects the current page. It is usually preceded by \vfil to push everything on the page toward the top, instead of having it loosely spread out.

Prologue

The core of this book was written in the summer of 1987. I was a postdoctoral fellow at Syracuse University and just beginning to learn TeX. As a way of better understanding the program, I put together some examples of its uses. The examples seemed to interest my colleagues, so I added some notes and an appendix, called the collection *An Absolute Beginner's Guide to Using TeX*, and gave away a few copies. That, I thought, was that.

But my colleagues showed the guide to their colleagues, who in turn showed it to theirs. The learn-by-example approach that it adopted was apparently appealing. In the four years between then and now, the guide has informally circulated among TeX users at several institutions, and requests for copies have regularly come in. It is partly in response to such requests that the guide, now considerably expanded, is being published.

This book is not a systematic exposition of the workings of TeX. It has illustrations of what can be done with TeX, but few explanations of how the program works; it has recipes that create formats of various kinds, but little analysis of their ingredients. It is all practice and no theory. This approach has some obvious drawbacks, but it has one significant advantage: it allows even the complete beginner to start using TeX right away, essentially by copying.

I have tried to make sure that the examples cover a wide range of features and that the Appendix includes descriptions of all common commands. Users who have no interest in the inner workings of TeX, and no desire to achieve unusual or extravagant typesetting effects, should find everything here that they need. But those who want more information on how the program works will have to consult other sources. The best of these is Donald Knuth's book on TeX, *The TeXbook*.

Long Island, New York   *Arvind Borde*
August 1991

ix

```
1  \pageno=-11
2  \rightline{\title Contents} % CAUTION: '\title' IS NOT A STANDARD COMMAND.
3  \vskip 2.5 true in
4  \noindent How to use this book\dotfill vii\break
5  {\sl The preset format of plain \TeX; simple spacing; centering.} \bigskip
6  \noindent Prologue\dotfill ix\break
7  {\sl Magnification; adjusting page size and position; paragraphs; page breaks.}
8  \bigskip
9  \noindent Contents\dotfill xi\break {\sl Making itemized lists; line breaks.}
10 \bigskip
11 \noindent Introduction\dotfill 1\break
12 {\sl Basic commands; command characters; typefaces; spacing;}\hfil\break
13 {\sl mathematics mode; processing the input; errors.} \bigskip
14 \noindent Examples \medskip
15 \item{I.}On writing simply\dotfill 21\break
16 {\sl Displaying text in narrow or broad format; shaping paragraphs.}
17 \medskip
18 \item{II.}$\sqrt2$ is irrational\dotfill 25\break
19 {\sl Displaying equations; fractions; powers; roots; footnotes.}
20 \medskip \item{III.}Cauchy horizons\dotfill 31\break
21 {\sl Set theoretic symbols; blank space inserts for diagrams.} \medskip
22 \item{IV.}A Spanish interlude\dotfill 35\break
23 {\sl 'Unusual' punctuation; accents; overlap commands.}
24 \medskip
25 \item{V.}Trapped surfaces in G\"odel's universe\dotfill 37\break
26 {\sl Matrices; aligning equations; indices; partial derivatives; footnotes.}
27 \medskip
28 \item{VI.}Sunil Gavaskar: a statistical tribute\dotfill 45\break
29 {\sl Tables.} \medskip
30 \item{VII.}On zeros of solutions of $\ddot x+F(t)x=0$\dotfill
31 53\break{\sl Derivatives  and integrals; aligning equations.} \medskip
```

NOTES

The commands \pageno, \rightline, \title, %, \vskip, \noindent and \sl have all been explained on previous pages.

1: Page numbering is actually automatic in TeX, and you usually do not need to reset the page number on every page. Here, however, the right- and left-hand pages come from separate computer files, so the page number on the right has to be increased by two each time a new page begins. A command can be constructed to do this automatically, but it seemed simpler to set numbers manually for the opening pages. On page 2, you will be shown a non-standard automatic page-numbering command.

4, 6, etc.: \dotfill fills vacant space on the line with dots. \break ends the line. The line just after is considered by TeX to be part of the same paragraph and is not indented. Therefore, \noindent is not necessary.

12: \hfil\break ends the current line. The \hfil fills the remaining portion of the line with white space (without it, the contents of the line would be spread semi-uniformly through its length), and the \break actually ends the line.

14, 17: \medskip gives some vertical space. It does not matter if you do not place it on a separate line.

15, . . . : This is how an itemized list is made. The main text of the list is indented by an amount equal to the current value of the paragraph indentation (see \parindent on the previous page), and the numbers or other markers that indicate items on the list are placed flush right in the 'margin' for the text. Material is considered part of the same entry until TeX reaches either the next \item or the end of the paragraph.

18: $\sqrt$ produces the 'square root' symbol. It is available only in the mathematics mode, i.e., between $ signs.

25: The accented character ö is produced by \"o.

30: '\ddot x' produces $\ddot{x}$ in the mathematics mode. There are many commands that work only within this mode, so you have to be careful about what you use where. Spacing is also different in this mode.

31: \break can occur in the middle of an input line, and it breaks the output line just as well as when it's at the end. TeX made its own decision that the page should break at this line: no special 'page break' commands were issued.

COMMENT

As you will have noticed by now, TeX offers you great freedom in arranging input as you wish, without it affecting the output. This makes editing and rearranging files extremely easy.

Contents

```
1  \item{VIII.}The many names of Dirac\dotfill                                      59\break
2  {\sl Hanging indentation.}
3  \medskip
4  \item{IX.}From Ramanujan's letters to Hardy\dotfill                              61\break
5  {\sl Details of typesetting equations.}
6  \medskip
7  \item{X.}Typography\dotfill                                                      65\break
8  {\sl Typeface styles and sizes.}
9  \medskip
10 \item{XI.}A letter\dotfill                                                       67\break
11 {\sl Definitions; letters.}
12 \medskip
13 \item{XII.}A memorandum\dotfill                                                  69\break
14 {\sl More definitions; storing variables; loop commands; memoranda.}
15 \medskip
16 \item{XIII.}A conversation\dotfill                                               71\break
17 {\sl Conditional commands; a simple script.}
18 \medskip
19 \item{XIV.}Fermat's last theorem\dotfill                                         73\break
20 {\sl Programming in \TeX.}
21 \medskip
22 \item{XV.}On boxing\dotfill                                                      75\break
23 {\sl Arranging material in horizontal and vertical boxes.}
24 \medskip
25 \item{XVI.}Playing around\dotfill                                                77\break
26 {\sl Framing text; shading boxes; other simpleminded effects.}
27 \medskip
28 \item{XVII.}Scenes from a magazine\dotfill                                       81\break
29 {\sl Simple aspects of magazine design.}
30 \bigskip
31 \noindent Acknowledgements\dotfill                                               87\break
32 {\sl Font switching; ragged right edges; suppressing hyphenation.}
33 \bigskip
34 \noindent References\dotfill                                                     89\break
35 {\sl Automatic numbering; lists within lists.}
36 \bigskip
37 \noindent  Appendix\dotfill                                                      91\break
38 {\sl An index and a glossary.}
39 \bigskip
40 \noindent Epilogue\dotfill                                                      161\break
41 {\sl The input for the input (or, how to cook a book).}
42 \pageno=-13
43 \bye
```

NOTES

COMMENT

As said at the bottom of the notes for the previous page, you can arrange input largely as you wish. In particular, multiple spaces in the input are interpreted as, at most, a single space. (Of course, there *is* a difference between no space and a single one.) In general, you will find that keeping the input file neat (as above) is not worth the extra effort. But a few devices, like placing vertical spacing commands on their own lines, do help in reading input files.

1: Itemized lists continue smoothly from one page to another, with no special action required from you.
31, 34, 37, 40: \noindent is needed after \bigskip because TeX thinks of such vertical skip commands as starting a new paragraph, and non-indented lines were wanted here.
42: The page number is set manually again here, before this page ends. *This is usually not necessary.* See the notes for line 1 on page x for an explanation.
43: \bye is the preferred way to end a file. It is an abbreviation for a combination of commands, with \end built in, but it does more than just abruptly end the TeX session. This is discussed in the Appendix. The present book was composed out of several separate computer files, so you'll see \bye again a few times before it's really good-bye.

```
 1 \font\title=cmssdc10 scaled 2488  % A NEW FILE BEGINS HERE.
 2 \magnification=\magstep1
 3 \baselineskip 22 true pt     \parskip=0pt plus3pt
 4 \hsize 5.5 true in \hoffset .125 true in
 5 \vsize 8.5 true in \voffset .1 true in
 6
 7 \rightline{\title Introduction} % WARNING: '\title' is not a standard command.
 8 \rightline{\sl Basic commands; command characters; typefaces; spacing;}
 9 \line{\hfil\sl mathematics mode; processing the input; errors.}
10 \vskip 2.5 true in
11 \vskip-2\baselineskip
12 \noindent \TeX---roughly pronounced 'Tekh'---is a program composed
13 by Donald Knuth for the ''creation of beautiful books.'' It is a clever and
14 powerful program, and a lot can be done with it. But it has a reputation for
15 being difficult. This is partly {\sl because\/} it is so powerful, but also
16 partly because \TeX\ enthusiasts sometimes try to tell you everything about
17 it right away: {\it all\/} the things that it can do and also how and why it
18 works. This can make the program appear rather formidable---a pity, for it is
19 really rather simple to use \TeX\ to carry out straightforward printing tasks.
20
21 This guide has been written to show you how easy it is to prepare simple
22 documents with \TeX. Page {\sl vii\/} describes how the guide is
23 meant to work. The page is short. \underbar{Read it.} Though the later
24 examples in the book are a little complicated, for most of it I will stick
25 to simple applications. All the sophisticated little details that I am leaving
26 out can be found in the engaging book on \TeX\ that Knuth has written.$^1$
27
28 \TeX\ is a {\sl typesetting\/} program: you use it to place text and other
29 material in precise positions on the printed page. To do this, you first have to
30 create a computer file that contains the material you want printed. You may use
31 {\it any\/} text editing or 'word processing' program you want for this. (I
32 am assuming that you know how to create and edit a file on your computer.
```

NOTES

1: \font allows you to define names for typefaces. See page *viii*. \title names the same large typeface as it did there, even though the expression on the right-hand side of the = is different here. See Example X.

2–5: These lines set up the page format that is imposed on the right-hand pages.

2: \magnification here is \magstep1, which magnifies the overall document (typefaces, spacing, etc.) by 1.2. Even higher magnifications, \magstep2, ..., \magstep5, are possible. Each step magnifies the previous one by 1.2. You cannot use different magnifications on different parts of the same document.

3: \baselineskip sets the gap between 'baselines' (very roughly, the bottoms of lines, though characters like 'y' descend below baselines) of successive lines. The default value is **12pt**, where **pt** stands for a *point*. One inch equals 72.27 points. **true** means 'ignore magnification'; without it, a specification of 22 points would give 26.4 ($= 22 \times 1.2$) points on the right-hand pages. \parskip sets the gap between paragraphs; the **plus** allows the gap to stretch, if needed. Stretchability of spaces is essential for TeX to align bottoms of pages and right margins.

4,5: Horizontal and vertical page specifications, as on page *viii*; **in** stands for an inch.

7–9: \rightline{X} and \line{\hfil X} are two different ways to set X on a line flush right. \sl gives slanted type.

10,11: The first \vskip gives 2.5 inches of vertical space from the bottom of the last line printed. For consistency with the 'dip' on earlier pages, the second \vskip moves back up two baselines (thus compensating for the two lines of subtitle here).

12,18: --- gives the long dash, —.

13: Observe how left and right quotes may be obtained in TeX.

15,22,28: \sl gives slanted type. \/ gives an 'italic correction', i.e., a small amount of extra space to prevent italic or slanted characters from leaning too far into the space of the next character.

17,31: \it gives italics.

23: \underbar underlines text (a style frowned on in serious typesetting). **Grouping** braces, { and }, are used to mark what text is to be underlined. These braces are used a little differently when switching typeface, as in {\sl vii\/} from the line above. This is discussed in the Appendix, under **arguments**.

26: ^ is the mathematics mode command for a power; it serves for reference numbers as well. The **$** signs switch the mathematics mode on/off.

Introduction

Basic commands; command characters; typefaces; spacing;

mathematics mode; processing the input; errors.

TEX—roughly pronounced 'Tekh'—is a program composed by Donald Knuth for the "creation of beautiful books." It is a clever and powerful program, and a lot can be done with it. But it has a reputation for being difficult. This is partly *because* it is so powerful, but also partly because TEX enthusiasts sometimes try to tell you everything about it right away: *all* the things that it can do and also how and why it works. This can make the program appear rather formidable—a pity, for it is really rather simple to use TEX to carry out straightforward printing tasks.

This guide has been written to show you how easy it is to prepare simple documents with TEX. Page *vii* describes how the guide is meant to work. The page is short. <u>Read it.</u> Though the later examples in the book are a little complicated, for most of it I will stick to simple applications. All the sophisticated little details that I am leaving out can be found in the engaging book on TEX that Knuth has written.[1]

TEX is a *typesetting* program: you use it to place text and other material in precise positions on the printed page. To do this, you first have to create a computer file that contains the material you want printed. You may use *any* text editing or 'word processing' program you want for this. (I am assuming

1

```
 1 If you do not, you will have to ask someone who does.) However, you must be
 2 careful not to use any {\sl formatting\/} commands that come with your editing
 3 program. For example, if you want a page to end at some point, you must use the
 4 \TeX\ command for this, not a command that may come with the editing program you
 5 are using. You can create the file on any computer you like, even if it
 6 does not itself have \TeX\ available on it. As you type material into this file,
 7 you also type into it the \TeX\ commands needed to get the format you want. The
 8 left-hand pages of this book show you what such a file looks like. It is only
 9 when the file is complete that you run it through \TeX. (If your file is stored
10 in a system that does not have \TeX\ loaded, you will have to transfer it at
11 this point to one that does.) The program will create for you a separate file
12 that you can send to your printer. The process is discussed again on page~17.
13
14 One of the most powerful features of \TeX\ is that it gives you a completely
15 free hand in defining your own commands. For example, if there is some
16 combination of commands that you find yourself using frequently, you can define
17 a single command that does the work of the entire set. There are several
18 packages of new commands and definitions (sometimes called 'macros') now
19 available for special purposes. In fact, what is usually called '\TeX' is itself
20 a combination of {\sl primitive\/} commands---strictly speaking, it is just
21 these primitives that make up \TeX---and a set of additional commands defined
22 in terms of the primitives. The correct name for the whole package is 'Plain
23 \TeX', but I will follow general usage for the most part and just say~'\TeX'.
24
25 %AN ADVANCED SET OF COMMANDS FOLLOW. THEY ARE NEEDED FOR PLACING PAGE NUMBERS IN
26 %THE TOP RIGHT MARGINS OF THE OUTPUT. IGNORE THESE LINES IF YOU ARE NEW TO \TeX.
27 \nopagenumbers
28 \def\newpageno {{\multiply\pageno by2 \advance\pageno by-1
29                 \rlap{\hbox to 1.125 true in{\hfil\bf\the\pageno}}}}
30 \headline{\hfil\it Introduction\newpageno}
31 %END OF FANCY STUFF; YOU CAN OPEN YOUR EYES AGAIN.
32
33 This guide will show you how to use the commands of Plain \TeX. These commands
34 may not always work in the same way, or be recognized at all, if you are using
```

NOTES

Several of the commands here have occurred before. See the previous pages for discussions of \sl, \bf and \it. The command \/ gives an italic correction, a little extra space at the end of slanted or italic type. \TeX produces the logo 'TEX'. The notes on the next page tell you more about typing such commands.

12, 23: ˜ gives a tie—a single space at which a line will not be broken. This is an extremely useful device: it binds together material that you do not want split. Here, it ensures that '17' will not appear at the beginning of a new line all by itself, nor will 'TEX'. It is a good idea to automatically type a tie at such points. The Appendix entry on line breaks contains a longer discussion of ties.

AN APOLOGY

The commands on lines 27–30 were put in only because something unusual was needed for numbering the right-hand pages of the rest of this book. The page numbers will now appear at the top of the right margin, in boldface, and they will only have odd values. The left-hand pages are numbered by a similar command, shown in the Epilogue. Separate commands are used for left and right pages, because—for most

of this book—they come from separate files. The formatting commands for the Appendix (reproduced in the Epilogue) show how the two may be combined into a single command.

Lines 25, 26 and 31 are comments (they are preceded by %). *All the commands on lines 27–30 are discussed at greater length later in this book, especially in the Appendix.* But here is a quick explanation:

27: \nopagenumbers shuts off normal page numbering. (Pages are normally numbered consecutively, and the numbers appear centered on the bottom. See page 1 for an example.)

28: A new command, \newpageno, is defined. The normal page number—represented by a standard TEX name, \pageno—is multiplied by 2 and then reduced by 1. This gives the correct value for the page number.

29: This line continues the definition of \newpageno; it sets up the required positioning, spacing and typeface, then extracts the new value of the page number from \pageno.

30: \headline sets the headline: here, it will consist of the word 'Introduction' in italics, set flush right, and with the new page number to its right. See the next page for some general remarks on headlines.

that you know how to create and edit a file on your computer. If you do not, you will have to ask someone who does.) However, you must be careful not to use any *formatting* commands that come with your editing program. For example, if you want a page to end at some point, you must use the TeX command for this, not a command that may come with the editing program you are using. You can create the file on any computer you like, even if it does not itself have TeX available on it. As you type material into this file, you also type into it the TeX commands needed to get the format you want. The left-hand pages of this book show you what such a file looks like. It is only when the file is complete that you run it through TeX. (If your file is stored in a system that does not have TeX loaded, you will have to transfer it at this point to one that does.) The program will create for you a separate file that you can send to your printer. The process is discussed again on page 17.

One of the most powerful features of TeX is that it gives you a completely free hand in defining your own commands. For example, if there is some combination of commands that you find yourself using frequently, you can define a single command that does the work of the entire set. There are several packages of new commands and definitions (sometimes called 'macros') now available for special purposes. In fact, what is usually called 'TeX' is itself a combination of *primitive* commands—strictly speaking, it is just these primitives that make up TeX—and a set of additional commands defined in terms of the primitives. The correct name for the whole package is 'Plain TeX', but I will follow general usage for the most part and just say 'TeX'.

This guide will show you how to use the commands of Plain TeX. These commands may not always work in the same way, or be recognized at all, if you are using some other package. For example, the widely used package

```
 1  some other package. For example, the widely used package {\sl La\TeX\/} has a
 2  rather different set of commands built out of \TeX's primitives. Illustrations
 3  of how new commands are defined are given from Example~X onward. With two
 4  exceptions, I will put off introducing special commands of my own till then.
 5  The exceptions are the command that names the large typeface used for section
 6  titles (defined at the very start of the input for page~1) and the command that
 7  gives the non-standard page numbering needed for these output pages (defined in
 8  the input, just before this paragraph). I have defined these commands---and used
 9  them---at the start, but the definitions are properly explained only much later.
10  The new commands that are defined in Examples X--XVII contain several that are
11  likely to be of general interest: commands for formatting letters and memoranda,
12  commands to draw boxes around text, etc. These general-purpose new commands
13  are also systematically listed in the Appendix.
14
15  Since this guide is supposed to teach by example, most of it will consist of
16  short sections that will illustrate what \TeX\ can do. Before you look at these
17  sections, you may find it useful to go over the rest of this introduction. It
18  describes, very briefly, some basic features of the program.
19  \bigskip
20  \centerline{$\star\quad\star\quad\star$}
21  \vfil\eject
```

NOTES

2,16: Unless followed immediately by a non-letter character, like punctuation (as on line 2), you need a second \ after a command like \TeX to prevent the space right after the command from being 'gobbled up'. This may sound strange, but the reason is simple: as it scans a command name, TeX needs to know when the name is over; by its rules, one indicator is a space, and so a space is taken here not as the instruction to *leave a space* but as an end-of-name indicator. Another way to indicate the end of a command name to TeX is to use braces; e.g., {\TeX}.

20: \centerline is used to center material. \star is a mathematics mode command; it gives a ⋆. $ signs switch on and off the mathematics mode. \quad gives a little space: it works both in and out of the mathematics mode.

GENERAL REMARKS ON HEADLINES

As said in the notes on the previous page, \headline sets the headline for the page: one line of material that will be repeated at the top of every page, till \headline is reset.

You have to be careful on two counts when setting headlines. Firstly, you should always explicitly specify the typeface. Otherwise, TeX will use whatever it was currently using when it paused from its normal page-making activities to set the headline.

The second thing you have to be careful about is subtler. TeX reads ahead and accumulates more than one page's worth of material before it chooses a good page break and sets the page. When it does the page-setting, it uses the most recently read instruction for the headline. Occasionally it will happen that TeX will encounter a new instruction in material that eventually ends up on the next page. It will then use the new instruction, which, though it will leave you marvelling at TeX's prescience, is probably not what you wanted. To avoid such problems, TeX offers a way of marking text and putting it aside for use *after* the page is set. Headlines are more appropriately set using this approach. See the discussion of \mark in the Appendix.

This discussion applies to the setting of footlines as well.

LaTeX has a rather different set of commands built out of TeX's primitives. Illustrations of how new commands are defined are given from Example X onward. With two exceptions, I will put off introducing special commands of my own till then. The exceptions are the command that names the large typeface used for section titles (defined at the very start of the input for page 1) and the command that gives the non-standard page numbering needed for these output pages (defined in the input, just before this paragraph). I have defined these commands—and used them—at the start, but the definitions are properly explained only much later. The new commands that are defined in Examples X–XVII contain several that are likely to be of general interest: commands for formatting letters and memoranda, commands to draw boxes around text, etc. These general-purpose new commands are also systematically listed in the Appendix.

Since this guide is supposed to teach by example, most of it will consist of short sections that will illustrate what TeX can do. Before you look at these sections, you may find it useful to go over the rest of this introduction. It describes, very briefly, some basic features of the program.

$\star \quad \star \quad \star$

```
 1 \noindent{\bf \S\ Command characters}\hfil\break
 2 A file that is to be processed by \TeX\ is typed using only those characters
 3 that are standard on computer keyboards. Most of these characters will be
 4 printed in the output as they appear on the screen. However, the following
 5 symbols have special uses as commands in \TeX:
 6
 7 \centerline{\tt \string\ \qquad \string{ \qquad \string} \qquad \$ \qquad \&
 8 \qquad \^ \qquad \string_ \qquad \% \qquad \~ \qquad \#}
 9
10 \noindent To have {\it these\/} printed in the output, as above, special
11 instructions must be issued. Input lines 7--8 and the notes below the input
12 box show you how this is done. Their basic functions are:
13 \smallskip
14 {\narrower \parindent 25 true pt
15 \item{\tt\string\  } to signal the start of all commands (except ones issued by
16 the 'command characters' being discussed here);
17 \item{\tt\string{ \quad \string} } to group expressions, so that the program
18 knows what commands apply to what portions of the input text;
19 \item{\tt\$ } to signal the start, and the end, of the mathematics mode;
20 \item{\tt\& } to display text, numbers, etc., in columns (as in a table, or in
21 a matrix): it signals a jump to the next column;
22 \item{\tt\^\ } to print superscripts in the mathematics mode;
23 \item{\tt\string_ } to print subscripts in the mathematics mode;
24 \item{\tt\% } to make comments in the input that you do not want appearing in
25 the output: the program % This typing is so #$&%! tiring; I wish I could stop.
26 stops scanning the input when it sees this sign and skips to the next line;
27 \item{\tt\~\ } to mark an unbreakable single space, so that the program knows
28 not to break a line there; and
29 \item{\tt\# } to issue generic commands, so that the program can later fill in
30 specific items from some list.
31 \smallskip}
32 \noindent You will see these symbols used throughout this guide. It is possible
33 to redefine things so that other characters play 'command' roles; this will be
34 discussed in the Appendix.
35 \vfil\eject
```

NOTES

1: We've seen \noindent, \bf and \hfil\break before. \S gives §. (The second \ ensures that a space will be left after §.)

7–8: \centerline centers material, as we've seen. \tt gives the 'typewriter' typeface used in this book to represent the commands that you type. \string is an interesting command; essentially, it represents verbatim the single item that immediately follows. This is a very useful feature when you want a command printed rather than obeyed. Throughout this guide, we'll need to print commands, and \string will give us one easy way. Here it is used to print the \ that precedes all commands, the characters { and }, and the _. \qquad is a spacing command that leaves a certain amount of horizontal space. The other commands on these two lines each produce the associated character. For example, \& gives &.

13: \smallskip is a companion to \medskip and \bigskip, but it leaves less vertical space than is left by those two.

14: \narrower contracts paragraphs of text on the right and left by the current value of the paragraph indentation. That indentation is temporarily reset here,

using \parindent, to 25 true (i.e., ignoring magnification) points. The left brace { opens a **group** that will confine both the effect of \narrower and the new value of \parindent. When the group is closed (line 31: see the note below), the old settings are restored.

15, 17, 19, etc.: \item produces lists; look at the input for the Contents pages.

17: \quad is like \qquad, but it leaves half as much space.

31: It is important here to have the closing brace (}) *after* \smallskip. Settings like \narrower are used by TEX after it reads the full input paragraph. The \smallskip tells the program that the paragraph is over and that it should now get on with setting it. Without such a paragraph-ending command prior to }, TEX would leave the group that confines the action of \narrower *without yet knowing the paragraph was over.* When it did realize this (i.e., that the paragraph was complete), \narrower would no longer be in effect. The discussion under **paragraphs** in the Appendix provides lists of paragraph settings and of things that end paragraphs.

§ Command characters

A file that is to be processed by TEX is typed using only those characters that are standard on computer keyboards. Most of these characters will be printed in the output as they appear on the screen. However, the following symbols have special uses as commands in TEX:

\qquad \\ \qquad { \qquad } \qquad $ \qquad & \qquad ^ \qquad _ \qquad % \qquad ~ \qquad #

To have *these* printed in the output, as above, special instructions must be issued. Input lines 7–8 and the notes below the input box show you how this is done. Their basic functions are:

\\   to signal the start of all commands (except ones issued by the 'command characters' being discussed here);

{   }   to group expressions, so that the program knows what commands apply to what portions of the input text;

$ to signal the start, and the end, of the mathematics mode;

&   to display text, numbers, etc., in columns (as in a table, or in a matrix): it signals a jump to the next column;

^   to print superscripts in the mathematics mode;

_   to print subscripts in the mathematics mode;

%   to make comments in the input that you do not want appearing in the output: the program stops scanning the input when it sees this sign and skips to the next line;

~   to mark an unbreakable single space, so that the program knows not to break a line there; and

to issue generic commands, so that the program can later fill in specific items from some list.

You will see these symbols used throughout this guide. It is possible to redefine things so that other characters play 'command' roles; this will be discussed in the Appendix.

```
 1  \noindent{\bf \S\ Typefaces}\hfil\break
 2  \TeX\ offers a variety of typefaces, most commonly these:\hfil\break
 3  \centerline{{\rm Roman} \quad {\sl Slanted} \quad {\it Italic}
 4  \quad {\bf Bold} \quad {\tt Typewriter}}
 5  Unless other commands are given, the typeface used is roman. Further styles are
 6  available in the mathematics mode. (See page~15.) It is possible to use a wider
 7  range of typefaces, but I will avoid this for the most part. Example~X
 8  illustrates how to obtain other typefaces and how to adjust typeface size. The
 9  Appendix contains a longer list of available styles (under 'fonts').
10  \bigskip
11  \noindent{\bf \S\ Spacing}\hfil\break
12  \TeX\ sets its own spacing between letters and words, chooses its own paragraph
13  indentations, and makes its own decisions about where to break lines and pages.
14  The program scans entire input paragraphs before choosing a spacing that is
15  consistent with certain preset parameters. (If your computer does not have a
16  large memory, your paragraphs cannot be unusually long.) The parameters may be
17  changed if needed. Units used to change spacing include {\sl inches} (in),
18  {\sl centimeters} (cm) and {\sl points} (pt), where 1$\,$in = 72.27$\,$pt.
19  \TeX\ also recognizes other units, but I will stick to these three.
20  Page~{\sl vii\/} illustrates the preset spacing of Plain \TeX. You have by now
21  already seen some examples of how this spacing can be changed---various spacings
22  were set in the input for pages~{\sl ix\/} and~1, for instance---and you will
23  see others later. The next two pages will tell you more about how you can
24  control the spacing of text.
25
26  (\TeX\ arranges the spacing of text, formulas, etc., by first
27  building horizontal and vertical {\sl boxes\/} of material---'hbox' and 'vbox'
28  arrays---and then putting them together using an invisible quantity called
29  {\sl glue}. Example~XV illustrates the uses of explicitly introduced boxes;
30  both topics, boxes and glue, are discussed in the Appendix.)
31  \vfil\eject
```

NOTES

Almost everything here has been discussed on earlier pages. For example, there are several ties (i.e., ~; see the notes for page 2) scattered about the page.

1, 11: \noindent suppresses TEX's normal paragraph indentation, \S gives § and \hfil\break fills what remains of the line it's on with white space, then breaks it (i.e., switches you to the next line).

3–4: \centerline centers material on a line. \rm, \sl, \it, \bf and \tt are typeface commands, representing roman, *slanted*, *italic*, **bold** and `typewriter` type, respectively. The default typeface of Plain TEX is roman. \quad is a spacing command that leaves a little horizontal space.

10: \bigskip leaves vertical space.

25: A blank line tells TEX that you're starting a new paragraph. Paragraphs are important entities in TEX:

TEX scans entire paragraphs before deciding how to set text; certain commands, like \narrower, apply to entire paragraphs; entries in itemized lists are considered to continue till the end of the paragraph. Because TEX sets text paragraph-by-paragraph instead of line-by-line, it offers some very powerful paragraph-shaping commands. Some of these will be shown in Examples I and VIII. A fuller discussion of **paragraphs** is given in the Appendix.

31: \vfil fills the rest of the page with white space. \eject ends the current paragraph and ejects the page. If you want a page to end in mid-paragraph, type '\vadjust{\vfil\eject}'. This will complete the current line, end the page, and then continue the same paragraph on the next page.

§ **Typefaces**

T_EX offers a variety of typefaces, most commonly these:

Roman   *Slanted*   *Italic*   **Bold**   `Typewriter`

Unless other commands are given, the typeface used is roman. Further styles are available in the mathematics mode. (See page 15.) It is possible to use a wider range of typefaces, but I will avoid this for the most part. Example X illustrates how to obtain other typefaces and how to adjust typeface size. The Appendix contains a longer list of available styles (under 'fonts').

§ **Spacing**

T_EX sets its own spacing between letters and words, chooses its own paragraph indentations, and makes its own decisions about where to break lines and pages. The program scans entire input paragraphs before choosing a spacing that is consistent with certain preset parameters. (If your computer does not have a large memory, your paragraphs cannot be unusually long.) The parameters may be changed if needed. Units used to change spacing include *inches* (in), *centimeters* (cm) and *points* (pt), where 1 in = 72.27 pt. T_EX also recognizes other units, but I will stick to these three. Page *vii* illustrates the preset spacing of Plain T_EX. You have by now already seen some examples of how this spacing can be changed—various spacings were set in the input for pages *ix* and 1, for instance—and you will see others later. The next two pages will tell you more about how you can control the spacing of text.

(T_EX arranges the spacing of text, formulas, etc., by first building horizontal and vertical *boxes* of material—'hbox' and 'vbox' arrays—and then putting them together using an invisible quantity called *glue*. Example XV illustrates the uses of explicitly introduced boxes; both topics, boxes and glue, are discussed in the Appendix.)

```
 1  \textindent{$\bullet$} \underbar{\sl SPACING BETWEEN WORDS\/}: When processing
 2  text (as opposed to mathematics), \TeX\ interprets one or more blank spaces as a
 3  {\it single\/} interword space. Thus, you need not worry about gaps        between
 4     words    in   the input. (See input lines 3--4.) If you need blank space, you
 5  can force horizontal spaces of varying lengths to appear, as shown in the spaces
 6  between the square brackets below:\hfil\break
 7  \centerline{[], [\negthinspace], [\thinspace], [\ ], [\quad], [\qquad].}
 8  (See input line 7.) The first of these is the 'normal' intercharacter space, the
 9  next a small 'negative' space, and the rest positive spaces of different
10  lengths. The commands that produced the last three ({\tt\string\ } followed
11  by a single blank space, {\tt\string\quad} and {\tt\string\qquad},
12  respectively) are frequently used to adjust spacing. If these commands are
13  not enough to give you what you want, a horizontal space of essentially
14  arbitrary length $l$ may be left by typing '{\tt\string\hskip} $l$', where $l$
15  must be given in units that \TeX\ recognizes. The program automatically leaves
16  an interword space between the last word on one input line and the first word on
17  the next. If you do not want a spa%
18  ce, put a {\tt\%} there.
19
20  Since \TeX\ is set up to create straight right margins, the interword spaces
21  are allowed to stretch and shrink. However, there is a minimum space that the
22  program leaves between words. You may also ask for elastic spaces; for example,
23  '{\tt\string\hskip\ 10pt plus 2pt minus 3pt}' gives a 10-point space that
24  can stretch by 2 points (and more, if needed) and shrink by~3.
25  \medskip\textindent{$\bullet$}
26  \underbar{\sl LINES\/}: \TeX\ will decide where to end a line and start a new
27  one. It will use the preset line length and interline spacing unless instructed
28  otherwise. (See the input for page 1, where such instructions were issued.) As
29  with horizontal spaces, it is possible to leave vertical spaces of certain
30  standard amounts. The commands for these are {\tt\string\smallskip},
31  {\tt\string\medskip} and {\tt\string\bigskip}. The effects of these commands are
32  shown between drawn horizontal lines on the next page, underneath a space
33  representing the interline spacing.\vfil\eject
```

NOTES

1: \textindent{*stuff*} indents text and places *stuff* in the indentation. $\bullet$ gives •. \underbar underlines text. \/ gives an *italic correction*, i.e., a little space just after italic or slanted type.

3, 4: Observe how successive blank spaces are ignored by TEX. Incidentally, TEX leaves slightly more space after some punctuation marks (such as periods) than it does normally between words.

7: \negthinspace gives a small 'negative' space, i.e., moves text back a bit. For example, 'æ' would be typeset by 'a\negthinspace e'. \thinspace gives just that, a thin space. For example, 'Di Stefano'

would be typeset by 'Di\thinspace Stefano'. \ followed by a space in the input gives an output space roughly equalling an interword space. \quad and \qquad give bigger spaces.

10, 11, 14, 23, etc.: \string causes what comes just after to be printed verbatim. \tt gives typewriter type.

25: \medskip gives a vertical space. Observe the complete freedom that TEX gives you in placing such commands where you want; they may appear on a separate line or on the same one as text above or below.

33: \vfil\eject was discussed on the previous page.

- *SPACING BETWEEN WORDS*: When processing text (as opposed to mathematics), TeX interprets one or more blank spaces as a *single* interword space. Thus, you need not worry about gaps between words in the input. (See input lines 3–4.) If you need blank space, you can force horizontal spaces of varying lengths to appear, as shown in the spaces between the square brackets below:

$$[], [], [], [ ], [\quad], [\qquad].$$

(See input line 7.) The first of these is the 'normal' intercharacter space, the next a small 'negative' space, and the rest positive spaces of different lengths. The commands that produced the last three (\ followed by a single blank space, `\quad` and `\qquad`, respectively) are frequently used to adjust spacing. If these commands are not enough to give you what you want, a horizontal space of essentially arbitrary length l may be left by typing '`\hskip` l', where l must be given in units that TeX recognizes. The program automatically leaves an interword space between the last word on one input line and the first word on the next. If you do not want a space, put a % there.

Since TeX is set up to create straight right margins, the interword spaces are allowed to stretch and shrink. However, there is a minimum space that the program leaves between words. You may also ask for elastic spaces; for example, '`\hskip 10pt plus 2pt minus 3pt`' gives a 10-point space that can stretch by 2 points (and more, if needed) and shrink by 3.

- *LINES*: TeX will decide where to end a line and start a new one. It will use the preset line length and interline spacing unless instructed otherwise. (See the input for page 1, where such instructions were issued.) As with horizontal spaces, it is possible to leave vertical spaces of certain standard amounts. The commands for these are `\smallskip`, `\medskip` and `\bigskip`. The effects of these commands are shown between drawn horizontal lines on the next page, underneath a space representing the interline spacing.

```
 1 \hrule width5cm\hfil\break
 2 \line{\hfill}
 3 \hrule width5cm\smallskip
 4 \hrule width5cm\medskip
 5 \hrule width5cm\bigskip
 6 \hrule width5cm
 7 \line{\hfill}\smallskip
 8 \noindent It is also possible to leave a vertical space of more or less
 9 arbitrary height $h$ by typing '{\tt\string\vskip} $h$', using units for $h$
10 that \TeX\ recognizes. These spaces can be made elastic, exactly as can
11 horizontal spaces. Line breaks are forced by typing
12 '{\tt\string\hfil\string\break}' or '{\tt\string\hfill\string\break}'. The
13 second command in each of these breaks the line; the first fills the remainder
14 of the line with white space. Try leaving out an {\tt\string\hfil} sometime to
15 see what happens. Of the two 'filling' commands, the second is stronger than the
16 first and is generally used to override a previously given spacing command. For
17 example, certain mathematical displays are automatically centered by \TeX;
18 they can be moved to the right (or to the left) by putting {\tt\string\hfill}
19 to the left (or to the right) of the equation---{\tt\string\hfil} will not work
20 there. (See the input for Equation~6 in Example~IX.)
21 \medskip\textindent{$\bullet$}
22 \underbar{\sl PARAGRAPHS\/}: A blank line is the signal for the program
23 to end a paragraph. The command {\tt\string\par} can be used for
24 the same purpose; look at the input for this paragraph (line~24).\par
25 Paragraphs are automatically indented and separated from the preceding text by
26 preset amounts. Again, these may be changed by special commands. (See the input
27 for pages~{\sl ix\/} and~1.)
28 \medskip\textindent{$\bullet$}
29 \underbar{\sl PAGES\/}: \TeX\ makes its own decisions about where to end pages
30 and start new ones. Page breaks may be forced in a manner similar to line
31 breaks. (See the bottom of the input for this page.) The vertical length of the
32 material printed on a page can be controlled by setting a 'vertical size', as
33 was done at the top of the input for page~1.
34 \medskip
35 More information about spacing can be found in the Appendix.
36 \vfil\eject
```

NOTES

1, 3–6: \hrule gives a horizontal rule, i.e., a ruled line. It can have height, width and depth. The default depth is 0pt, the height is .4pt and the width is the current horizontal size. (This 'current' size is either the full page width, or a different width if the rule appears inside some other structure, like a table.) If any of these are explicitly specified, as width is here, those default values are overridden.

2, 7: \line{\hfill} makes a blank line, filled with glorious white space. \hfill is like \hfil, only stronger. It is normally used to override other spacing commands, such as those involving \hfil. It was actually not needed here, but it does no harm and it seemed time to introduce it.

24: \par ends paragraphs. In fact, TEX internally places the command at the end of every paragraph, even one ended by a blank line. This is useful in a number of situations; for example, one can insert something at the end of every paragraph merely by redefining \par. Example XIII illustrates this.

It is also possible to leave a vertical space of more or less arbitrary height h by typing '\vskip h', using units for h that TeX recognizes. These spaces can be made elastic, exactly as can horizontal spaces. Line breaks are forced by typing '\hfil\break' or '\hfill\break'. The second command in each of these breaks the line; the first fills the remainder of the line with white space. Try leaving out an \hfil sometime to see what happens. Of the two 'filling' commands, the second is stronger than the first and is generally used to override a previously given spacing command. For example, certain mathematical displays are automatically centered by TeX; they can be moved to the right (or to the left) by putting \hfill to the left (or to the right) of the equation—\hfil will not work there. (See the input for Equation 6 in Example IX.)

- *PARAGRAPHS*: A blank line is the signal for the program to end a paragraph. The command \par can be used for the same purpose; look at the input for this paragraph (line 24).

Paragraphs are automatically indented and separated from the preceding text by preset amounts. Again, these may be changed by special commands. (See the input for pages *ix* and 1.)

- *PAGES*: TeX makes its own decisions about where to end pages and start new ones. Page breaks may be forced in a manner similar to line breaks. (See the bottom of the input for this page.) The vertical length of the material printed on a page can be controlled by setting a 'vertical size', as was done at the top of the input for page 1.

More information about spacing can be found in the Appendix.

```
 1 \noindent{\bf \S\ Mathematics mode}\hfil\break
 2 Mathematical formulas in text must be typed between {\tt\$} signs, and formulas
 3 to be displayed (i.e., centered on a separate line) between double
 4 {\tt\$} signs.
 5 \smallskip\textindent{$\bullet$}
 6 \underbar{\sl TYPE\/}: The normal typeface is called $math$ $italic$, similar
 7 to {\it text italic\/} but not identical to it. (Can you spot the difference?)
 8 It is possible to print text in other typefaces within mathematical
 9 expressions; see Example~IX, Equations~6, 9, 12 and~13. Other available
10 typefaces are ${\cal CALLIGRAPHIC}$ (only for uppercase letters),
11 $\scriptstyle Script$ and $\scriptscriptstyle Scriptscript$ (used for indices
12 and other small-size expressions). The normal-size typeface is called 'text
13 style', and a larger typeface used for displayed equations is called 'display
14 style'. You can ask for parts of a formula to appear in specific styles if you
15 do not like what \TeX\ automatically provides. (See Equation 1c in Example V.)
16 Greek letters are also available ($\phi$, $\epsilon$, $\gamma$, $\Gamma$, etc.),
17 as are a variety of special symbols (e.g., $\cup$, $\bigcup$, $\infty$, $\sum$,
18 $\emptyset$, $\in$). Lists of symbols are given in the Appendix.
19 \smallskip\textindent{$\bullet$}
20 \underbar{\sl SPACING\/}: The spacing rules that \TeX\ follows here cause it to
21 arrange characters as it thinks best for formulas. This is not always the
22 best spacing for words: e.g., $sufferi  n  g$. The program ignores all blank
23 spaces in input formulas (see the 'suffering' input, line 22). This allows you
24 to arrange the input any way you want without affecting the output spacing.
25 Horizontal spacing can be adjusted, as shown in the gaps between square
26 brackets below:
27 $$[],\;[\!],\;[\,],\;[\>],\;[\;],\;[\quad],\;[\qquad].$$
28 The first of these shows the normal spacing, the second a 'negative thin
29 space', and the rest positive spaces. Spacing in mathematical expressions is
30 discussed further in the Appendix. \TeX\ will try to fit an entire displayed
31 formula on a single line, so it is best to break long expressions yourself
32 at some appropriate point. Multi-line systems of expressions can be displayed
33 in many ways; see Examples V, VII and IX.
34 \vfil\eject
```

NOTES

5, 6, etc.: A $ sign switches on (or off) the mathematics mode, as discussed before.

10, 11: \cal, \scriptstyle, etc., provide special typefaces for use in the mathematics mode, as explained on the facing page.

16–18: The effects of ϕ, ..., $\in$ are easy to spot by looking at the facing page. Though separate pairs of $ signs are not strictly needed for each command (i.e., $\phi, \epsilon, \gamma, \Gamma$ also works), it is preferable to use separate pairs for some mathematical expressions. See the discussion under **mathematics: punctuation** in the Appendix.

27: \!, \,, \> and \; are all spacing commands.

Their effects are shown on the facing page. The $$ signs are used to start and end the mathematics 'display' mode. Displayed mathematical expressions are put on a separate line, and are automatically centered with extra space left above and below.

___

COMMENT

TeX does not find it easy to break formulas between lines; in fact, displayed formulas are never automatically split over two lines. Therefore, you must help the program if you are using long formulas. The Appendix contains a discussion of such matters under **mathematics: line breaks**.

§ **Mathematics mode**

Mathematical formulas in text must be typed between $ signs, and formulas to be displayed (i.e., centered on a separate line) between double $ signs.

- *TYPE*: The normal typeface is called *math italic*, similar to *text italic* but not identical to it. (Can you spot the difference?) It is possible to print text in other typefaces within mathematical expressions; see Example IX, Equations 6, 9, 12 and 13. Other available typefaces are $\mathcal{CALLIGRAPHIC}$ (only for uppercase letters), $\mathscr{Script}$ and $\mathscr{Scriptscript}$ (used for indices and other small-size expressions). The normal-size typeface is called 'text style', and a larger typeface used for displayed equations is called 'display style'. You can ask for parts of a formula to appear in specific styles if you do not like what TeX automatically provides. (See Equation 1c in Example V.) Greek letters are also available (ϕ, ϵ, γ, Γ, etc.), as are a variety of special symbols (e.g., $\cup$, $\bigcup$, ∞, $\sum$, $\emptyset$, $\in$). Lists of symbols are given in the Appendix.

- *SPACING*: The spacing rules that TeX follows here cause it to arrange characters as it thinks best for formulas. This is not always the best spacing for words: e.g., $suffering$. The program ignores all blank spaces in input formulas (see the 'suffering' input, line 22). This allows you to arrange the input any way you want without affecting the output spacing. Horizontal spacing can be adjusted, as shown in the gaps between square brackets below:

$$[], [\![], [\,], [\:], [\;], [\quad], [\qquad].$$

The first of these shows the normal spacing, the second a 'negative thin space', and the rest positive spaces. Spacing in mathematical expressions is discussed further in the Appendix. TeX will try to fit an entire displayed formula on a single line, so it is best to break long expressions yourself at some appropriate point. Multi-line systems of expressions can be displayed in many ways; see Examples V, VII and IX.

```
1  \noindent{\bf \S\ Processing the input}\hfil\break
2  \TeX\ likes the input file to have a name of the type '{\it filename}.tex' and
3  for the file to end with {\tt\string\end} (or {\tt\string\bye}, as discussed
4  on page {\sl xii\/} and in the Appendix). If your file does not end
5  this way, the program will flash an $\ast$ at you after it processes the file,
6  and it will expect you to type '{\tt\string\end}' in response.
7
8  To get \TeX\ to process a file, you have to type something like
9  '{\tt tex \it filename\/}'. The command varies from system to system, and you
10 will have to ask your local expert what is to be used on yours. The file is
11 processed page by page, and error messages are flashed if errors are found.
12 Errors are discussed briefly below and at greater length in the Appendix.
13 As \TeX\ prepares pages, it stores them in a file called '{\it filename}.dvi',
14 where {\sl dvi\/} stands for {\sl device-independent}. The
15 {\sl dvi\/} file contains explicit printing instructions for your printing
16 device to follow, and it is from this file that your document will be printed.
17 {\sl Dvi\/} files are discussed further in the Appendix (under 'dvi').
18
19 Once the {\sl dvi\/} file is made, it can be printed. Different {\tt print}
20 commands are used on different systems, and you will have to ask locally for the
21 one to be used on yours.
22 \bigskip
23 \noindent{\bf \S\ Errors}\hfil\break
24 If \TeX\ flashes an error message at you, press {\tt h} to get more information
25 and {\tt e} to re-edit your file. If your errors are 'local' and do not affect
26 too much of what follows, it is generally more efficient to run the file through
27 the program fully, noting each error and then hitting the {\tt return} (or
28 {\tt enter}) key to go on, before re-editing. If you are doing only
29 straightforward typesetting, your errors (if any) are also likely to be
30 obvious ones, like missing {\tt\$} signs, or opening and closing braces
31 ({\tt\string{} and {\tt\string}}), or misspelled commands.
32
33 Until you get used to them, you may find \TeX's error messages confusing.
34 Common error messages are discussed in the Appendix (under 'errors').
35 \vfil\eject
```

§ **Processing the input**

TEX likes the input file to have a name of the type '*filename*.tex' and for the file to end with \end (or \bye, as discussed on page *xii* and in the Appendix). If your file does not end this way, the program will flash an * at you after it processes the file, and it will expect you to type '\end' in response.

To get TEX to process a file, you have to type something like 'tex *filename*'. The command varies from system to system, and you will have to ask your local expert what is to be used on yours. The file is processed page by page, and error messages are flashed if errors are found. Errors are discussed briefly below and at greater length in the Appendix. As TEX prepares pages, it stores them in a file called '*filename*.dvi', where *dvi* stands for *device-independent*. The *dvi* file contains explicit printing instructions for your printing device to follow, and it is from this file that your document will be printed. *Dvi* files are discussed further in the Appendix (under 'dvi').

Once the *dvi* file is made, it can be printed. Different **print** commands are used on different systems, and you will have to ask locally for the one to be used on yours.

§ **Errors**

If TEX flashes an error message at you, press **h** to get more information and **e** to re-edit your file. If your errors are 'local' and do not affect too much of what follows, it is generally more efficient to run the file through the program fully, noting each error and then hitting the **return** (or **enter**) key to go on, before re-editing. If you are doing only straightforward typesetting, your errors (if any) are also likely to be obvious ones, like missing $ signs, or opening and closing braces ({ and }), or misspelled commands.

Until you get used to them, you may find TEX's error messages confusing. Common error messages are discussed in the Appendix (under 'errors').

```
1  \noindent{\bf \S\ General comments}\hfil\break
2  The introductory remarks on the last few pages are sketchy; the Appendix has a
3  more complete list of rules and commands. You may make mistakes at the start,
4  but with practice you will soon get the hang of it. The examples in
5  the following sections will show you some of the things that can be done with
6  \TeX. If you are using a version of \TeX\ with more advanced commands than those
7  of Plain \TeX, everything may not work out exactly as shown here. In that case,
8  you will have to experiment a bit.
9
10 There are often several ways to get a format, but I will stick only
11 to a few basic rules and will generally not show variations.
12 {\it To make the input easier to follow, I will mostly leave out the various
13 small refinements that \TeX\ is capable of (e.g., fine spacing adjustments) if
14 they appear to interfere with the main points being illustrated.} As a result,
15 the output pages are not always as elegant as they could be, but they should
16 give you some idea of the possibilities in \TeX.
17
18 {I have also resisted defining new commands at the start, even though they would
19 have made the job of formatting this book much easier. Only in the later
20 examples and in the Appendix do I fully allow myself that convenience. The
21 commands introduced there should suggest to you how it is possible to set up
22 frameworks in which practically all formatting commands are hidden behind a few
23 simple ones. Once set up, such frameworks allow you to concentrate on the
24 content of your document without cluttering it with large numbers of
25 {\tt\string\hfil}s and {\tt\string\noindent}s. If you use \TeX\ regularly, it
26 would be a good idea for you to set up such a framework of your own for tasks
27 that you routinely do. \TeX\ may more accurately be thought of as a powerful
28 {\it language\/} geared towards typesetting, and only when you use it as
29 such, to construct formats for yourself, will you be using its full power.
30 \parfillskip0pt\par}
31 \vfil\break
```

NOTES

18–30: The last paragraph here was enclosed in braces. This was because one of TEX's paragraph settings was being tampered with, as the next note discusses.

30: \parfillskip tells TEX how to arrange the last line of a paragraph. The normal setting has a fil (as in, say, \hfil) built into it, so that white space will be put at the end as necessary. Resetting it to 0pt forces the paragraph to end at the right margin. Other values will cause it to end elsewhere. \par is then put in to make sure that TEX knows that the paragraph is complete before it leaves the group that confines the effect of \parfillskip.

It is worth noting that this (i.e., controlling the *last* line of a paragraph) is possible only because TEX typesets entire paragraphs at a time, instead of merely proceeding line-by-line.

31: \vfil fills the rest of the page with white space; at this point \break acts as a page break command, rather like \eject, not a line break one. See the discussion of \break in the Appendix.

§ General comments

The introductory remarks on the last few pages are sketchy; the Appendix has a more complete list of rules and commands. You may make mistakes at the start, but with practice you will soon get the hang of it. The examples in the following sections will show you some of the things that can be done with TEX. If you are using a version of TEX with more advanced commands than those of Plain TEX, everything may not work out exactly as shown here. In that case, you will have to experiment a bit.

There are often several ways to get a format, but I will stick only to a few basic rules and will generally not show variations. *To make the input easier to follow, I will mostly leave out the various small refinements that TEX is capable of (e.g., fine spacing adjustments) if they appear to interfere with the main points being illustrated.* As a result, the output pages are not always as elegant as they could be, but they should give you some idea of the possibilities in TEX.

I have also resisted defining new commands at the start, even though they would have made the job of formatting this book much easier. Only in the later examples and in the Appendix do I fully allow myself that convenience. The commands introduced there should suggest to you how it is possible to set up frameworks in which practically all formatting commands are hidden behind a few simple ones. Once set up, such frameworks allow you to concentrate on the content of your document without cluttering it with large numbers of `\hfils` and `\noindents`. If you use TEX regularly, it would be a good idea for you to set up such a framework of your own for tasks that you routinely do. TEX may more accurately be thought of as a powerful *language* geared towards typesetting, and only when you use it as such, to construct formats for yourself, will you be using its full power.

```
1  \line{\hfil\title Examples} % WARNING: '\title' IS NOT A STANDARD COMMAND.
2  \headline{\hfil}
3  \vskip 2.5 true in
4  \centerline{\bf I. ON WRITING SIMPLY}
5  \centerline{\sl Displaying text in narrow or broad format; shaping paragraphs.}
6  \bigskip
7  \noindent In an essay on the decline of the English language, published in
8  1946,$^2$ George Orwell translated a passage from {\sl Ecclesiastes\/} into
9  ``modern English of the worst sort.'' Here is the original passage:
10 \smallskip
11 {\narrower \noindent
12 \sl I returned, and saw under the sun, that the race is not to the swift, nor
13 the battle to the strong, neither yet bread to the wise, nor yet riches to
14 men of understanding, nor yet favour to men of skill; but time and chance
15 happeneth to them all.\smallskip}
16 \noindent And here is Orwell's 'translation':\smallskip
17 {\leftskip=1cm \rightskip=.8cm \noindent
18 \it Objective consideration of contemporary phenomena compels the conclusion
19 that success or failure in competitive activities exhibits no tendency to be
20 commensurate with innate capacity, but that a considerable element of the
21 unpredictable must invariably be taken into account.\smallskip}
22 \noindent Orwell went on to say that, though his translation was a parody, the
23 sort of writing it represented was ``gaining ground in modern English.''
```

NOTES

1: \line puts material on one line. \hfil fills a line with white space. \title is a private command, defined on page 1. *It will not work without this definition.* % is a comment character: it makes TeX ignore the rest of the line.

2: \headline sets a headline. Here, the headline is filled with white space to erase the setting carried over from the previous page.

3: \vskip allows you to jump vertically.

4, 5: \centerline centers material. \bf and \sl give **bold** and *slanted* type respectively.

6: \bigskip gives a vertical jump.

7, 11, etc.: \noindent suppresses paragraph indentation.

8: ^{2} gives a superscript 2. This is only available in the mathematics mode; the $ signs switch you to and from this mode.

9: Observe how quotes are obtained.

10, 15, etc.: \smallskip gives a small vertical jump.

11: \narrower gives text narrowed by an amount equal to the paragraph indentation. Within the new margins, paragraphs are set just as before: the first line is automatically indented, etc. \noindent works as an indentation suppressor even if placed on the line above the one where the paragraph text begins.

12: \sl gives slanted type.

15: The paragraph is ended with \smallskip, and then the \narrower setting and the slanted typeface are switched off by the closing brace (}).

17: \leftskip and \rightskip give you total control over paragraph margins—something you've hitherto only dreamed of. Positive values bring the edges in, as here. On the next page you'll see what negative values do.

18: \it gives italics.

21: The paragraph that has just ended must be explicitly terminated (done here with \smallskip) before the group that encloses the new margin commands ends (with }). Several of the parameters that shape a paragraph use the values they have at the very end of the paragraph. If they are given values at the start, and if the group that confines these new values ends before the paragraph does, the parameters are reset to their old values. The old values will then be the ones used to form the paragraph. This is discussed a little more in the Appendix, under **paragraphs**.

Examples

I. ON WRITING SIMPLY

Displaying text in narrow or broad format; shaping paragraphs.

In an essay on the decline of the English language, published in 1946,[2] George Orwell translated a passage from *Ecclesiastes* into "modern English of the worst sort." Here is the original passage:

> *I returned, and saw under the sun, that the race is not to the swift, nor the battle to the strong, neither yet bread to the wise, nor yet riches to men of understanding, nor yet favour to men of skill; but time and chance happeneth to them all.*

And here is Orwell's 'translation':

> *Objective consideration of contemporary phenomena compels the conclusion that success or failure in competitive activities exhibits no tendency to be commensurate with innate capacity, but that a considerable element of the unpredictable must invariably be taken into account.*

Orwell went on to say that, though his translation was a parody, the sort of writing it represented was "gaining ground in modern English." He was

```
 1 | He was right. Here are the simple and direct opening lines of a
 2 | great~novel:$^3$\smallskip
 3 | {\leftskip=-.5cm\rightskip=-.5cm\noindent {\sl Ten weeks before he died,
 4 | Mr.~Mohun Biswas, a journalist of Sikkim Street, St James, Port of Spain, was
 5 | sacked. He had been ill for some time. In less than a year he had spent more
 6 | than nine weeks at the Colonial Hospital and convalesced at home for even
 7 | longer. When the doctor advised him to take a complete rest the {\rm Trinidad
 8 | Sentinel} had no choice. It gave Mr.~Biswas three months' notice and continued,
 9 | up to the time of his death, to supply him every morning with a free copy of
10 | the paper.}\smallskip}
11 | \noindent And here, more typical of the sort of writing we are likely to come
12 | across today (especially in academic journals), are the opening lines of a
13 | literary critic's essay on this novel:$^4$\smallskip
14 | \parshape=5 2.64true in .47true in 1.65true in 2.45true in
15 | 1.33true in 3.09true in .75true in 4.25true in 1.17true in 3.34true in
16 | {\it \parindent=0pt One is tempted, in reading
17 | V.S.~Naipaul's {\sl A House for Mr.~Biswas}, to transform the routine mission
18 | of a realtor with more lucrative claims on his time and custom, into the
19 | heraldic rheto\-ric of an older dispensation: ''The House of Bi\-swas.'' For
20 | realists schooled, like Naipaul, in the tactical trivialities of the quotidian,
21 | the move will doubtless seem ill-advised, grandiose.}\smallskip
22 | \noindent Doubtless.
23 | \headline{\hfil\it Example I\newpageno} %'\newpageno' IS NOT A STANDARD COMMAND.
24 | \vfil\eject
```

NOTES

2, 4, 8, 17: Ties (i.e., ~) are employed here to keep words together, for a variety of reasons. On line 2, a tie is used to ensure that the last word does not stray onto a line by itself: on an earlier run, with different spacings, the rest of the sentence had stayed on the previous page and only 'novel' had made its way to this one; that was when the tie went in. The other instances of the use of ties are for more obvious reasons: it is awkward to have initials or 'Mr.' on one line and the name on the next. Ties have also been discussed on page 2.

3: Negative values for \leftskip and \rightskip will push the edges out. You can also combine a negative and a positive value for that elegant one-edge-in/ one-edge-out effect.

14–15: For even more control, there's \parshape. The first number, say n, specifies the number of lines to be shaped; the rest are to be given in pairs (and there must be n pairs). The first number in each pair specifies the indentation from the left margin; the second, the line length. If there are fewer pairs than the number of lines in the paragraph, the extra lines repeat the pattern given by the last pair, till the paragraph is over. If there are too many pairs, the extra ones are ignored. This is a useful command for magazine and newsletter design: text can be shaped as you want, or irregular gaps can be created to accommodate irregularly shaped photographs or pictures. The default setting, \parshape=0, is automatically restored at the end of every paragraph.

16: One way to suppress paragraph indentation is to set \parindent to 0. You must remember to 'group' correctly if you do this (i.e., use { and }) to confine the effects of the new setting.

19: \- is called a *discretionary hyphen*; it suggests possible hyphenations to TeX at places that it may not have picked on its own. In this case, the suggestions were made purely to make the lines fit the odd shape of the paragraph.

23: This reestablishes the headline. See the discussion on pages 2 and 4.

Example I   **23**

right. Here are the simple and direct opening lines of a great novel:[3]

Ten weeks before he died, Mr. Mohun Biswas, a journalist of Sikkim Street, St James, Port of Spain, was sacked. He had been ill for some time. In less than a year he had spent more than nine weeks at the Colonial Hospital and convalesced at home for even longer. When the doctor advised him to take a complete rest the Trinidad Sentinel *had no choice. It gave Mr. Biswas three months' notice and continued, up to the time of his death, to supply him every morning with a free copy of the paper.*

And here, more typical of the sort of writing we are likely to come across today (especially in academic journals), are the opening lines of a literary critic's essay on this novel:[4]

One is

tempted, in reading V.S. Naipaul's

A House for Mr. Biswas, to transform the

routine mission of a realtor with more lucrative claims on

his time and custom, into the heraldic rheto-

ric of an older dispensation: "The House of

Biswas." For realists schooled, like Naipaul,

in the tactical trivialities of the quotidian, the

move will doubtless seem ill-advised, grandiose.

Doubtless.

```
 1 | \centerline{\bf II. $\sqrt2$ IS IRRATIONAL}
 2 | \centerline{\sl Displaying equations; fractions; powers; roots; footnotes.}
 3 | \headline{\hfil\it Example II\newpageno} %'\newpageno' IS NOT STANDARD.
 4 | \bigskip
 5 | \noindent The numbers 1, 2, 3, \dots\ are called {\sl natural numbers}. A number
 6 | is called {\sl rational\/} if it can be written as $m/n$ (where $m$ and $n$ are
 7 | natural numbers) and {\sl irrational\/} if it cannot. $\root n\of a$, where
 8 | $n$ is a natural number, is defined to be a positive number $b$ such that
 9 | $$b^n = a, \qquad {\rm i.e.,}\;\;\overbrace{b\times\cdots\times
10 | b}^{n\;\rm times}=a.$$
11 | \bigbreak
12 | \noindent{\it THEOREM 1\/}: If $q > 1$, then $q^n > q$, where $n$ is any natural
13 | number $\geq 2$.\hfil\break
14 | {\it PROOF\/}: Multiply both sides of $q > 1$ by $q$. This gives $q^2 > q$.
15 | Multiplying once more by $q$ gives $q^3 > q^2$ and, therefore, $q^3 > q$.
16 | Continuing in this way, the result follows.\thinspace$\clubsuit$
17 | \footnote\dag{The symbol $\clubsuit$ will mark the end of a proof. The usual
18 | symbol is a rectangle; the entry under 'rule' in the Appendix shows how to
19 | create it.}
20 | \bigbreak
21 | Now, suppose that a natural number $n$ can be written as $n=m_1\times m_2$,
22 | where $m_1$ and $m_2$ are both natural numbers not equal to 1. Then $n$ is
23 | called {\sl composite}, and $m_1$ and $m_2$ are called {\sl factors\/} of $n$.
24 | If a natural number $p$ ($\not= 1$) cannot be written in this way, it is called
25 | {\sl prime}. Examples of composite numbers are $6\,(= 2 \times 3)$ and $12\,(=
26 | 3\times4\,,or=2\times6)$. Examples of prime numbers are 2, 3, 7 and 1013.
27 | \bigbreak
28 | \noindent{\it THEOREM 2\/}: Any natural number $n$ greater than 1 can be written
29 | as a product of prime factors, i.e., as $n = p_1\times p_2\times
30 | \cdots\times p_k$, where the $p_i$ are all prime. This factorization is
31 | unique.\hfil\break
32 | {\it PROOF\/}: If $n$ is prime, we are done. If it is composite, then
33 | $n = m_1 \times m_2$. Since we have $m_1 > 1$ and $m_2 > 1$, it follows exactly
34 | as in Theorem~1 that $n > m_1$ and $n > m_2$. This process can be repeated for
35 | $m_1$ and for $m_2$: either they are prime, or they too can be decomposed into
```

NOTES

COMMENT

The next page discusses the use of $ signs in the notes.

1: `$\sqrt x$` gives $\sqrt{x}$.

3: `\headline` gives headlines. See pages 2 and 4.

5: `\dots` gives . . . .

6, etc.: All variables are enclosed in $ signs, even when they appear in text. This ensures consistency of typeface (the $ signs switch on/off *math italics*).

7: `\root` and `\of` allow you to express arbitrary roots in the mathematics mode. The structure of the command is `$\root n\of{x}$`, which gives $\sqrt[n]{x}$. The braces are necessary only when more than one quantity is to go under the radical.

9–10: The double $ signs surrounding the expression switch on, then off, the 'displayed math' mode. This automatically puts the expression on a separate line, puts space above and below it and centers it. ^ gives superscripts. `\rm` is needed before some words to switch to roman typeface in the middle of the mathematics mode. The braces limit what appears in roman type. `\;` is a mathematics spacing command, giving you a little extra space. `\overbrace` gives just that: the structure of the command used here is `$$\overbrace{A}^{B}$$`, which puts a brace above A, and then B above the brace. `\qquad` is a spacing command, giving a little horizontal space. `$\times$` gives × and `$\cdots$` gives $\cdots$.

11, 20, etc.: `\bigbreak` suggests a possible page break to TeX. If it is not a good place to break the page, TeX will leave a vertical space equal to a `\bigskip`.

13: `$\geq$` gives $\geq$.

16: `\thinspace` leaves a little bit of space, about this[ ]much. `$\clubsuit$` gives ♣.

17: `\footnote` gives you footnotes. You need to supply two pieces of information: the symbol used to mark the footnote, and the footnote text. The command for the symbol here, `\dag`, gives †. The footnote text is enclosed in braces just after.

21, etc.: _ gives a subscript.

24: `\not` is a mathematics mode command that negates the relation that follows.

26: Note how the word 'or' gets printed.

Example II   **25**

II. $\sqrt{2}$ IS IRRATIONAL

Displaying equations; fractions; powers; roots; footnotes.

The numbers 1, 2, 3, ... are called *natural numbers.* A number is called *rational* if it can be written as m/n (where m and n are natural numbers) and *irrational* if it cannot. $\sqrt[n]{a}$, where n is a natural number, is defined to be a positive number b such that

$$b^n = a, \qquad \text{i.e.,} \quad \overbrace{b \times \cdots \times b}^{n \text{ times}} = a.$$

THEOREM 1: If $q > 1$, then $q^n > q$, where n is any natural number ≥ 2.

PROOF: Multiply both sides of $q > 1$ by q. This gives $q^2 > q$. Multiplying once more by q gives $q^3 > q^2$ and, therefore, $q^3 > q$. Continuing in this way, the result follows. ♣ †

Now, suppose that a natural number n can be written as $n = m_1 \times m_2$, where m_1 and m_2 are both natural numbers not equal to 1. Then n is called *composite*, and m_1 and m_2 are called *factors* of n. If a natural number p ($\neq 1$) cannot be written in this way, it is called *prime*. Examples of composite numbers are $6 \, (= 2 \times 3)$ and $12 \, (= 3 \times 4, \, or \, = 2 \times 6)$. Examples of prime numbers are 2, 3, 7 and 1013.

THEOREM 2: Any natural number n greater than 1 can be written as a product of prime factors, i.e., as $n = p_1 \times p_2 \times \cdots \times p_k$, where the p_i are all prime. This factorization is unique.

PROOF: If n is prime, we are done. If it is composite, then $n = m_1 \times m_2$. Since we have $m_1 > 1$ and $m_2 > 1$, it follows exactly as in Theorem 1 that

---

† The symbol ♣ will mark the end of a proof. The usual symbol is a rectangle; the entry under 'rule' in the Appendix shows how to create it.

```
 1 │ smaller factors. Since $n$ was finite, the process must end with a
 2 │ decomposition of $n$ into prime factors.
 3 │ \bigbreak
 4 │ Next,\footnote{$^\star$}{This portion of the proof is taken from {\sl What is
 5 │ Mathematics?\/} by R.~Courant and H.~Robbins, Oxford University Press, 1941.}
 6 │ suppose that $n$ admits two prime factorizations, i.e.,
 7 │ $$n=p_1\times\cdots\times p_k=q_1\times\cdots\times q_l,\eqno(1)$$
 8 │ where the $p_i$ and the $q_j$ are all prime. Let us suppose that $n$ is the
 9 │ {\it smallest\/} such number (i.e., one that admits distinct factorizations).
10 │ Then the smallest of the $p_i$ cannot equal the smallest of the $q_j$; we may
11 │ assume that these smallest factors are $p_1$ and $q_1$ and that $p_1<q_1$. Let
12 │ $$n'=n-(p_1\times q_2\times \cdots\times q_l).\eqno(2)$$
13 │ Then we have
14 │ $$n'=\cases{p_1(p_2\times\cdots\times p_k-q_2\times\cdots\times q_l)&
15 │ using the first factorization of $p$,\cr
16 │ &\cr
17 │ (q_1-p_1)(q_2\times\cdots\times q_l)& using the second factorization.\cr}$$
18 │ \smallskip\noindent
19 │ Let $m=q_2\times\cdots\times q_l$. Since $m<n'<n$, $m$ and $n'$ will have
20 │ unique prime factorizations. Now, $p_1$ is a factor of $n'=(q_1-p_1)m$,
21 │ but it cannot be one of the factors of $m$ since it is less than all the $q_j$.
22 │ So, it must be a factor of $(q_1-p_1)$; i.e., $q_1-p_1=gp_1$, or $q_1=(g+1)p_1$.
23 │ This is not possible.\thinspace$\clubsuit$
24 │ \bigbreak
25 │ \noindent{\it COROLLARY\/}: If a prime $p$ is a factor of a product $a\times b$,
26 │ then it is a factor of $a$ or of $b$.
27 │ \vfil\eject
```

NOTES

COMMENT

Most of the commands here were discussed on the previous page. Mathematics mode commands are enclosed between explicit $ signs when listed in these notes. The $ signs are just reminders: when using the mathematics mode you must not sandwich every command thus, just entire formulas, as in the box above.

4: $\star$ gives ⋆. \footnote here is slightly different from the previous page. The ⋆ marking it is raised to superscript status by ^. Braces { and } are used to mark where the commands defining the symbol end, and where the footnote text begins. In that text, typeface can be changed just as for normal text.

5: The ~ symbols are **ties**. They leave an interword space and they keep the words or characters on either side together: line breaks cannot occur there. See pages 2 and 22.

7: \eqno is used to number displayed equations. To get numbers on the left, use \leqno (this is shown in Example VII).

7, 12, etc.: Double $ signs are used to start, and end, displayed mathematics formulas. Such displays are automatically centered on a new line, and extra space is left above and below. Several entries in the Appendix—see, for example, mathematics: displays and mathematics: spacing—further discuss this mode.

14–17: \cases allows you to make aligned multi-line displays. Each line of the display has two parts. The first part is in mathematics mode, the second in ordinary text (for comments). The two parts are separated by an &, and each line ends with a \cr (for 'carriage return'). If you don't have, say, a comment for some line, you don't have to enter anything. But the & is necessary, regardless. For example, the display in Equation 2 is actually a three-line display with a blank middle line. (This was done for better vertical spacing.) The structure here is characteristic of aligned displays (like matrices and tables) in TeX: & plays a 'tabbing' function, moving you from entry to entry, and \cr ends lines.

Example II **27**

$n > m_1$ and $n > m_2$. This process can be repeated for m_1 and for m_2: either they are prime, or they too can be decomposed into smaller factors. Since n was finite, the process must end with a decomposition of n into prime factors.

Next,[*] suppose that n admits two prime factorizations, i.e.,

$$n = p_1 \times \cdots \times p_k = q_1 \times \cdots \times q_l, \tag{1}$$

where the p_i and the q_j are all prime. Let us suppose that n is the *smallest* such number (i.e., one that admits distinct factorizations). Then the smallest of the p_i cannot equal the smallest of the q_j; we may assume that these smallest factors are p_1 and q_1 and that $p_1 < q_1$. Let

$$n' = n - (p_1 \times q_2 \times \cdots \times q_l). \tag{2}$$

Then we have

$$n' = \begin{cases} p_1(p_2 \times \cdots \times p_k - q_2 \times \cdots \times q_l) & \text{using the first factorization of } p, \\ (q_1 - p_1)(q_2 \times \cdots \times q_l) & \text{using the second factorization.} \end{cases}$$

Let $m = q_2 \times \cdots \times q_l$. Since $m < n' < n$, m and n' will have unique prime factorizations. Now, p_1 is a factor of $n' = (q_1 - p_1)m$, but it cannot be one of the factors of m since it is less than all the q_j. So, it must be a factor of $(q_1 - p_1)$; i.e., $q_1 - p_1 = gp_1$, or $q_1 = (g+1)p_1$. This is not possible. ♣

COROLLARY: If a prime p is a factor of a product $a \times b$, then it is a factor of a or of b.

---

[*] This portion of the proof is taken from *What is Mathematics?* by R. Courant and H. Robbins, Oxford University Press, 1941.

```
 1 | \noindent{\it THEOREM 3\/}: Let $m$ and $n$ be natural numbers. Suppose that
 2 | $\root n\of m=p/q$, where $p$ and $q$ are natural numbers such that $q$ is
 3 | not a factor of $p$. Then  $q = 1$.\hfil\break
 4 | {\it PROOF\/}: Suppose that $q \not= 1$. Then we have
 5 | $$\root n\of m={p\over q} = {p_1\times\cdots\times p_k\over q_1\times
 6 | \cdots\times q_l},\eqno(3)$$
 7 | where $p_1,\ldots,p_k$ and $q_1,\ldots,q_l$ are the prime factors of $p$
 8 | and $q$ respectively. If any factor in the numerator equals a factor in the
 9 | denominator, the two may be cancelled. It is assumed that this has been
10 | done. Then, raising Equation~3 to the $n$th power, we get
11 | $$m={(p_1\times\cdots\times p_k)^n\over(q_1\times\cdots\times q_l)^n},$$
12 | or
13 | $$(q_1\times\cdots\times q_l)^nm=(p_1\times\cdots\times p_k)^n.$$
14 | Since $q_1$ is a factor of the left-hand side, it must be a factor of one of
15 | the $p_i$ on the right-hand side. This is impossible.
16 | Therefore, we must have $q = 1$.\thinspace$\clubsuit$
17 | \bigbreak
18 | \noindent{\it COROLLARY\/}: $\sqrt2$ is irrational.\hfil\break
19 | {\it PROOF\/}: Suppose $\sqrt2=p/q$ where $p$ and $q$ are natural numbers.
20 | By Theorem~3, $q=1$. By Theorem 1, $p<p^2$. But $p^2=2$. Therefore,
21 | $p$ is a natural number less than 2, i.e., $p = 1$. That is not
22 | possible, and so $\sqrt2$ must be irrational.\thinspace$\clubsuit$
23 | \vfil\eject
```

NOTES

5: \over gives fractions. The structure is simple: ${Numerator\over Denominator}$, where the numerator and denominator may be long expressions.

All the other commands used here have been previously explained.

5, 11, etc.: See the discussion of mathematics displays on the previous page.

ABOUT POWERS

The superscript command, ^, makes only the character just next to it a superscript; subsequent characters stay as part of the main expression. See line 13. If you want a *long expression* as a superscript you must type '^{*long expression*}'. This holds for subscripts as well.

Typing x^{y^z} is the correct way to get a power in a power; {x^y}^z gives an ambiguous-looking expression (the size of z is wrong and the expression can look a little like what you get from x^{yz}). In general, you may need to experiment a little to pick forms that best express what you want to say and that are easy to read. (Compare for yourself, as an example, the effect of $(x^y)^z$ with that of ${(x^y)}^z$.)

Example II   **29**

THEOREM 3: Let m and n be natural numbers. Suppose that $\sqrt[n]{m} = p/q$, where p and q are natural numbers such that q is not a factor of p. Then $q = 1$.

PROOF: Suppose that $q \neq 1$. Then we have

$$\sqrt[n]{m} = \frac{p}{q} = \frac{p_1 \times \cdots \times p_k}{q_1 \times \cdots \times q_l}, \tag{3}$$

where $p_1, \ldots, p_k$ and $q_1, \ldots, q_l$ are the prime factors of p and q respectively. If any factor in the numerator equals a factor in the denominator, the two may be cancelled. It is assumed that this has been done. Then, raising Equation 3 to the nth power, we get

$$m = \frac{(p_1 \times \cdots \times p_k)^n}{(q_1 \times \cdots \times q_l)^n},$$

or

$$(q_1 \times \cdots \times q_l)^n m = (p_1 \times \cdots \times p_k)^n.$$

Since q_1 is a factor of the left-hand side, it must be a factor of one of the p_i on the right-hand side. This is impossible. Therefore, we must have $q = 1$.♣

COROLLARY: $\sqrt{2}$ is irrational.

PROOF: Suppose $\sqrt{2} = p/q$ where p and q are natural numbers. By Theorem 3, $q = 1$. By Theorem 1, $p < p^2$. But $p^2 = 2$. Therefore, p is a natural number less than 2, i.e., $p = 1$. That is not possible, and so $\sqrt{2}$ must be irrational. ♣

```
 1  \centerline {\bf III. CAUCHY HORIZONS}
 2  \centerline{\sl Set theoretic symbols; blank space inserts for diagrams.}
 3  \headline{\hfil\it Example III\newpageno}%`\newpageno' IS NOT STANDARD.
 4  \bigskip \noindent
 5  Let $\cal M$ be a time-orientable space-time (i.e., a space-time that admits a
 6  global choice of future time direction). A {\sl timelike (null) curve\/}
 7  in $\cal M$ is defined to be a $C^1$ curve whose tangent is everywhere timelike
 8  (null). A {\sl full\/} timelike (null) curve is one with no endpoints. Then, for
 9  any $p\in\cal M$, the {\sl chronological future (past)\/} of $p$ is defined by
10
11  \smallskip
12  \centerline{$I^{\pm}(p)=\{q\in{\cal M}\mid\exists$ a future(past)-directed
13  timelike curve from $p$ to $q\}$.}
14  \smallskip \noindent
15  This definition may be extended to arbitrary ${\cal A}\subset{\cal M}$:
16  $$I^{\pm}({\cal A})=\bigcup_{p\in{\cal A}}I^{\pm}(p).$$
17  \indent Now, let $\cal S\subset\cal M$ be an achronal (i.e., no two points on
18  it can be connected by a timelike curve) spacelike hypersurface without edge.
19  Define the {\sl future (past) domain of dependance\/} of $\cal S$ as follows:
20  \medskip
21  {\narrower\itemitem{$D^{\pm}(\cal S) =$}$\{p\in{\cal M}\mid\forall$
22  full timelike or null curves $\rho$ through $p$, $\rho\cap{\cal S}\not=
23  \emptyset$, with $\cal S$ lying to the past (future) of $p$ along $\rho\}$.
24  \medskip}
25  \noindent For a spacelike hypersurface $\cal S$, it may be possible that
26  $I^{\pm}({\cal S}) - D^{\pm}({\cal S}) \not= \emptyset$; i.e., there might
27  be points that lie to the future (past) of $\cal S$ which do not lie in
28  $D^{\pm}(\cal S)$. In such cases, $D^{\pm}(\cal S)$ will have a non-empty future
29  (past) boundary called the {\sl future (past) Cauchy horizon\/} defined by
30  \smallskip
31  \centerline{$H^{\pm}({\cal S}) =
32  \overline{D^{\pm}({\cal S})} - I^{\mp}(D^{\pm}({\cal S}))$.}  \smallskip
33  \noindent All these sets are illustrated in Fig.\ 1.
34  \pageinsert
35     The content of the insert is on the next page.
36  \endinsert
37  They are interpreted as follows: the surface $\cal S$ can be regarded as an
38  initial value surface on which the initial state of some system (which may be
39  the space-time geometry itself) may be specified. $D^+(\cal S)$ represents
40  the region in which the future development of the system can be determined
```

NOTES

COMMENT

Mathematics mode commands that are explained below will mostly be explicitly enclosed in $ signs to serve as a reminder that the commands will not work outside this mode. In the input above, each command is not enclosed in $ signs, just entire formulas.

5: \cal gives calligraphic type in the mathematics mode. This style is available only for uppercase letters. If there are more parts to the expression than just the characters you want in this typeface, you must isolate the characters with braces, as is done in several expressions on this page. If you don't, you'll get wonderfully wacky effects: see \cal in the Appendix.

9: $\in$ gives $\in$.

12–13: $\pm$ gives $\pm$, $\{$ gives {, $\mid$ gives |, $\exists$ gives $\exists$ and $\}$ gives }.

15: $\subset$ gives $\subset$.

16: \bigcup gives a big union symbol. The normal subscript command, _, is used here to put something below the symbol. In Example VII there is a discussion of how to move 'subscripts' and 'superscripts' from the top to the side, or from the side to the top.

21–24: \narrower and \itemitem are used here to display a definition. It was needed that everything to the right of the = align along the same left margin, and \itemitem gave an easy way to do that. \item would have worked as well, but \itemitem gives twice as much indentation.

21–23: $\forall$ gives $\forall$, ρ gives ρ, $\cap$ gives $\cap$ and $\emptyset$ gives $\emptyset$.

32: \overline puts a line over whatever is grouped in braces just after; $\mp$ gives $\mp$.

34–36: \pageinsert inserts a page's worth of stuff into the next page. This is useful for including pictures and diagrams. \endinsert ends the insertion.

Example III **31**

III. CAUCHY HORIZONS

Set theoretic symbols; blank space inserts for diagrams.

Let $\mathcal{M}$ be a time-orientable space-time (i.e., a space-time that admits a global choice of future time direction). A *timelike (null) curve* in $\mathcal{M}$ is defined to be a C^1 curve whose tangent is everywhere timelike (null). A *full* timelike (null) curve is one with no endpoints. Then, for any $p \in \mathcal{M}$, the *chronological future (past)* of p is defined by

$$I^{\pm}(p) = \{q \in \mathcal{M} \mid \exists \text{ a future(past)-directed timelike curve from } p \text{ to } q\}.$$

This definition may be extended to arbitrary $\mathcal{A} \subset \mathcal{M}$:

$$I^{\pm}(\mathcal{A}) = \bigcup_{p \in \mathcal{A}} I^{\pm}(p).$$

Now, let $\mathcal{S} \subset \mathcal{M}$ be an achronal (i.e., no two points on it can be connected by a timelike curve) spacelike hypersurface without edge. Define the *future (past) domain of dependance* of $\mathcal{S}$ as follows:

$$D^{\pm}(\mathcal{S}) = \{p \in \mathcal{M} \mid \forall \text{ full timelike or null curves } \rho \text{ through } p, \rho \cap \mathcal{S} \neq$$
$$\emptyset, \text{ with } \mathcal{S} \text{ lying to the past (future) of } p \text{ along } \rho\}.$$

For a spacelike hypersurface $\mathcal{S}$, it may be possible that $I^{\pm}(\mathcal{S}) - D^{\pm}(\mathcal{S}) \neq \emptyset$; i.e., there might be points that lie to the future (past) of $\mathcal{S}$ which do not lie in $D^{\pm}(\mathcal{S})$. In such cases, $D^{\pm}(\mathcal{S})$ will have a non-empty future (past) boundary called the *future (past) Cauchy horizon* defined by

$$H^{\pm}(\mathcal{S}) = \overline{D^{\pm}(\mathcal{S})} - I^{\mp}(D^{\pm}(\mathcal{S})).$$

All these sets are illustrated in Fig. 1.

They are interpreted as follows: the surface $\mathcal{S}$ can be regarded as an initial value surface on which the initial state of some system (which may be the space-time geometry itself) may be specified. $D^{+}(\mathcal{S})$ represents the region in which the future development of the system can be determined

```
 1 | \pageinsert
 2 | \centerline{\bf Figure 1}
 3 | \vfil
 4 | \item{\bf 1a.}{Two-dimensional Minkowski space; $ds^2 = -dt^2 + dx^2$.
 5 | $\cal S$ is the $t=1$ surface. Here $D^{\pm}({\cal S}) = I^{\pm}(\cal S)$.
 6 | Also shown are the sets $I^{\pm}(p)$ for some $p\in \cal M$.}
 7 | \vfil
 8 | \item{\bf 1b.}{Two-dimensional Minkowski space again. $\cal S$ is given
 9 | by $t = -\sqrt{1+x^2}$. Here $D^-({\cal S}) = I^-({\cal S})$, but
10 | $D^+({\cal S}) \not= I^+({\cal S})$. Therefore, $H^+({\cal S})
11 | \not=\emptyset$.}
12 | \vfil
13 | \item{\bf 1c.}{A two-dimensional space-time with the cylinder $R\times S^1$
14 | as the manifold; $ds^2 = -d\psi\,dt - t(d\psi)^2$, $-\infty < t < \infty$,
15 | $0\leq\psi\leq 2\pi$. Here $t=-2$ is a spacelike hypersurface and $t=0$
16 | is a future Cauchy horizon for it. This Cauchy horizon is compact.}
17 | \endinsert
```

NOTES

This is the text of the `\pageinsert` from the previous page. It was typed as part of the main body of the document, with an `\endinsert` to mark where the insertion ended. TeX responds to these commands by taking the material between them and inserting it on the next page. The insertion can be a blank page, obtained thus:

```
\pageinsert
\vfil
\endinsert
```

Or it can have material in it, as it does here.

The figure captions were typed with white space left, via `\vfil`, for diagrams. The diagrams themselves were drawn elsewhere (some of the rudimentary graphical features that come with LaTeX were used) and were pasted into the blank space by the publisher. It is also possible to electronically 'import' graphics files from other sources and place them in blank spaces during printing via a command called `\special` (which, roughly, instructs the printer to do special things). But the exact procedures vary from system to system, so you will have to ask locally to find out how this may be achieved on yours.

9: This is how `\sqrt` can be made to cover longer expressions.

14: ψ gives ψ and ∞ gives ∞. The command `\,` allows you to fine-tune spacing; it gives a little extra space here between $d\psi$ and dt.

15: $\leq$ gives $\leq$.

COMMENT

$ signs in the notes indicate which commands work only in the mathematics mode.

Example III **33**

Figure 1

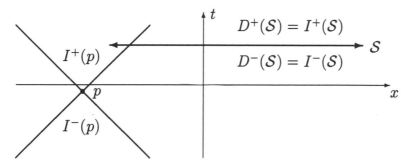

1a. Two-dimensional Minkowski space; $ds^2 = -dt^2 + dx^2$. $\mathcal{S}$ is the $t = 1$ surface. Here $D^{\pm}(\mathcal{S}) = I^{\pm}(\mathcal{S})$. Also shown are the sets $I^{\pm}(p)$ for some $p \in \mathcal{M}$.

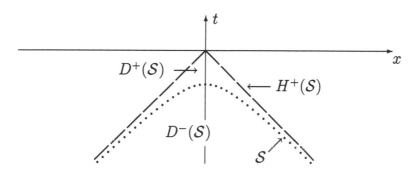

1b. Two-dimensional Minkowski space again. $\mathcal{S}$ is given by $t = -\sqrt{1 + x^2}$. Here $D^{-}(\mathcal{S}) = I^{-}(\mathcal{S})$, but $D^{+}(\mathcal{S}) \neq I^{+}(\mathcal{S})$. Therefore, $H^{+}(\mathcal{S}) \neq \emptyset$.

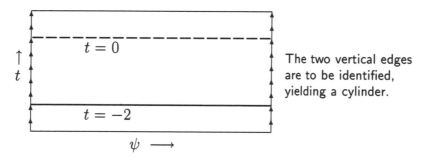

1c. A two-dimensional space-time with the cylinder $R \times S^1$ as the manifold; $ds^2 = -d\psi\, dt - t(d\psi)^2$, $-\infty < t < \infty$, $0 \leq \psi \leq 2\pi$. Here $t = -2$ is a spacelike hypersurface and $t = 0$ is a future Cauchy horizon for it. This Cauchy horizon is compact.

```
1  from the initial data. There are analogous, but time-reversed,
2  interpretations of~$D^-(\cal S)$.
3
4  Cauchy horizons represent a breakdown of our ability to predict the future,
5  even given a complete knowledge of the present. The existence of space-times
6  that do not possess any surfaces $\cal S$ such that
7  $D^{\pm}({\cal S}) = I^{\pm}({\cal S})$ (i.e., that possess nontrivial
8  Cauchy horizons) appears to have first been noticed and explicitly discussed
9  by Roger Penrose.$^5$ The properties of Cauchy horizons were then extensively
10 investigated by Stephen Hawking. His results are given in Ref.~6. There are
11 suggestions that space-times that contain such Cauchy horizons are highly
12 special and physically unrealistic. Studies of compact Cauchy horizons (such
13 as the one in Fig.~1c) bear this out.$^{7,8}$
14
15 \line{\hfil}
16 \smallbreak
17 \hrule height1pt
18 \smallskip
19 \hrule height1pt
20 \line{\hfil}
21 \bigskip
22 \centerline{\bf IV. A SPANISH INTERLUDE}
23 \centerline{\sl 'Unusual' punctuation; accents; overlap commands.}
24 \headline{\hfil\it Example IV\newpageno} %'\newpageno' IS NOT STANDARD.
25 \bigskip
26 \noindent Some years ago, Donald Knuth wrote a delightful book about a new
27 number system (called by him the system of 'surreal numbers') that had been
28 invented by John Conway. The book is in the form of a novella.$^9$ A woman and a
29 man retreat to a deserted place to 'find themselves'. There, they accidentally
30 discover the rules for constructing Conway's numbers. They are intrigued,
31 and they begin to explore the properties of these new numbers. As they do,
32 their interest grows and they become steadily more excited. And, very soon,
33 this excitement is not only intellectual.
34
35 Knuth's book is probably the first description of a mathematical advance that
36 has sex in it. The relevant passage is interesting and is quoted below,
37 translated into Spanish:\footnote{$^\ast$}{The translation was made by Luca
38 Bombelli.}
39
```

NOTES

2, 10, 13: Ties are used, once again, in several places. See pages 2, 22 and 26 for a discussion.

15: \line{\hfil} gives you a line filled with white space.

16: \smallbreak suggests a page break to TeX. If the suggestion is not taken at this point, then a space equal to a \smallskip is left.

17, 19: The two \hrule commands give horizontal lines of height 1 point across the page .

18: \smallskip gives the gap between the lines.

20–21: Another blank line, followed by a vertical space given by \bigskip.

24: \headline is changed here in mid-page, and the page headline changes in response. (TeX sets the headline to be whatever the most recently encountered \headline command orders. See the discussion on page 4.) \newpageno is a special command, needed for the format of this book. See page 2.

37: Another \footnote; nothing new here.

39: The page break fell between paragraphs here, but no extra space was left at the bottom of this page or at the top of the next one.

Example IV   **35**

from the initial data. There are analogous, but time-reversed, interpretations of $D^-(\mathcal{S})$.

Cauchy horizons represent a breakdown of our ability to predict the future, even given a complete knowledge of the present. The existence of space-times that do not possess any surfaces $\mathcal{S}$ such that $D^\pm(\mathcal{S}) = I^\pm(\mathcal{S})$ (i.e., that possess nontrivial Cauchy horizons) appears to have first been noticed and explicitly discussed by Roger Penrose.[5] The properties of Cauchy horizons were then extensively investigated by Stephen Hawking. His results are given in Ref. 6. There are suggestions that space-times that contain such Cauchy horizons are highly special and physically unrealistic. Studies of compact Cauchy horizons (such as the one in Fig. 1c) bear this out.[7,8]

IV. A SPANISH INTERLUDE

'Unusual' punctuation; accents; overlap commands.

Some years ago, Donald Knuth wrote a delightful book about a new number system (called by him the system of 'surreal numbers') that had been invented by John Conway. The book is in the form of a novella.[9] A woman and a man retreat to a deserted place to 'find themselves'. There, they accidentally discover the rules for constructing Conway's numbers. They are intrigued, and they begin to explore the properties of these new numbers. As they do, their interest grows and they become steadily more excited. And, very soon, this excitement is not only intellectual.

Knuth's book is probably the first description of a mathematical advance that has sex in it. The relevant passage is interesting and is quoted below, translated into Spanish:*

---

* The translation was made by Luca Bombelli.

```
1  \item{B:}{Alicia, estoy descubriendo un nuevo aspecto de tu personalidad hoy.
2  Realmente derribas el mito de que las mujeres no valen para las
3  mate\-m\'aticas.}
4  \item{A:}{!'Pues muchas gracias, amable caballero!}
5  \item{B:}{S\'e que suena como una locura, pero trabajar contigo en estas
6  cosas creativas me hace sentir como un potro salvaje. Uno pensar\'\i a
7  que tanto trabajar de seso apagar\'\i a cualquier deseo f\'\i sico,
8  pero en realidad hace mucho tiempo que no me sentia as\'\i.}
9  \item{A:}{Si quieres que te diga la verdad, yo tambi\'en.}
10 \item{B:}{Mira la puesta de sol, es igual que el poster que compramos aquella
11 vez. Y mira el agua.}
12 \item{A:}{(Corriendo) Vamos.}\vskip1pt
13 \line{\llap{$\heartsuit\heartsuit$}\hfil\dots\dots\dots\hfil
14 \rlap{$\heartsuit\heartsuit$}}
15 \item{B:}{!'Jol\'\i n! Nunca hab\'\i a dormido tan bien.}
16 \item{A:}{Lo mismo digo yo. Es estupendo despertar y estar realmente
17 despierta, no solamente ``despierta de caf\'e.''}
18 \item{B:}{?'Donde hab\'\i amos quedado ayer, antes de que perdi\'eramos
19 la cabeza y nos olvid\'aramos por completo de las matem\'aticas?}
20
21 \line{}\smallbreak
22 \hrule height1pt\smallskip\hrule height1pt
23 \line{}\bigskip
24 \centerline{\bf V. TRAPPED SURFACES IN G\"ODEL'S UNIVERSE}
25 \centerline{\sl Matrices; aligning equations; indices; partial
26 derivatives; footnotes.}
27 \headline{\hfil\it Example V\newpageno} %'\newpageno' IS NOT A STANDARD COMMAND.
28 \bigskip
29 \noindent In 1949, Kurt G\"odel presented a cosmological solution of Einstein's
30 equation with some very curious properties.$^{10}$ G\"odel appears to have
31 discovered this solution in the course of an investigation of the idealistic
32 conception of time, i.e., of whether or not ``reality consists of an infinity
33 of layers of `now'.'' In his model it (i.e., reality) does not. Firstly, through
34 every point in it there passes a closed timelike curve. Secondly, it is simply
```

NOTES

1–19: These lines show how you can use \item to typeset a small script. Example XIII shows you another way. The script is in Spanish; it ought to be fairly simple for you to spot how the various unusual punctuation and accent symbols are obtained.

3: \- is a *discretionary hyphen*. See page 22. It suggests a hyphenation to TeX that the program may not have tried on its own. It was inserted here after an initial run when TeX had trouble finding good spacing for the line. \'a gives á.

4: The combination !' is interpreted by TeX as the single character ¡. Line 18 shows how ¿ is obtained. See the discussion of ligatures in the Appendix.

6, 7, 8, etc.: Accenting an *i* is tricky: the dot has to be stripped off first, using \i, which gives ı. Then it can be accented as usual, say with \'.

13–14: \llap takes whatever is in braces just after the command, and puts it to the left of the point where the command occurs. Here, that means the left margin. This is called an 'overlap' command, because it can be used to get text to overlap. $\heartsuit$ gives ♡. \rlap works like \llap, but it puts stuff to the right. It gives an easy way to put material in the right margin. Both commands are briefly discussed again in the Appendix. \line is used to keep everything on the same line.

24, 29, 30: \" produces an accent, as shown on the output page.

27: \headline is reset again. And, once again, a warning: \newpageno is a specially defined command; it cannot be used without the definition from page 2.

Example V **37**

B: Alicia, estoy descubriendo un nuevo aspecto de tu personalidad hoy. Realmente derribas el mito de que las mujeres no valen para las matemáticas.

A: ¡Pues muchas gracias, amable caballero!

B: Sé que suena como una locura, pero trabajar contigo en estas cosas creativas me hace sentir como un potro salvaje. Uno pensaría que tanto trabajar de seso apagaría cualquier deseo físico, pero en realidad hace mucho tiempo que no me sentia así.

A: Si quieres que te diga la verdad, yo también.

B: Mira la puesta de sol, es igual que el poster que compramos aquella vez. Y mira el agua.

A: (Corriendo) Vamos.

♡♡ . . . . ♡♡

B: ¡Jolín! Nunca había dormido tan bien.

A: Lo mismo digo yo. Es estupendo despertar y estar realmente despierta, no solamente "despierta de café."

B: ¿Donde habíamos quedado ayer, antes de que perdiéramos la cabeza y nos olvidáramos por completo de las matemáticas?

V. TRAPPED SURFACES IN GÖDEL'S UNIVERSE

Matrices; aligning equations; indices; partial derivatives; footnotes.

In 1949, Kurt Gödel presented a cosmological solution of Einstein's equation with some very curious properties.[10] Gödel appears to have discovered this solution in the course of an investigation of the idealistic conception of time, i.e., of whether or not "reality consists of an infinity of layers of 'now'." In his model it (i.e., reality) does not. Firstly, through every point in it

```
1  connected. It follows from these properties that the model does not admit any
2  spacelike hypersurfaces. 'Reality' here does not contain even a {\it single\/}
3  layer of 'now'.
4
5  Some features of G\"odel's solution are discussed in Ref.~6, and I will use
6  the conventions and notation that are used there. The manifold on which
7  G\"odel's metric is defined is $I\!\!R^4$. Coordinates $(t', x, y, z)$ may be
8  chosen such that each coordinate $\in (-\infty,\infty)$ and with the metric
9  given by
10 $$ds^2=-{dt'}^2+dx^2-(1/2)\exp{(2\sqrt2\omega x)}dy^2+dz^2-2\exp{(\sqrt2\omega
11 x)}dt'dy,$$
12 where $\omega$ = constant $>0$. This metric satisfies the equation
13 $$G_{ab}+{\Lambda}g_{ab}=8\pi T_{ab},\qquad\hbox{with}\qquad T_{ab}=
14 \varrho U_aU_b,$$
15 if $({\partial\,\over\partial t'})^a=U^a$ and $\omega^2=-\Lambda=4\pi\varrho$.
16
17 G\"odel's solution has another interesting property: there is a space-time
18 based on it that contains 'marginally trapped surfaces'. The notion of a {\sl
19 trapped surface\/} was introduced in 1965, by Roger Penrose, to characterize
20 a system that is undergoing gravitational collapse.$^{11}$ It may be defined
21 as a compact spacelike two-surface without boundary, such that both systems of
22 future-directed null geodesics that emanate orthogonally from it have positive
23 convergence $\rho$. A {\sl marginally trapped surface\/} is defined similarly,
24 but with $\rho\geq 0$. It was discovered by Stephen Hawking that trapped
25 surfaces exist in some expanding cosmological models as well.$^{12}$ (These
26 models may be regarded as undergoing gravitational collapse in the reverse
27 time direction.) It is intriguing that a non-collapsing space-time,
28 like G\"odel's, should also contain such a structure.
29
30 The existence of marginally trapped surfaces is most easily seen if new
31 coordinates $(t, r, \phi , z)$ are defined,$^6$ with $-\infty< t <\infty$,
32 $0\leq r<\infty$, \hbox{$0\leq\phi\leq 2\pi$}, and $-\infty<z<\infty$,
```

NOTES

COMMENT

\$ signs in the notes indicate which commands work only in the mathematics mode.

5: The tie, ~, keeps the Ref. and the 6 together. See pages 2, 22 and 26.

7: $\!$ gives a small 'negative' space in the mathematics mode; i.e., it moves material backward. The combination on this line leads to the partial overlap of I and R.

10: $\exp$ gives 'exp' (i.e., using roman type). Such functions are generally typeset that way in formulas. ω gives ω.

13–15: Λ gives Λ, ϱ gives ϱ, π gives π and ∂ gives ∂. Words that you want appearing in regular text typeface, with regular text spacing, must be put in an \hbox. \, is a spacing command.

23–24: ρ gives ρ and $\geq$ gives $\geq$.

31–32: ϕ gives ϕ, ∞ gives ∞ and $\leq$ gives $\leq$.

32: The line break, and the page break, originally

occurred in mid-formula at a $\leq$. (A relation symbol is one of the very few places where TeX will break a formula. See the discussion under **mathematics: line breaks** in the Appendix.) To prevent an awkward page break like this, the formula that was broken is now enclosed in an \hbox, as shown. The contents of an \hbox are never divided over two lines. In this case, the entire box was moved by TeX to the next line, and so to the next output page.

EQUATION ALIGNMENTS

The next page introduces you to \eqalignno. The command aligns systems of equations and allows you to number them. The structure follows the general pattern of alignments in TeX: entries are separated by an & and lines end with a \cr. The equations on the next page are aligned along the =, with the entries on the left set flush right against it and those on the right set flush left. The last entry on each line is the equation number. The entry is optional. Such displays of equations continue automatically from one page to the next, if needed.

Example V **39**

there passes a closed timelike curve. Secondly, it is simply connected. It follows from these properties that the model does not admit any spacelike hypersurfaces. 'Reality' here does not contain even a *single* layer of 'now'.

Some features of Gödel's solution are discussed in Ref. 6, and I will use the conventions and notation that are used there. The manifold on which Gödel's metric is defined is $I\!\!R^4$. Coordinates (t', x, y, z) may be chosen such that each coordinate $\in (-\infty, \infty)$ and with the metric given by

$$ds^2 = -dt'^2 + dx^2 - (1/2)\exp{(2\sqrt{2}\omega x)}dy^2 + dz^2 - 2\exp{(\sqrt{2}\omega x)}dt'dy,$$

where $\omega = $ constant > 0. This metric satisfies the equation

$$G_{ab} + \Lambda g_{ab} = 8\pi T_{ab}, \qquad \text{with} \qquad T_{ab} = \varrho U_a U_b,$$

if $(\frac{\partial}{\partial t'})^a = U^a$ and $\omega^2 = -\Lambda = 4\pi\varrho$.

Gödel's solution has another interesting property: there is a space-time based on it that contains 'marginally trapped surfaces'. The notion of a *trapped surface* was introduced in 1965, by Roger Penrose, to characterize a system that is undergoing gravitational collapse.[11] It may be defined as a compact spacelike two-surface without boundary, such that both systems of future-directed null geodesics that emanate orthogonally from it have positive convergence ρ. A *marginally trapped surface* is defined similarly, but with $\rho \geq 0$. It was discovered by Stephen Hawking that trapped surfaces exist in some expanding cosmological models as well.[12] (These models may be regarded as undergoing gravitational collapse in the reverse time direction.) It is intriguing that a non-collapsing space-time, like Gödel's, should also contain such a structure.

The existence of marginally trapped surfaces is most easily seen if new coordinates (t, r, ϕ, z) are defined,[6] with $-\infty < t < \infty$, $0 \leq r < \infty$,

```
 1 | by the following transformations:
 2 | $$\eqalignno{\exp{(\sqrt2\omega x)} & = \cosh{2r}+\cos\phi\,\sinh{2r}, &(1a)\cr
 3 | \omega y\exp{(\sqrt2\omega x)} & = \sin\phi\,\sinh{2r}, & (1b) \cr
 4 | \tan{\textstyle{1\over2}}(\phi + \omega t - (\sqrt2)t') & = \exp(-2r)
 5 | \tan{\scriptstyle{1\over2}}\phi, & (1c) \cr
 6 | \noalign{\hbox{and}}
 7 | z&=z.&(1d)\cr}$$
 8 | In these coordinates, the metric $g_{ab}$ has components given by
 9 | $$g_{\mu\nu}={2\over\omega^2}
10 | \pmatrix{-1&0&\sqrt2\sinh^2\!r&0\cr
11 | 0&1&0&0\cr
12 | \sqrt2\sinh^2\!r&0&-\sinh^2\!r(\sinh^2r-1)&0\cr
13 | 0&0&0&{\omega^2\over2}\cr}^{\P}\eqno(2a)$$
14 | \vfootnote\P{I.e., $ds^2={2\over{\omega^2}}(-dt^2+dr^2-
15 | \sinh^2\!r(\sinh^2\!r-1)d\phi^2+2\sqrt2\sinh^2\!rd\phi\,dt)+dz^2$.}
16 | and the inverse metric has components
17 | $$g^{\mu\nu}={\omega^2\over2}
18 | \left[\matrix{-(1-\sinh^2\!r)/\cosh^2\!r&0&\sqrt2/\cosh^2\!r&0\cr
19 | 0&1&0&0\cr     \sqrt2/\cosh^2\!r&0&1/\sinh^2\!r\cosh^2\!r&0\cr
20 | 0&0&0&2/\omega^2}\right].\eqno(2b)$$
21 | Then, the only nonzero
22 | $${\Gamma}^{\lambda}_{\phantom{a}\mu\nu}=\textstyle{1\over2}g^{\lambda
23 | \rho}\{\partial_{\nu}g_{\rho\mu}+\partial_{\mu}g_{\rho\nu}-
24 | \partial_{\rho}g_{\mu\nu}\}$$ are
25 | $$\eqalign{\Gamma^t_{tr}&=2\tanh r,\cr
26 | \Gamma^r_{t\phi}&=\sqrt2\sinh r\cosh r,\cr
27 | \Gamma^{\phi}_{tr}&={\sqrt2\over\sinh r\cosh r},\cr}
28 | \qquad\eqalign{\Gamma^t_{r\phi}&=\sqrt2\tanh r\sinh^2\!r,\cr
29 | \Gamma^r_{\phi\phi}&=\sinh r\cosh r(2\sinh^2\!r-1),\cr
30 | \Gamma^{\phi}_{r\phi}&=2\tanh r.\cr}$$
31 | \smallskip \noindent
32 | From these equations, it is easy to check that the closed curve given by
33 | $$t=\hbox{constant}, \quad r=\log(1+\sqrt2), \quad \phi=\phi(p) \quad
34 | {\rm and} \quad z={\rm constant}\eqno(3)$$
```

NOTES

COMMENT

There is a general discussion of equation alignments and of \eqalignno on the previous page.

2, 3, 4, etc.: $\cosh$, $\sinh$, etc., are used to set the corresponding functions in roman type; $\,$ is used to adjust spacing.

4–5: Note how \textstyle and \scriptstyle affect the size of the fractions.

6: \noalign inserts something nonaligned—here, an \hbox containing the word 'and'—into an alignment.

9–13: μ and ν give μ and ν. $\pmatrix$ creates a matrix with large parentheses. The structure of the command is similar to that of equation alignments: entries are separated by &, lines ended by \cr. Most of the other commands on these lines have been discussed earlier. $\!$ is used to make fine spacing adjustments. Towards the end of line 13, the command \P gives ¶, which is then placed as an exponent. You will see why just below. The last command, \eqno, allows you to specify an equation number.

14: \vfootnote gives you a sort of floating footnote, i.e., one not tied to any specific part of the main document. The footnote symbol chosen here is also a ¶, so that it has the effect of being a footnote to the matrix.

18–20: A matrix with square brackets is obtained by typing \matrix and specifying square brackets before and after. \left and \right make the brackets grow to the size of the display. The other commands here are either ones to produce names of functions in roman typeface, or spacing commands, or all Greek.

22: Γ gives Γ. \phantom is an interesting command: it leaves the exact space that would have been occupied by the material in braces, but doesn't print the material. Here we have a phantom subscript the size of the letter 'a', then two visible subscripts. This positions subscripts where they were needed. Compare the first occurrence of Γ with the ones in the display below. \textstyle produces smaller fractions than would normally occur in a display.

25–30: \eqalign is another alignment command. It does not permit the numbering of individual equations, nor does it allow the alignment to continue onto a second page. But it allows multiple alignments in the same display. Each alignment is created separately using & and \cr in the usual way, then put between the same $$ pair as the others. Here, two sets of aligned equations are placed side-by-side, separated by a \qquad's worth of horizontal space. Other commands on these lines were explained earlier.

Example V **41**

$0 \leq \phi \leq 2\pi$, and $-\infty < z < \infty$, by the following transformations:

$$\exp\left(\sqrt{2}\omega x\right) = \cosh 2r + \cos\phi \sinh 2r, \qquad (1a)$$

$$\omega y \exp\left(\sqrt{2}\omega x\right) = \sin\phi \sinh 2r, \qquad (1b)$$

$$\tan\tfrac{1}{2}(\phi + \omega t - (\sqrt{2})t') = \exp(-2r)\tan\tfrac{1}{2}\phi, \qquad (1c)$$

and

$$z = z. \qquad (1d)$$

In these coordinates, the metric g_{ab} has components given by

$$g_{\mu\nu} = \frac{2}{\omega^2}\begin{pmatrix} -1 & 0 & \sqrt{2}\sinh^2 r & 0 \\ 0 & 1 & 0 & 0 \\ \sqrt{2}\sinh^2 r & 0 & -\sinh^2 r(\sinh^2 r - 1) & 0 \\ 0 & 0 & 0 & \frac{\omega^2}{2} \end{pmatrix}^{\P} \qquad (2a)$$

and the inverse metric has components

$$g^{\mu\nu} = \frac{\omega^2}{2}\begin{bmatrix} -(1 - \sinh^2 r)/\cosh^2 r & 0 & \sqrt{2}/\cosh^2 r & 0 \\ 0 & 1 & 0 & 0 \\ \sqrt{2}/\cosh^2 r & 0 & 1/\sinh^2 r \cosh^2 r & 0 \\ 0 & 0 & 0 & 2/\omega^2 \end{bmatrix}. \qquad (2b)$$

Then, the only nonzero

$$\Gamma^\lambda{}_{\mu\nu} = \tfrac{1}{2}g^{\lambda\rho}\{\partial_\nu g_{\rho\mu} + \partial_\mu g_{\rho\nu} - \partial_\rho g_{\mu\nu}\}$$

are

$$\Gamma^t_{tr} = 2\tanh r, \qquad\qquad \Gamma^t_{r\phi} = \sqrt{2}\tanh r \sinh^2 r,$$

$$\Gamma^r_{t\phi} = \sqrt{2}\sinh r \cosh r, \qquad \Gamma^r_{\phi\phi} = \sinh r \cosh r(2\sinh^2 r - 1),$$

$$\Gamma^\phi_{tr} = \frac{\sqrt{2}}{\sinh r \cosh r}, \qquad\qquad \Gamma^\phi_{r\phi} = 2\tanh r.$$

From these equations, it is easy to check that the closed curve given by

$$t = \text{constant}, \quad r = \log(1 + \sqrt{2}), \quad \phi = \phi(p) \quad \text{and} \quad z = \text{constant} \qquad (3)$$

$\P$ I.e., $ds^2 = \frac{2}{\omega^2}(-dt^2 + dr^2 - \sinh^2 r(\sinh^2 r - 1)d\phi^2 + 2\sqrt{2}\sinh^2 r\, d\phi\, dt) + dz^2$.

```
1   is a nongeodesic null curve whose acceleration $a^b$ ($=N^c\nabla\!_cN^b$,
2   where $N^b=({\partial\>\over\partial p})^b$ and $\nabla\!_c$ is the
3   covariant derivative) has components given by\hfil\break
4   \centerline{$(0,\,\sinh r\cosh r\,(2\sinh^2\!r-1)\dot\phi^2,\,0,\,0)$,}
5   where '$\dot{\;}$' refers to a derivative with respect to $p$.
6   In the region $r < \log(1+\sqrt2)$, the two-surfaces given by $t$ = constant,
7   $r$ = constant, will be spacelike. These surfaces may be compactified by
8   identifying, say, $z=0$ with $z=1$. The resulting two-surfaces will have
9   topology $S^1\times S^1$. The components of the tangents to the two systems
10  of null geodesics that emanate orthogonally from these surfaces may be
11  written as
12  $$\eqalign{N^t_{\pm}&={1-\sinh^2\!r\over\cosh^2\!r},\cr
13  N^r_{\pm}&=\pm{(1-\sinh^2\!r)^{1/2}\over\cosh^2\!r},\cr
14  N^{\phi}_{\pm}&={-\sqrt2\over\cosh^2\!r} \quad {\rm and}\cr
15  N^z_{\pm}&=0.\cr}\eqno(4)$$
16  And the convergence of these two systems may be computed to be
17  $$\eqalignno{\rho_{\pm}\equiv -\nabla\!_aN^a_{\pm}&={-1\over\sqrt{-g}}
18  {\partial(\sqrt{-g}N^{\mu}_{\pm})\over \partial x^\mu}\cr
19  &=\mp\left[{2\sinh^2\!r-1\over\sinh r\sqrt{1-\sinh^2\!r}}\right],\cr}$$
20  where $x^\mu$ represents the coordinates. Then, for $r$ given by
21  $\sinh^2\!r=1/2$, both systems have zero convergence. This is the marginally
22  trapped surface.
23  \vfil\eject
```

NOTES

COMMENT

$ signs in the notes indicate which commands work only in the mathematics mode.

1–2: ∇ gives ∇; ∂ gives ∂; \! fine-tunes spacing: it gives a 'negative thin space', i.e., it moves material back slightly.

4: There are several fine-spacing commands here. Explicit spaces are often needed just before parentheses, since TeX can interpret such combinations as functions and therefore move things together slightly.

4, 5: $\dot$ places a dot above whatever follows next.

12–15: An entire set of equations that are aligned by \eqalign can be numbered by \eqno, even if the individual equations cannot. If you need individual numbers desperately, you will have to try tricks (like introducing a column of numbers as a separate alignment and adjusting spacing to make them line up correctly with the equations).

17–19: ρ gives ρ, $\pm$ gives $\pm$, $\equiv$ gives $\equiv$, ∇ gives ∇, ∂ gives ∂, μ gives μ, $\mp$ gives $\mp$ and $\sinh$ gives 'sinh'. The \left, \right method for square matrix brackets works with any displayed formula, as here. You can also use parentheses instead, or other 'delimiters'; see **mathematics: delimiters** in the Appendix.

PRELIMINARY NOTES ON TABLES

Simple tables are not hard to do in TeX, but complicated ones, especially with rules, can get messy. The tables shown on the next few pages will illustrate all of the basic principles, but building tables from scratch each time in this way is not the recommended procedure, especially if you use tables frequently. Instead, you should use specially defined commands that will take away much of the drudgery. The entry **tables** in the Appendix shows you a sample table command; you can copy that and use it if you wish. Also, there are now several 'table-making' packages available from groups that supply TeX-related products that will allow you to make fancy tables without too much labor.

\halign is the command that underlies alignments in TeX. Tables may be made by directly using it, or by using another command built on it called \settabs. \halign requires you to enter a 'preamble', a sort of sample line that sets the appearance of the rest of the table. \settabs requires instead either an explicit specification of the number of columns (in which case it gives columns of equal width), or a sample line whose entries' individual widths represent the desired width of each column.

All these approaches are illustrated on the next few pages.

Example V **43**

is a nongeodesic null curve whose acceleration a^b ($= N^c \nabla_c N^b$, where $N^b = (\frac{\partial}{\partial p})^b$ and ∇_c is the covariant derivative) has components given by

$$(0, \sinh r \cosh r \, (2 \sinh^2 r - 1) \dot{\phi}^2, 0, 0),$$

where "˙" refers to a derivative with respect to p. In the region $r < \log(1+\sqrt{2})$, the two-surfaces given by $t = $ constant, $r = $ constant, will be spacelike. These surfaces may be compactified by identifying, say, $z = 0$ with $z = 1$. The resulting two-surfaces will have topology $S^1 \times S^1$. The components of the tangents to the two systems of null geodesics that emanate orthogonally from these surfaces may be written as

$$
\begin{aligned}
N^t_\pm &= \frac{1 - \sinh^2 r}{\cosh^2 r}, \\
N^r_\pm &= \pm \frac{(1 - \sinh^2 r)^{1/2}}{\cosh^2 r}, \\
N^\phi_\pm &= \frac{-\sqrt{2}}{\cosh^2 r} \quad \text{and} \\
N^z_\pm &= 0.
\end{aligned}
\tag{4}
$$

And the convergence of these two systems may be computed to be

$$
\begin{aligned}
\rho_\pm \equiv -\nabla_a N^a_\pm &= \frac{-1}{\sqrt{-g}} \frac{\partial(\sqrt{-g} N^\mu_\pm)}{\partial x^\mu} \\
&= \mp \left[\frac{2 \sinh^2 r - 1}{\sinh r \sqrt{1 - \sinh^2 r}} \right],
\end{aligned}
$$

where x^μ represents the coordinates. Then, for r given by $\sinh^2 r = 1/2$, both systems have zero convergence. This is the marginally trapped surface.

```
 1  \centerline{\bf VI. SUNIL GAVASKAR: A STATISTICAL TRIBUTE%
 2  \footnote\ddag{\rm This section contains unexplained references to cricket.
 3  Those who follow the game will know what they mean; those who do not are
 4  unlikely to care. The statistics are correct up to 1987.}}
 5  \centerline{\sl Tables.}
 6  \headline{\hfil\it Example VI\newpageno} %'\newpageno' IS NOT STANDARD.
 7  \bigskip
 8  \noindent Towards the end of 1983, the Indian batsman Sunil Gavaskar scored
 9  his 8,115$^{\rm th}$ Test run to become the highest scorer in the history of
10  international cricket. He was averaging at the time a little over 50 runs
11  for every completed inning. Before the year was over he had also made his
12  30$^{th}$ Test century, breaking Bradman's record of 29 set in 1948.
13
14  Gavaskar was then 34. He had been in international cricket for 13 years, and
15  he had played 99 times for India in this period. He had consistently opened
16  the batting and had faced some of the fastest bowlers in the history of the
17  game. The West Indian pace attack, in particular, had been exceptionally
18  fierce over most of the period that he had played. And against them his
19  record had been particularly good:
20  \bigskip
21  \vbox{\baselineskip=16 true pt\settabs7\columns
22  \+&&&\hfil{\bf Table 1}&\cr
23  \+&&\it Tests&\it Runs&\it Avg.&\it 100s\cr
24  \+&&\sl 27&\sl 2749&\sl 65.45&\sl 13\cr}
25  \bigskip
26  \noindent After this arduous and highly successful career, it seemed reasonable
27  to suppose that he would want to retire.
28
29  For a while, it did look as though he had lost some of his determination. A
30  series of low scores in 1984-85 followed his successes of 1983:
31  \bigskip
32  \vbox{\baselineskip=15pt
33  \halign{\hfil\sl#&\quad\hfil\it#\hfil&\quad#\hfil\cr
34  \multispan3\hfil\bf Table 2\hfil\cr
35  Country&Year&Scores:\cr Pakistan&1984&48, 37, 35.\cr
36  England&1984-85&27, 5, 1, 65, 13, 17, 3, 9.\cr}}
```

NOTES

COMMENT

See the notes on the previous page for a preliminary discussion of tables.

1: The % prevents the single space that TeX normally automatically places at the end of an input line.

2: \footnote is set from within \centerline here, without a problem.

9, 12: Since superscripts are part of the mathematics mode, anything that uses them will appear in math italics. But you can explicitly ask for another typeface. See the 'th' superscript on these two lines.

21–24: \vbox makes sure that the material in the box (i.e., whatever follows immediately after, enclosed in braces) is not split over two pages. If you wish, you can set separate specifications within the box, as with \baselineskip here; they will not leak out and affect text outside. Seven columns are specified here for \settabs, with the first two and last one left empty. This is done to give narrower columns. (The method creates columns of equal width that occupy the whole available horizontal space). It also has the pleasant side-effect here of roughly centering the table. Each row in this method must begin with a \+ and end with \cr. As with all other alignments in TeX, & takes you from column to column. Once a \cr is seen, all remaining columns on that line are automatically left blank. Entries are set flush left by default. The title at the top is really column 4, set flush right by \hfil.

33–36: The first line in \halign is the 'preamble'. You can specify typeface and position as well as text that is to be repeated throughout some column. Here, the first column will be set flush right and in slanted type, the second centered and in italics, the third flush left in the default roman typeface. The \quad commands effectively leave space between columns, for they otherwise sit touching. The width of columns here is variable, being determined for each column by the widest entry in it.

34: \multispan spans the number of columns specified, allowing you flexibility for long entries or for setting titles. Typeface commands given in entries will override those in the preamble and stronger spacing commands (i.e., \hfill rather than \hfil) will override the spacing specified there.

Example VI **45**

VI. SUNIL GAVASKAR: A STATISTICAL TRIBUTE‡

Tables.

Towards the end of 1983, the Indian batsman Sunil Gavaskar scored his 8,115[th] Test run to become the highest scorer in the history of international cricket. He was averaging at the time a little over 50 runs for every completed inning. Before the year was over he had also made his 30th Test century, breaking Bradman's record of 29 set in 1948.

Gavaskar was then 34. He had been in international cricket for 13 years, and he had played 99 times for India in this period. He had consistently opened the batting and had faced some of the fastest bowlers in the history of the game. The West Indian pace attack, in particular, had been exceptionally fierce over most of the period that he had played. And against them his record had been particularly good:

Table 1

Tests	*Runs*	*Avg.*	*100s*
27	2749	65.45	13

After this arduous and highly successful career, it seemed reasonable to suppose that he would want to retire.

For a while, it did look as though he had lost some of his determination. A series of low scores in 1984-85 followed his successes of 1983:

Table 2

Country	*Year*	Scores:
Pakistan	*1984*	48, 37, 35.
England	*1984-85*	27, 5, 1, 65, 13, 17, 3, 9.

---

‡ This section contains unexplained references to cricket. Those who follow the game will know what they mean; those who do not are unlikely to care. The statistics are correct up to 1987.

```
 1 | \bigskip  \noindent
 2 | In seven Test matches he had made 260 runs at an average of 23.64. In late 1985,
 3 | he asked to be dropped in the batting order against Sri Lanka and made 51, 0,
 4 | 52, 19, 49 and 15 not out. It seemed as if his career must surely be over.
 5 |
 6 | But Gavaskar had gone through lean periods before, and he had always been able
 7 | to pull himself out. He did so once more. Returning as opener against Australia
 8 | in 1985-86, he made 166 not out, 6, 8, and 172. He subsequently scored two
 9 | more centuries, continued to maintain an overall average of 50 and, in early
10 | 1987, he became the first player to cross 10,000 Test runs.
11 |
12 | Though it is clear that these are exceptional achievements, their full magnitude
13 | may not immediately be apparent. By 1971, the year Gavaskar started playing
14 | Test cricket, over 15 international players (from England, Australia and the
15 | West Indies) had accumulated career run aggregates of 4,500 or more, whereas
16 | only 3 Indian batsmen (Umrigar, Manjrekar and Borde) had scored more than 3,000.
17 | Umrigar, at the top of the Indian list, had a total run aggregate that was
18 | almost exactly half the international record (see Table~3). He was also the only
19 | Indian batsman who had made more than 10 centuries. No Indian batsman who had
20 | played for any real length of time had averaged over 50.
21 | \midinsert
22 |    The insert ended up at the top of the next page, so the input is there.
23 | \endinsert
24 | In such circumstances, not much was seriously expected from Indian batsmen.
25 | I went to the same high school that Gavaskar did (though I was many years his
26 | junior and did not know him, except by his reputation as a successful member
27 | of the Indian schoolboy's team), and it would have been considered the purest
28 | fantasy there had anyone suggested that an Indian batsman would one day
29 | score as many runs as Hammond or as many centuries as Bradman. It is against
30 | a background of low expectations, and of satisfaction with middle-level
31 | success, that Gavaskar has played out most of his~career.
32 | \vfil\eject
```

NOTES

1: The \bigskip here was part of the main file between the bottom of the table (on the previous page) and the text just after. It so happened that TeX broke the page there. When this happens, no extra space is left at the top of the new page.

16: No relation.

21–23: \midinsert tries to place material exactly where it finds it. Failing that, as here, it puts it at the top of the next page. Another type of insertion, \topinsert, always puts material at the top of the first available page. For all these inserts, the end of the material to be inserted is marked by \endinsert.

31: The tie, ~, is used to prevent an isolated word on the last line. See pages 2, 22 and 26.

GENERAL REMARKS ON RULED TABLES

TeX-wise, this has been an unremarkable page. That is good, for the one just after will seem to you very un-unremarkable—especially if you are new to TeX.

However, the table there isn't different in principle from the second table on the previous page. The big difference is the presence of 'rules', i.e., drawn lines. Since TeX normally inserts space between lines of text, that mechanism has to be switched off using the command \offinterlineskip. To prevent lines of text from touching, a \strut is introduced on each line. This is an invisible symbol of zero width but nonzero height and depth, and it serves to hold apart the lines by a fixed distance. The vertical rules in the table are built into the preamble as table entries; horizontal rules (as well as any other material that must ignore the column alignment) are put into a \noalign. A final command that is useful in ruled tables, as well as others, is \omit. This, at the start of any given entry, will override the preamble specifications for that entry, allowing you to specify something else. It has clear uses if you need to make exceptions to some general pattern.

Example VI   **47**

In seven Test matches he had made 260 runs at an average of 23.64. In late 1985, he asked to be dropped in the batting order against Sri Lanka and made 51, 0, 52, 19, 49 and 15 not out. It seemed as if his career must surely be over.

But Gavaskar had gone through lean periods before, and he had always been able to pull himself out. He did so once more. Returning as opener against Australia in 1985-86, he made 166 not out, 6, 8, and 172. He subsequently scored two more centuries, continued to maintain an overall average of 50 and, in early 1987, he became the first player to cross 10,000 Test runs.

Though it is clear that these are exceptional achievements, their full magnitude may not immediately be apparent. By 1971, the year Gavaskar started playing Test cricket, over 15 international players (from England, Australia and the West Indies) had accumulated career run aggregates of 4,500 or more, whereas only 3 Indian batsmen (Umrigar, Manjrekar and Borde) had scored more than 3,000. Umrigar, at the top of the Indian list, had a total run aggregate that was almost exactly half the international record (see Table 3). He was also the only Indian batsman who had made more than 10 centuries. No Indian batsman who had played for any real length of time had averaged over 50.

In such circumstances, not much was seriously expected from Indian batsmen. I went to the same high school that Gavaskar did (though I was many years his junior and did not know him, except by his reputation as a successful member of the Indian schoolboy's team), and it would have been considered the purest fantasy there had anyone suggested that an Indian batsman would one day score as many runs as Hammond or as many centuries as Bradman. It is against a background of low expectations, and of satisfaction with middle-level success, that Gavaskar has played out most of his career.

```
1  \midinsert
2  $$\vbox{\offinterlineskip
3  \halign{&\vrule#&\strut\ #\ \cr
4  \multispan{13}\hfil\bf Table 3\hfil\cr
5  \noalign{\medskip}
6  \noalign{\hrule}
7  height3pt&\omit&&\omit&&\omit&&\omit&&\omit&&\omit&\cr
8  &\hfil\bf Comment\hfil&&\hfil\bf Player\hfil&&\hfil\bf T\hfil&&
9  \hfil\bf R\hfil&&\hfil\bf Avg.\hfil&&\hfil\bf 100s\hfil&\cr
10 height3pt&\omit&&\omit&&\omit&&\omit&&\omit&&\omit&\cr
11 \noalign{\hrule}
12 height3pt&\omit&&\omit&&\omit&&\omit&&\omit&&\omit&\cr
13 &\it Highest\hfil&&{}&&{}&&{}&&{}&&{}&\cr
14 &\it scorer till 1970\hfil&&W.R. Hammond (Eng.)\hfil&&
15 \hfil85&&7249&&58.45&&22&\cr
16 &\it Highest\hfil&&{}&&{}&&{}&&{}&&{}&\cr
17 &\it Indian scorer till 1970\hfil&&P.R. Umrigar\hfil&&
18 \hfil59&&3631&&42.22&&12&\cr
19 height3pt&\omit&&\omit&&\omit&&\omit&&\omit&&\omit&\cr
20 \noalign{\hrule}
21 height3pt&\omit&&\omit&&\omit&&\omit&&\omit&&\omit&\cr
22 &\it Second highest\hfil&&{}&&{}&&{}&&{}&&{}&\cr
23 &\it scorer till 1987\hfil&&G. Boycott (Eng.)\hfil&&
24 \hfil108&&8114&&47.22&&22&\cr
25 &\it Second highest\hfil&&{}&&{}&&{}&&{}&&{}&\cr
26 &\it Indian scorer till 1987\hfil&&G.R. Viswanath\hfil&&
27 \hfil91&&6080&&41.93&&14&\cr
28 height3pt&\omit&&\omit&&\omit&&\omit&&\omit&&\omit&\cr
29 \noalign{\hrule}\noalign{\medskip}
30 \multispan3\hfil Sources:\ &\multispan{10}--{\it Playfair Cricket
31 Annual,}\hfil\cr\noalign{\smallskip}
32 \multispan3\hfil&\multispan{10}\ {Queen Anne Press (1986).}\hfil\cr
33 \noalign{\smallskip}
34 \multispan3\hfil&\multispan{10}--{\it The Encyclopaedia of Indian
35 Cricket,}\hfil\cr\noalign{\smallskip}
36 \multispan3\hfil&\multispan{10}\ {L.N. Mathur, Rajhans Prakashan
37 (1965).}\hfil\cr}}$$
38 \endinsert
```

NOTES

COMMENT

Read the general comments on the previous pages, if you are new to tables. This page only shows the input for the table on the right, not the text.

1: Neither the **$$** nor the **\vbox** are crucial to the success of this table, but they are useful. The **$$** switches on the mathematics display mode and centers material (the closing pair occurs on line 37). If such a display mechanism is used the **\vbox** is necessary, for it will shield the inside of the table from the effects of the mathematics mode. It will also prevent material from being split over two pages.

3: The preamble in this **\halign** is 'open ended': it starts with an **&**, which leads the program to read it over and over again as the model for all table entries. In general, a line like **A&& B& C\cr** in a preamble will be read by TeX as **A& B& C& B& C& B**.... In such cases, the number of columns is decided by the longest line in the table. The table entries here will alternate between fixed ones containing just a vertical ruled line, a **\vrule**, and ones where information is put into the slots provided by the **#**. The latter entries are all preceded by a **\strut**.

4: **\multispan** spans the number of columns specified, here all 13 (the vertical rules are regarded as columns too). The **\hfil** commands on either side will center the title.

5, 6, etc.: **\noalign** allows you to introduce material that ignores the table alignment.

7, etc.: The **\omit** on these formidable-looking lines will make it possible to ignore preamble specifications, like **\strut**. Here, all these lines do is introduce 3pt of extra space above and below every horizontal line.

13, 16, 22, 25: These lines place an entry in the first non-rule column, and nothing in the other columns.

30, 34, etc.: These lines have two entries: the first spans 3 columns, the second 10. So, though the lines are outside the ruled table, they are still part of the overall alignment.

Example VI **49**

Table 3

Comment	Player	T	R	Avg.	100s
Highest scorer till 1970	W.R. Hammond (Eng.)	85	7249	58.45	22
Highest Indian scorer till 1970	P.R. Umrigar	59	3631	42.22	12
Second highest scorer till 1987	G. Boycott (Eng.)	108	8114	47.22	22
Second highest Indian scorer till 1987	G.R. Viswanath	91	6080	41.93	14

Sources: –*Playfair Cricket Annual,*
Queen Anne Press (1986).
–*The Encyclopaedia of Indian Cricket,*
L.N. Mathur, Rajhans Prakashan (1965).

Seen against this background, the extent of Gavaskar's achievement is all the more remarkable. Up to mid-1987, seven players had scored more than 7,000 runs in Test cricket. Apart from the two names in Table 3, they were Greg Chappell (7110) of Australia, Cowdrey (7624) of England and Lloyd (7515) and Sobers (8032) of the West Indies. And then, after Boycott, there was the 2,000-run jump to Gavaskar. Eight batsmen had made between 20 and 25 centuries, and then came Sobers (26), Bradman (29) of Australia and Gavaskar (34).

Partly, of course, this success was due to the steadily rising standards in Indian cricket, and the steadily improving overall performances, since 1970. But that is not the complete story. In some ways, the better standards and the resulting higher expectations existed *because* of the goals that Gavaskar had set. Also, a glance at the last entry in Table 3 shows that the second most successful Indian batsman was a considerable distance behind. This gap between Gavaskar and the other Indian batsmen was dramatically seen

```
 1  Seen against this background, the extent of Gavaskar's achievement is all the
 2  more remarkable. Up to mid-1987, seven players had scored more than 7,000 runs
 3  in Test cricket. Apart from the two names in Table~3, they were Greg Chappell
 4  (7110) of Australia, Cowdrey (7624) of England and Lloyd (7515) and Sobers
 5  (8032) of the West Indies. And then, after Boycott, there was the 2,000-run
 6  jump to Gavaskar. Eight batsmen had made between 20 and 25 centuries, and then
 7  came Sobers (26), Bradman (29) of Australia and Gavaskar~(34).
 8
 9  Partly, of course, this success was due to the steadily rising standards in
10  Indian cricket, and the steadily improving overall performances, since 1970.
11  But that is not the complete story. In some ways, the better standards and
12  the resulting higher expectations existed {\it because\/} of the goals that
13  Gavaskar had set. Also, a glance at the last entry in Table~3 shows that the
14  second most successful Indian batsman was a considerable distance behind.
15  This gap between Gavaskar and the other Indian batsmen was dramatically
16  seen in the last Test match that he played, against Pakistan in Bangalore in
17  1987. Set to make 221 to win on a difficult wicket, India lost by 16 runs.
18  Their second inning scorecard, shown in Table~4, speaks for itself.\bigskip
19  \centerline{\bf Table 4}
20  \nobreak\medskip
21  \noindent\hfil \vbox{\baselineskip=13.5pt
22  \settabs\+Extras (22b, 51b)\quad&c Yousseff b Tauseef\quad&ABC&\cr % SAMPLE
23  \+S. Gavaskar        &c Rizwan b Qasim      &\hfill       96&\cr
24  \+K. Srikkanth       &lbw b Akram           &\hfill        6&\cr
25  \+M. Amarnath        &c Youssef b Akram     &\hfill        0&\cr
26  \+D. Vengsarkar      &b Tauseef             &\hfill       19&\cr
27  \+K. More            &lbw b Tauseef         &\hfill        3&\cr
28  \+M. Azharuddin      &c and b Qasim         &\hfill       26&\cr
29  \+R. Shastri         &c and b Qasim         &\hfill        4&\cr
30  \+Kapil Dev          &b Qasim               &\hfill        2&\cr
31  \+R. Binny           &c Youssef b Tauseef&\hfill          15&\cr
32  \+S. Yadav           &b Tauseef             &\hfill        4&\cr
33  \+M. Singh           &not out               &\hfill        2&\cr
34  \+Extras (22b, 51b)&                        &\hfill       27&\cr
35  \+\bf Total          &                 &\bf\hfill 204&\cr}
36  \vfil\eject
```

NOTES

The paragraphs at the top of the input were actually printed on the preceding page. The input is shown here for reasons of space. The table on this page shows you one way to take advantage of the way TeX ignores most spaces in the input. Laying the table out in this way can help you keep track of what entry goes where.

19: The title for this table is placed outside the `\vbox` containing the alignment.

20: `\nobreak\medskip` discourages a page break at the `\medskip` between the title and the table.

21: Yet another way to center material is to place `\noindent\hfil` before it. This only works if done right at the start of a paragraph, and if the paragraph ends just after the material. (The normal paragraph-ending process in TeX effectively has a built-in `\hfil` that balances the one you explicitly introduce.)

22–35: This is another way to make a table with `\settabs`. Instead of stating the number of columns, a sample line is typed at the start, with the width of each sample entry greater than the widest actual entry in that column. The table will then set columns to these widths. Otherwise, the structure is like that of previously discussed alignments, with `&` as a 'tab' marker and `\cr` ending lines.

COMMENT

By default, alignments in Plain TeX are arranged so that columns touch. The gap between columns is determined by a 'parameter' called `\tabskip`. The normal value for it in Plain TeX is `0pt`, but it can be reset if you want to alter the appearance of tables made with `\halign`. (Unless you want to change TeX's default settings for all such tables, you should make sure that new settings are placed within braces so as to confine their effects to that group.)

Further, by specifying a variable size for `\tabskip`, say, '`\tabskip=20pt plus 5pt minus 5pt`', you can make tables constructed with `\halign` fill a given horizontal space. If, for example, the space is 4 inches wide, you would type '`\halign to 4in{`' and then continue as before. Of course, the new setting for `\tabskip` must have enough stretchability (the number after `plus`) to properly fill the necessary space.

Example VI   **51**

in the last Test match that he played, against Pakistan in Bangalore in 1987. Set to make 221 to win on a difficult wicket, India lost by 16 runs. Their second inning scorecard, shown in Table 4, speaks for itself.

Table 4

S. Gavaskar	c Rizwan b Qasim	96
K. Srikkanth	lbw b Akram	6
M. Amarnath	c Youssef b Akram	0
D. Vengsarkar	b Tauseef	19
K. More	lbw b Tauseef	3
M. Azharuddin	c and b Qasim	26
R. Shastri	c and b Qasim	4
Kapil Dev	b Qasim	2
R. Binny	c Youssef b Tauseef	15
S. Yadav	b Tauseef	4
M. Singh	not out	2
Extras (22b, 5lb)		27
Total		**204**

```
1  \centerline{\bf VII. ON ZEROS OF SOLUTIONS OF $\ddot x + F(t)x = 0$}
2  \centerline{\sl Derivatives and integrals; aligning equations.}
3  \headline{\hfil\it Example VII\newpageno}%'\newpageno' IS NOT STANDARD.
4  \bigskip
5  \noindent The equation $${d^2\!x\over dt^2} + F(t)x = 0 \leqno{\rm(i)}$$
6  describes the behavior of many different systems. If $F={\rm constant}>0$,
7  it describes an ordinary harmonic oscillator. It also describes the motion
8  of a charged particle in an axially symmetric electromagnetic field. (Here,
9  $F$ may not be constant, or even positive.$^{13}$) In both situations we are
10 interested in oscillatory solutions, i.e., solutions where $x$ passes
11 repeatedly through~0. Another equation that is of this type is the geodesic
12 focusing equation for causal geodesics in space-time. This may be seen by
13 introducing a new variable $y=(\dot x/x)$.$^{14}$ Then,
14 $$\dot y\equiv {dy\over dt}=-y^2-F(t). \leqno{\rm(ii)}$$
15 This equation has the form of the geodesic focusing equation.$^{14,15}$ The
16 solutions of interest here (for a number of applications) are ones where there
17 exist $t_1$ and $t_2$, with $t_1 < t_2$, such that $y\rightarrow\infty$ as
18 $t\rightarrow t^+_1$ and $y\rightarrow -\infty$ as $t\rightarrow t^-_2$
19 (or, equivalently, solutions of Equation~(i) with two zeros). The following
20 result establishes a condition for such a solution to exist.$^{15}$
21
22 \proclaim Theorem. Let $F(t)$ be continuous. Suppose that
23 \item{\rm a)} there is some $t_0$ such that $F(t_0)\neq 0$, and
24 \item{\rm b)} there is some $b>0$ such that, for any $t_1<t_0$ and
25 $t_2>t_0$, there are closed intervals $I_1<t_1$ (i.e., $\sup I_1<t_1$)
26 and $I_2>t_2$ (i.e., $\inf I_2>t_2$) of length $\geq b$ with
27 $$ \int\limits_t^{t_0}\!F(t')\,dt'\geq0\qquad\forall\>t\in I_1$$ and
```

NOTES

$ signs in the notes indicate which commands work only in the mathematics mode.

1: \ddot is a math accent: $\ddot x$ gives $\ddot x$.

5: \! is used to fine-tune spacing: it brings the x in a little. \leqno puts equation numbers on the left. Both are mathematics mode commands. \rm asks for the numbers to appear in roman type.

13–14: \dot is another math accent: $\dot x$ gives $\dot x$. $\equiv$ gives $\equiv$.

17: $\rightarrow$ gives $\rightarrow$; ∞ gives ∞.

22: \proclaim is an example of a 'high level' command, with most primitive operations subsumed into its definition. On seeing the command, TeX reads ahead till the first period. Everything up to that period is set in boldface (the assumption being that this is the theorem title). It then sets everything beyond that (till the end of the paragraph) in slanted type. Definitions like these make it possible for you to enjoy the full benefits of the power of TeX, without cluttering your file with large numbers of explicit typesetting commands. *That should be your ultimate goal.*

23: \rm is used here and in the line below to force roman type on the \item labels. $\neq$ gives $\neq$.

25: $\sup$ gives 'sup'.

26: $\inf$ gives 'inf' and $\geq$ gives $\geq$.

27: $\int$ gives $\int$. \limits place the integration limits above and below the integral sign. The next page will show you their normal positions. Conversely, if there is some operator that places 'superscripts' and 'subscripts' directly above and below, \nolimits will bring them down, to the side. See mathematics: operations in the Appendix.

As for the other commands on this line, $\!$ and $\,$ fine-tune spacing and $\forall$ gives $\forall$.

Example VII   **53**

VII. ON ZEROS OF SOLUTIONS OF $\ddot{x} + F(t)x = 0$

Derivatives and integrals; aligning equations.

The equation

(i)
$$\frac{d^2x}{dt^2} + F(t)x = 0$$

describes the behavior of many different systems. If $F = $ constant > 0, it describes an ordinary harmonic oscillator. It also describes the motion of a charged particle in an axially symmetric electromagnetic field. (Here, F may not be constant, or even positive.[13]) In both situations we are interested in oscillatory solutions, i.e., solutions where x passes repeatedly through 0. Another equation that is of this type is the geodesic focusing equation for causal geodesics in space-time. This may be seen by introducing a new variable $y = (\dot{x}/x)$.[14] Then,

(ii)
$$\dot{y} \equiv \frac{dy}{dt} = -y^2 - F(t).$$

This equation has the form of the geodesic focusing equation.[14,15] The solutions of interest here (for a number of applications) are ones where there exist t_1 and t_2, with $t_1 < t_2$, such that $y \to \infty$ as $t \to t_1^+$ and $y \to -\infty$ as $t \to t_2^-$ (or, equivalently, solutions of Equation (i) with two zeros). The following result establishes a condition for such a solution to exist.[15]

Theorem. *Let $F(t)$ be continuous. Suppose that*

a) *there is some t_0 such that $F(t_0) \neq 0$, and*

b) *there is some $b > 0$ such that, for any $t_1 < t_0$ and $t_2 > t_0$, there are closed intervals $I_1 < t_1$ (i.e., $\sup I_1 < t_1$) and $I_2 > t_2$ (i.e., $\inf I_2 > t_2$) of length $\geq b$ with*

$$\int_t^{t_0} F(t')\, dt' \geq 0 \qquad \forall\, t \in I_1$$

```
 1 │   $$ \int\limits_{t_0}^t\!F(t')\,dt'\geq0\qquad\forall\>t\in I_2.$$
 2 │ \smallskip
 3 │ Then, there is a solution of Equation~(i) with two zeros.
 4 │
 5 │ \noindent{\bf Proof:} We will work with Equation~(ii) instead of with (i)
 6 │ directly. Since $F(t_0)\ne0$, there will be an interval $[t_1\,,t_2]$ containing
 7 │ $t_0$ such that $F(t)\ne0$ on $[t_1\,,t_2]$. Consider a solution of
 8 │ Equation~(ii) with $y(t_0)=0$. We will have
 9 │ $$\delta=\min\Bigg\{\int_{t_1}^{t_0}y^2dt, \;\int_{t_0}^{t_2}y^2dt\Bigg\}>0$$
10 │ for this solution.\hfil\break
11 │ \indent We first show that $y(t)\rightarrow-\infty$ at some $t>t_0$.
12 │ It will follow, in an identical manner, that $y(t)\rightarrow\infty$ at some
13 │ $t<t_0$.\hfil\break
14 │ \indent By condition (b), there will be a sequence of intervals $I_i$ of length
15 │ $\geq b$, with $\inf I_1>t_2$ and $\inf I_{i+1}>\sup I_i$, $\forall\,i$, such
16 │ that
17 │ $$\int_{t_0}^tF(t')dt'\geq0 \qquad \forall\;t\in I_i.$$
18 │ Equation (ii) may be formally integrated to yield, for the solution with
19 │ $y(t_0)=0$,
20 │ $$\leqalignno{y(t)&=-\int_{t_0}^ty^2dt'-\int_{t_0}^tF(t')dt'
21 │ \leq-\int_{t_2}^ty^2dt'-\int_{t_0}^tF(t')dt'-\delta\cr
22 │ \noalign{\bigskip}
23 │ &<-\int_{t_2}^ty^2dt'-{\delta\over2}\qquad\forall\,t\in I_i.&{\rm(iii)}\cr
24 │ \noalign{\smallskip}
25 │  \hbox{Define}
26 │  \smallskip}
27 │ \alpha(t)&=-\int_{t_2}^ty^2dt'-{\delta\over2}<0.\cr
28 │ \noalign{\smallskip}
29 │  \hbox{Then}
30 │  \smallskip}
31 │ \dot\alpha(t)&=-y^2<-\Bigg[-\int_{t_2}^ty^2dt'-{\delta\over2}\Bigg]^2
32 │ =-\alpha^2,\qquad t\in I_i.\cr}$$
```

NOTES

COMMENT

$ signs in the notes indicate which commands work only in the mathematics mode.

1: $\geq$ gives $\geq$.

7: $\ne$ gives $\neq$ and $\,$ fine-tunes spacing.

9: δ gives δ, $\min$ gives 'min'. The output from this line also shows you what the normal positions are of integral limits.

9, 31: \Bigg gives a large size of whatever 'delimiter' the command immediately precedes. On these lines the delimiters are {, }, [and]. There are several such prefixing commands: \big, \Big, \bigg and \Bigg; they produce delimiters of increasing size. They are all mathematics mode commands. (Big delimiters may also be produced using the prefix commands \left

and \right, as discussed on page 41 and in the Appendix under mathematics: delimiters.)

14: \indent forces a paragraph indentation in a situation that would not normally be indented (the previous line ends with \hfil\break, so TeX considers this still part of the same paragraph).

20–32: \leqalignno works like \eqalignno, but with equation numbers placed on the left. As with all alignments, entries are aligned with respect to the & and lines end with a \cr.

22, 24–26, etc.: \noalign allows you to temporarily escape the alignment; the \hbox is used to avoid math italics.

23: $\forall$ gives $\forall$, $\,$ fine-tunes spacing and $\in$ gives $\in$.

27: α gives α.

Example VII **55**

and

$$\int\limits_{t_0}^{t} F(t')\,dt' \geq 0 \qquad \forall\, t \in I_2.$$

Then, there is a solution of equation (i) with two zeros.

Proof: We will work with Equation (ii) instead of with (i) directly. Since $F(t_0) \neq 0$, there will be an interval $[t_1, t_2]$ containing t_0 such that $F(t) \neq 0$ on $[t_1, t_2]$. Consider a solution of Equation (ii) with $y(t_0) = 0$. We will have

$$\delta = \min\left\{ \int_{t_1}^{t_0} y^2\,dt,\ \int_{t_0}^{t_2} y^2\,dt \right\} > 0$$

for this solution.

We first show that $y(t) \to -\infty$ at some $t > t_0$. It will follow, in an identical manner, that $y(t) \to \infty$ at some $t < t_0$.

By condition (b), there will be a sequence of intervals I_i of length $\geq b$, with $\inf I_1 > t_2$ and $\inf I_{i+1} > \sup I_i$, $\forall\, i$, such that

$$\int_{t_0}^{t} F(t')\,dt' \geq 0 \qquad \forall\, t \in I_i.$$

Equation (ii) may be formally integrated to yield, for the solution with $y(t_0) = 0$,

$$y(t) = -\int_{t_0}^{t} y^2\,dt' - \int_{t_0}^{t} F(t')\,dt' \leq -\int_{t_2}^{t} y^2\,dt' - \int_{t_0}^{t} F(t')\,dt' - \delta$$

(iii) $$\qquad < -\int_{t_2}^{t} y^2\,dt' - \frac{\delta}{2} \qquad \forall\, t \in I_i.$$

Define

$$\alpha(t) = -\int_{t_2}^{t} y^2\,dt' - \frac{\delta}{2} < 0.$$

Then

$$\dot{\alpha}(t) = -y^2 < -\left[-\int_{t_2}^{t} y^2\,dt' - \frac{\delta}{2} \right]^2 = -\alpha^2, \qquad t \in I_i.$$

```
1  In each $I_i$, with lower bound $a_i$, this can be integrated to give
2  $$\eqalignno{-\alpha^{-1}\!(t)+\alpha^{-1}\!(a_i)&<-(t-a_i).\cr
3  \noalign{\hbox{Therefore,}}
4  \alpha(t)&<[\alpha^{-1}\!(a_i)+(t-a_i)]^{-1}.\cr}$$
5  Now, $\alpha$ is a nonincreasing function of $t$. Also, in each $I_i$,
6  $y(t)<-(\delta/2)$. So, $-\int_{I_i}y^2dt<-(\delta^2b/4)$. If there are $n$ of
7  the $I_i$ in $(t_2,\,t)$, we will have $\alpha(t)<-(nb\delta^2/4)$. Thus,
8  $\alpha$ is not bounded below.\hfil\break
9  \indent Pick an interval $I_i$ such that $\alpha(a_i)<-b^{-1}$. In this
10 interval, $\alpha^{-1}\!(a_i)+(t-a_i)$ will range from $\alpha^{-1}\!(a_i)<0$ to
11 $\alpha^{-1}\!(a_i)+b>0$. Therefore, there must be some $\bar t$ such that
12 $\alpha\rightarrow-\infty$ as $t\rightarrow\bar t$. Then, $y$ cannot be finite
13 everywhere; inspection of Equation~(ii) shows that it must diverge to
14 $-\infty$.\hfil\break
15 \indent The second half of the result follows in the same
16 way.$\clubsuit$
17 \vfil\eject
```

Example VII   **57**

In each I_i, with lower bound a_i, this can be integrated to give

$$-\alpha^{-1}(t) + \alpha^{-1}(a_i) < -(t - a_i).$$

Therefore,

$$\alpha(t) < [\alpha^{-1}(a_i) + (t - a_i)]^{-1}.$$

Now, α is a nonincreasing function of t. Also, in each I_i, $y(t) < -(\delta/2)$. So, $-\int_{I_i} y^2 dt < -(\delta^2 b/4)$. If there are n of the I_i in (t_2, t), we will have $\alpha(t) < -(nb\delta^2/4)$. Thus, α is not bounded below.

Pick an interval I_i such that $\alpha(a_i) < -b^{-1}$. In this interval, $\alpha^{-1}(a_i) + (t - a_i)$ will range from $\alpha^{-1}(a_i) < 0$ to $\alpha^{-1}(a_i) + b > 0$. Therefore, there must be some $\bar{t}$ such that $\alpha \to -\infty$ as $t \to \bar{t}$. Then, y cannot be finite everywhere; inspection of Equation (ii) shows that it must diverge to $-\infty$.

The second half of the result follows in the same way.♣

```
 1 | \centerline{\bf VIII. THE MANY NAMES OF DIRAC}
 2 | \centerline{\sl Hanging indentation.}
 3 | \headline{\hfil\it Example VIII\newpageno} %`\newpageno' IS NOT STANDARD.
 4 | \bigskip
 5 | {\baselineskip 18 true pt
 6 | \noindent Paul Adrien Maurice Dirac was one of the greatest of
 7 | twentieth-century physicists. Here is a list of his books, taken from
 8 | \hbox{\it Books in Print, 1984--85\/}: \bigskip % \hbox blocks a line break.
 9 | \hangindent=.5cm\hangafter=1
10 | \noindent{\bf Dirac, P.,} {\it The Development of Quantum Theory}. J. Robert
11 | Oppenheimer Memorial Prize Acceptance Speech. \dots
12 | \vskip1pt
13 | \hangindent=.5cm\hangafter=1
14 | \noindent{\bf Dirac, P.A.,} {\it The Principles of Quantum Mechanics}. 4th ed.
15 | (International Series of Monographs on Physics). \dots\hfil\break
16 | --- {\it Spinors in Hilbert Space}. \dots
17 | \vskip 1pt
18 | \hangindent=.5cm\hangafter=1
19 | \noindent{\bf Dirac, Pam, et al.,} {\it Directions in Physics: Lectures
20 | Delivered During a Visit to Australia \& New Zealand}. \dots
21 | \vskip 1pt
22 | \hangindent=.5cm\hangafter=1
23 | \noindent{\bf Dirac, Paul A.,} {\it General Theory of Relativity}. \dots
24 | \bigskip
25 | \centerline{$\diamond \qquad \diamond \qquad \diamond$}
26 | \bigskip
27 | \hangindent=-2.25 true in \hangafter=1
28 | \noindent Visiting the University of Wisconsin in 1929, Dirac was interviewed
29 | for the {\it Wisconsin State Journal}. Here are excerpts:
30 | \medskip{\sl
31 | \hangindent=-2.25 true in \hangafter=-3
32 | \noindent I been hearing about a fellow they have up at the U.\ this spring---a
33 | mathematical physicist, or something they call him---who is pushing Sir Isaac
34 | Newton, Einstein and all the others off the front page. So I thought I better
35 | go up and interview him for the benefit of State Journal readers, same as I do
36 | all other top notchers. His name is Dirac and he is an Englishman.
37 | \smallskip \hangindent=3 true in \hangafter=-4
38 | \noindent ``Professor,'' says I, ``I notice you have quite a few letters in
39 | front of your last name. Do they stand for anything in particular?''
40 | ``No,'' says he. ``You mean I can write my own ticket?'' ``Yes,'' says he.
41 | ``Will it be all right if I say that P.A.M. stands for Poincar\'e Aloysius
42 | Mussolini?'' ``Yes,'' says he. ``Fine,'' says I, ``We are getting along great!''
43 | \par}} \bye
```

NOTES

TeX's 'hanging indentation' commands follow certain conventions: \hangindent specifies the amount of indentation. A positive value indents from the left and a negative value from the right. \hangafter specifies which lines are to be indented. Suppose that the number assigned to \hangafter is n. If $n>0$, the indentation will begin *after* the first n lines; if $n<0$, the first n lines are indented. The commands have to be explicitly issued for every paragraph that is to be indented this way. The normal paragraph indentation for the first line persists in addition to the effects of these commands; if you want to suppress it, you have to use \noindent.

5: A smaller value is picked for \baselineskip; the group begun here ends after \par on line 43.

9–23: This shows one of the most common uses of hanging indentation. \hangafter has the value 1, which starts indentation after the first line.

27: \hangindent is negative (the indentation will now be from the right margin) and \hangafter positive. The actual example on the output page isn't hugely compelling (the paragraph shape is about what it would have been even without any special commands), but you can try your own experiments if you're not convinced.

31, 37: \hangafter is negative now; you can see clearly in the output the effects of this, combined with a positive and a negative \hangindent.

43: \par ends the paragraph here before you exit the group that confines some of the new settings. \bye is the preferred way to go at the end of a file. See the notes for the last input line on page *xii*.

Example VIII　　**59**

VIII. THE MANY NAMES OF DIRAC

Hanging indentation.

Paul Adrien Maurice Dirac was one of the greatest of twentieth-century physicists. Here is a list of his books, taken from *Books in Print, 1984–85*:

Dirac, P., *The Development of Quantum Theory.* J. Robert Oppenheimer Memorial Prize Acceptance Speech. . . .

Dirac, P.A., *The Principles of Quantum Mechanics.* 4th ed. (International Series of Monographs on Physics). . . .
— *Spinors in Hilbert Space.* . . .

Dirac, Pam, et al., *Directions in Physics: Lectures Delivered During a Visit to Australia & New Zealand.* . . .

Dirac, Paul A., *General Theory of Relativity.* . . .

◇　　◇　　◇

Visiting the University of Wisconsin in 1929, Dirac was interviewed for the *Wisconsin State Journal.* Here are excerpts:

I been hearing about a fellow they have up at
the U. this spring—a mathematical physicist,
or something they call him—who is pushing
Sir Isaac Newton, Einstein and all the others off the front page. So I thought I
better go up and interview him for the benefit of State Journal readers, same
as I do all other top notchers. His name is Dirac and he is an Englishman.

"Professor," says I, "I notice you
have quite a few letters in front
of your last name. Do they stand
for anything in particular?" "No,"
says he. "You mean I can write my own ticket?" "Yes," says he. "Will it be
all right if I say that P.A.M. stands for Poincaré Aloysius Mussolini?" "Yes,"
says he. "Fine," says I, "We are getting along great!"

```
1  \input tbeoutmac \pageno=31  % A NEW FILE STARTS HERE.
2  \headline{\hfil\it Example IX\newpageno}
3  %NOTE: `\newpageno' is not a standard command; see page 2.
4
5  \centerline{\bf IX. FROM RAMANUJAN'S LETTERS TO HARDY}
6  \centerline{\sl Details of typesetting equations.}  \medskip
7  \noindent In early 1913, Srinivasa Ramanujan, a largely self-taught
8  mathematician, began writing letters to G.H. Hardy at Cambridge telling him of
9  theorems that he had discovered. The letters contain around 120 results, stated
10 without proof. Here are some of these, from a selection made by Hardy:$^{16}$
11 $$\displaylines{
12 (1)\quad 1 - {3!\over(1!2!)^3}x^2 + {6!\over(2!4!)^3}x^4 - \cdots \hfill \cr
13 \hfill = \biggl( \sum_{n=0}^\infty {x^n\over(n!)^3} \biggr)
14 \biggl(1 - {x\over(1!)^3} + {x^2\over(2!)^3} - \cdots \biggr) \cr
15 \noalign{\vfil}
16 (2)\hfill 1 + \sum\nolimits_{n=1}^\infty (-1)^n (1+4n) \left\{ \prod_{j=1}^{n}
17 {2j-1\over 2j} \right\}^{\!3} = {2\over\pi} \hfill \cr
18 \noalign{\vfil}
19 (3)\hfill 1 + 9\left( {1\over 4} \right)^4 + 17\left( {1\cdot5\over4\cdot8}
20 \right)^4 + 25\left( {1\cdot5\cdot9\over4\cdot8\cdot12} \right)^4 + \cdots =
21 {2^{3}\over2} \over \pi^{1/2} \{ \Gamma( {3\over4} ) \}^2} \hfill \cr
22 \noalign{\vfil}
23 (4)\hfill 1 - 5\bigg( {1\over2} \bigg)^{\!5} + 9\bigg( {1\cdot3\over2\cdot4}
24 \bigg)^{\!5} - 13\bigg( {1\cdot3\cdot5\over2\cdot4\cdot6} \bigg)^{\!5} +
25 \cdots = {2 \over \{ \Gamma( {3\over4} ) \}{\vphantom{\big(}}^4} \hfill \cr
26 \noalign{\vfil}
27 (5)\hfill \int^{\raise2pt\hbox{$\infty$}}_{\lower2pt\hbox{$\scriptstyle0$}}
28 {dx \over (1+x^2)(1+r^2x^2)(1+r^4x^2)\ldots} =
29 {\pi \over 2\sum_{j=0}^\infty (r^0\cdots r^n)} \hfill \cr
30 \noalign{\vfil}
31 (6)\quad \hbox{If}\; \alpha \beta = \pi^2, \> \hbox{then} \hfill \cr
32 \hfil \alpha^{-{1\over4}} \Bigg\lgroup 1 + 4\alpha\int^{\infty}_0 {xe^{-\alpha
33 x^2} \over e^{2\pi x} - 1} dx \Bigg\rgroup = \beta^{-{1\over4}} \Bigg\lgroup 1 +
34 4\beta\int^{\infty}_0 {xe^{-\beta x^2} \over e^{2\pi x} - 1} dx \Bigg\rgroup \cr
35 \noalign{\vfil}
36 (7)\,{\bf \int\limits^{\infty}_0\! {1+({x\over b+1})^2 \over 1 + ({x\over a})^2}
37 \cdot {1 + ({x\over b+2})^2 \over 1 + ({x\over a+1})^2} \cdots dx =
38 {\sqrt\pi\over2} {\Gamma(a+{1\over2}) \Gamma(b+1) \Gamma(b-a+{1\over2})
39 \over \Gamma(a) \Gamma(b+{1\over2}) \Gamma(b-a+1)}} \hfill \cr
40 \noalign{\eject}
```

NOTES

IF YOU HAVE NOT SEEN MATHEMATICS IN TEX BEFORE, YOU MAY FIND THIS PAGE CONFUSING; LOOK AT EARLIER EXAMPLES FIRST. A new file starts here. `\input tbeoutmac` inputs the same format commands as were used for page 1. The strange starting value for `\pageno` is related to the new page numbering command on page 2.

11,...: `\displaylines` displays sets of equations, presenting each centered on a separate line. (So you do not have to put `$$` signs around each one). `\hfill` moves equations to the left or to the right; `\hfil` will not work here. Brackets, parentheses, etc., are prefaced by `\left`, `\right`, `\biggl`, etc. These fix the sizes of such 'delimiters': `\big`, `\Big`, `\bigg` and `\Bigg` give specific sizes, with the additional l or r denoting a left or right delimiter; `\left` and `\right` give delimiters that grow automatically with the vertical size of the equation. See mathematics: delimiters in the Appendix.

13, 16, 29: `$\sum$` gives $\sum$. The positions of limits depend on where the symbol occurs: compare Equations 1 and 5. On line 16, `\nolimits` moves limits off the top (Equation 2). `$\prod$` gives $\prod$.

15, etc.: `\noalign` allows you to put in material that will ignore alignment imposed by `\displaylines`.

17, 23, 24: `$\!$` gives a small 'negative' space. Here, it allows precise positioning of exponents.

25: `\vphantom` makes a space of no width, but height equal here to a '\big('; it fools TEX into placing the exponent higher. Compare Equations 3 and 4.

27: `\raise` and `\lower` each do just that to material in a box. The default style inside the box is `\textstyle`. Compare the limits on the integral.

32: `\hfil` isn't strong enough to right-justify here: see Equation 6 on the facing page.

32–34: `\lgroup`, `\rgroup` give 'square' parentheses.

36: `\bf` changes only some characters to boldface. `\limits` moves the limits to the top of the integral.

Example IX   **61**

IX. FROM RAMANUJAN'S LETTERS TO HARDY

Details of typesetting equations.

In early 1913, Srinivasa Ramanujan, a largely self-taught mathematician, began writing letters to G.H. Hardy at Cambridge telling him of theorems that he had discovered. The letters contain around 120 results, stated without proof. Here are some of these, from a selection made by Hardy:[16]

(1) $\quad 1 - \dfrac{3!}{(1!2!)^3}x^2 + \dfrac{6!}{(2!4!)^3}x^4 - \cdots$

$$= \left(\sum_{n=0}^{\infty} \frac{x^n}{(n!)^3} \right) \left(1 - \frac{x}{(1!)^3} + \frac{x^2}{(2!)^3} - \cdots \right)$$

(2) $\quad 1 + \sum_{n=1}^{\infty} (-1)^n (1+4n) \left\{ \prod_{j=1}^{n} \frac{2j-1}{2j} \right\}^3 = \dfrac{2}{\pi}$

(3) $\quad 1 + 9\left(\dfrac{1}{4}\right)^4 + 17\left(\dfrac{1\cdot 5}{4\cdot 8}\right)^4 + 25\left(\dfrac{1\cdot 5\cdot 9}{4\cdot 8\cdot 12}\right)^4 + \cdots = \dfrac{2^{\frac{3}{2}}}{\pi^{1/2}\{\Gamma(\frac{3}{4})\}^2}$

(4) $\quad 1 - 5\left(\dfrac{1}{2}\right)^5 + 9\left(\dfrac{1\cdot 3}{2\cdot 4}\right)^5 - 13\left(\dfrac{1\cdot 3\cdot 5}{2\cdot 4\cdot 6}\right)^5 + \cdots = \dfrac{2}{\{\Gamma(\frac{3}{4})\}^4}$

(5) $\quad \displaystyle\int_0^{\infty} \dfrac{dx}{(1+x^2)(1+r^2x^2)(1+r^4x^2)\cdots} = \dfrac{\pi}{2\sum_{j=0}^{\infty}(r^0\cdots r^n)}$

(6) If $\alpha\beta = \pi^2$, then

$$\alpha^{-\frac{1}{4}}\left[1 + 4\alpha \int_0^{\infty} \frac{xe^{-\alpha x^2}}{e^{2\pi x}-1}dx \right] = \beta^{-\frac{1}{4}}\left[1 + 4\beta \int_0^{\infty} \frac{xe^{-\beta x^2}}{e^{2\pi x}-1}dx \right]$$

(7) $\displaystyle\int_0^{\infty} \dfrac{1+(\frac{x}{b+1})^2}{1+(\frac{x}{a})^2} \cdot \dfrac{1+(\frac{x}{b+2})^2}{1+(\frac{x}{a+1})^2} \cdots \mathbf{dx} = \dfrac{\sqrt{\pi}}{2} \dfrac{\Gamma(a+\frac{1}{2})\Gamma(b+1)\Gamma(b-a+\frac{1}{2})}{\Gamma(a)\Gamma(b+\frac{1}{2})\Gamma(b-a+1)}$

```
 1  (8)\hfill 4\int^{\infty}_0 {xe^{-x\surd5} \over \cosh x} dx \phantom{a} =
 2  \hphantom{a} {1 \over \displaystyle 1 + {1^2\hfill \over \displaystyle 1 +
 3  {1^2 \over \textstyle 1 + {2^2 \over \textstyle 1 + {2^2 \over 1 +
 4  {3^2 \over 1 + {3^2 \over 1 + \cdots}}}}}} \hfill \cr
 5  \noalign{\vfil}
 6  (9)\hfill{\rm If}\hfill\qquad\cr
 7  \underbrace{\overbrace{u = {x\over1+} {x^5\over1+} {x^{10}\over1+}
 8  {x^{15}\over1+\cdots} \quad {\rm and} \quad v = {x^{1\over5}\over1+} {x\over1+}
 9  {x^2\over1+} {x^3\over1+\cdots}}}, \cr    {\rm then}\cr
10  v^5 = u{1-2u+4u^2-3u^3+u^4 \over 1+3u+4u^2+2u^3+u^4} \cr
11  \noalign{\vfil}
12  (10)\hfill {1\over1+} {e^{-2\pi}\over1+} {e^{-4\pi}\over1+\cdots} =
13  \left\{ \sqrt{\smash{\Biggl( {5+\surd5\over2} \Biggr)} \vphantom{\bigg(}}-
14  {\surd5+1\over2} \right\} e^{{2\over5} \pi} \hfill \cr
15  \noalign{\vfil}
16  (11)\hfill {1\over1+} {e^{-2\pi\surd5}\over1+} {e^{-4\pi\surd5}\over1+\cdots}
17  = \Bigg[ {\surd5\over1+\root5\of{\Big\{ 5^{3/4} \big( {\surd5-1\over2} \big)
18  ^{5/2} - 1 \Big\}}} - {\sqrt5+1\over2} \Bigg] e^{2\pi/\surd5} \hfill\cr
19  \noalign{\vfil}
20  (12)\;{\rm If}\;F(k)=1+\big( {\textstyle{1\over2}} \big)^2k + \big(
21  {\textstyle{1\cdot3\over2\cdot4}} \big)^2 k^2 + \cdots\;{\rm and}\;
22  F(1-k) = \sqrt{210}F(k), {\rm\ then} \hfill \cr
23  \noalign{\smallskip}
24  \qquad\qquad k = (\sqrt2-1)^4 (2-\sqrt3)^2 (\sqrt7-\sqrt6)^4 (8-3\sqrt7)^2
25  \hfill\cr
26  \hfill \times (\sqrt{10}-3)^4 (4-\sqrt{15})^4 (\sqrt{15}-\sqrt{14})^2
27  (6-\sqrt{35})^2 \qquad \cr
28  \noalign{\vfil}
29  (13)\;\hbox{The number of numbers between}\;A\;{\rm and}\;x\;\hbox{which
30  are either squares, or}\hfill\cr
31  \qquad\hbox{sums of two squares is}\hfill\cr
32  K \int^x_A {dt\over\surd(\log t)} + \theta(x), \cr \noalign{\smallskip}
33  \qquad{\rm where}\; K = 0.764 \ldots\ {\rm and}\; \theta(x)\; \hbox{is very
34  small compared to the integral.}\hfill\cr}$$
35  \vfil\eject
```

NOTES

COMMENT

Like the previous page, this one is mathematics-heavy. If this is your very first glimpse of TeX, turn the page right away and pretend you didn't see anything. $ signs in the notes on this page and the previous one serve as reminders that certain commands work only in the mathematics mode.

1–4: `\phantom{a}` creates a blank space of height, depth and width equal to that of a. `\hphantom` works similarly, but the space it makes has zero height. Compare with `\vphantom` from line 25 on the previous page. On the right of Equation 8, the sizes of the numerators and denominators can be adjusted by asking for `\displaystyle` or `\textstyle`. Without that, the sizes automatically become very small (`\scriptscriptstyle`). The normal centering of numerators and denominators can be adjusted by using `\hfill`. If the vertical spacing seems cramped here (as it is), extra space can be left by using a `\vphantom`.

6–10: Roman typeface has to be explicitly asked for with `\rm`, if text is to appear. `\qquad` is put on line 6 to balance the space occupied by '(9)' on the left of the output line, so that 'If' is roughly centered.

13: `\smash` has the opposite effect of `\vphantom`: it assigns zero height to whatever it acts on. In conjunction with `\vphantom` it can be used to completely control vertical spacing. Here, the natural height of the formula is set to zero by `\smash` and a height equal to that of '\bigg(' is assigned to it by `\vphantom`. The resulting vertical spacing under the radical sign in the output is awful, but something drastic was needed to attract your attention to the power of the `\smash`-`\vphantom` combination.

16–18: The right-hand side of Equation 11 might have benefitted from adjustments to the size of the square bracket.

29–34: Longer amounts of text are best introduced in an `\hbox`. This will restore the default spacing rules for text (`\rm` by itself changes typeface, but keeps mathematics mode spacing rules like the suppression of all blank spaces). Line breaks for text in an `\hbox` have to be introduced by hand.

Example IX **63**

$$(8) \qquad 4\int_0^\infty \frac{xe^{-x\sqrt{5}}}{\cosh x}dx = \cfrac{1}{1+\cfrac{1^2}{1+\cfrac{1^2}{1+\cfrac{2^2}{1+\cfrac{2^2}{1+\cfrac{3^2}{1+\frac{3^2}{1+\cdots}}}}}}}$$

(9)
If

$$u = \frac{x}{1+}\frac{x^5}{1+}\frac{x^{10}}{1+}\frac{x^{15}}{1+\cdots} \quad \text{and} \quad v = \frac{x^{\frac{1}{5}}}{1+}\frac{x}{1+}\frac{x^2}{1+}\frac{x^3}{1+\cdots},$$

then

$$v^5 = u\frac{1-2u+4u^2-3u^3+u^4}{1+3u+4u^2+2u^3+u^4}$$

$$(10) \qquad \frac{1}{1+}\frac{e^{-2\pi}}{1+}\frac{e^{-4\pi}}{1+\cdots} = \left\{\sqrt{\left(\frac{5+\sqrt{5}}{2}\right)} - \frac{\sqrt{5}+1}{2}\right\}e^{\frac{2}{5}\pi}$$

$$(11) \quad \frac{1}{1+}\frac{e^{-2\pi\sqrt{5}}}{1+}\frac{e^{-4\pi\sqrt{5}}}{1+\cdots} = \left[\frac{\sqrt{5}}{1+\sqrt[5]{\left\{5^{3/4}\left(\frac{\sqrt{5}-1}{2}\right)^{5/2}-1\right\}}} - \frac{\sqrt{5}+1}{2}\right]e^{2\pi/\sqrt{5}}$$

(12) If $F(k) = 1 + \left(\frac{1}{2}\right)^2 k + \left(\frac{1\cdot3}{2\cdot4}\right)^2 k^2 + \cdots$ and $F(1-k) = \sqrt{210}F(k)$, then

$$k = (\sqrt{2}-1)^4(2-\sqrt{3})^2(\sqrt{7}-\sqrt{6})^4(8-3\sqrt{7})^2$$

$$\times(\sqrt{10}-3)^4(4-\sqrt{15})^4(\sqrt{15}-\sqrt{14})^2(6-\sqrt{35})^2$$

(13) The number of numbers between A and x which are either squares, or

sums of two squares is

$$K\int_A^x \frac{dt}{\sqrt{(\log t)}} + \theta(x),$$

where $K = 0.764\ldots$ and $\theta(x)$ is very small compared to the integral.

```
 1  \centerline{\bf X. TYPOGRAPHY}
 2  \centerline{\sl Typeface styles and sizes.}
 3  \headline{\hfil\it Example X\newpageno} %'\newpageno' IS NOT A STANDARD COMMAND
 4  \bigskip
 5  \font\sans=cmss10
 6  \font\sansbf=cmssbx10
 7  \font\nice=cmdunh10
 8  \font\lrm=cmr7 scaled\magstep1
 9  \font\bbf=cmbx5 scaled\magstep3
10
11  \nice
12  \noindent Typography is a conservative art: The style that is called ''modern''
13  in English typographic terminology is two hundred years old. The first types in
14  the modern style were cut late in the 18th century, toward the close of the age
15  of enlightenment and the beginning of the industrial revolution. The principal
16  originators of the style were Giambattista Bodoni, a printer and punch-cutter
17  of Parma, and Fermin Didot, a typefounder member of an illustrious Parisian
18  printing family. These were contemporaries of Thomas Jefferson, and if today we
19  regard Jefferson as a man modern in many respects, it may not be too far-fetched
20  to call the types of his time ''modern'' as well.
21  \medskip \lrm
22  \noindent {\bbf -- Charles A. Bigelow,}\hfil\break
23  in an introduction to {\sans Computer Modern Typefaces} by
24  {\sansbf Donald Knuth}, \hfil\break
25  \rm \copyright\ 1986 by Addison-Wesley Publishing Company, Inc. \hfil\break
26  Reprinted with permission of the publisher.
27  \vfil\eject
```

NOTES

ON FONTS

This example shows you how to gain access to typefaces that are not generally 'loaded' with TeX. Though the terminology is not always used in this exact way, a *typeface* usually refers to a particular style of type, and a *font* of type to a typeface of fixed size. Sizes are typically measured in *points*. Thus, *10-point Times-Roman* is an example of a font of type, of size 10 points in the roman style used by the London Times newspaper. Variations are possible within a font: *bold*, *italic* and the newer *slanted* being among the most common. TeX comes with some standard fonts automatically available: roman (with its bold, italic and slanted variations), typewriter, and several sets of mathematical symbols. All these fonts come from the Computer Modern family, created principally by Donald Knuth. In addition to the fonts mentioned just above, there are other Computer Modern fonts that you can gain access to, as discussed below.

5–9: Each of these lines shows a typical `\font` command, used to assign a name to a font. The command must contain the *external* name of the font on the right of the = (i.e., the name under which information about the font is stored in a separate file) and the name you will use in your document on the left. Font information is usually stored in two files: the first, a *metric* file, contains information about the sizes of each character in the font; the second, information about its shape appropriate to the level of resolution

of the particular viewing or printing device you are using. If you use an external name for which metric information is not available, you will get an error message when TeX processes your document. If you use a font that TeX knows about but which your printer cannot draw, you will get an error message only when you issue a 'print' command.

5: This defines the name `\sans` for the 10-point Computer Modern sans serif font.

6, 7: Similar to line 5; the fonts being 'loaded' are 10-point Computer Modern sans serif bold-extended and 10-point Computer Modern 'dunhill' (after the style popularized by the cigarette of that name).

8–9: These load 7-point roman and 5-point bold-extended fonts respectively, each magnified by a scale factor. `\magstep1` magnifies by 1.2 and `\magstep3` by 1.2^3 (=1.728). You can also explicitly specify a size by saying `at`, as was done on page *viii*.

11: Sets the text that follows in the typeface named `\nice`. Since no grouping symbols are used (i.e., no { or }), this typeface will persist till it is explicitly changed.

21: Changes the default typeface to `\lrm`.

22–25: Changes the typeface to `\bbf`, `\sans` and `\sansbf` for limited portions of text, then makes `\rm` (which usually stands for 10-point roman) the default typeface again.

A LIST OF COMPUTER MODERN FONTS IS GIVEN IN THE APPENDIX, UNDER fonts.

Example X **65**

X. TYPOGRAPHY
Typeface styles and sizes.

Typography is a conservative art: The style that is called "modern" in English typographic terminology is two hundred years old. The first types in the modern style were cut late in the 18th century, toward the close of the age of enlightenment and the beginning of the industrial revolution. The principal originators of the style were Giambattista Bodoni, a printer and punch-cutter of Parma, and Fermin Didot, a typefounder member of an illustrious Parisian printing family. These were contemporaries of Thomas Jefferson, and if today we regard Jefferson as a man modern in many respects, it may not be too far-fetched to call the types of his time "modern" as well.

— **Charles A. Bigelow,**

in an introduction to **Computer Modern Typefaces** by **Donald Knuth,**

© 1986 by Addison-Wesley Publishing Company, Inc.

Reprinted with permission of the publisher.

```
 1 \centerline{\bf XI. A LETTER}
 2 \centerline{\sl Definitions; letters.}
 3 \headline{\hfil\it Example XI\newpageno} %`\newpageno' IS NOT A STANDARD COMMAND
 4 \bigskip
 5
 6 \def\letterhead {\hrule height 1pt
 7     \medskip
 8     \rightline{\vbox{\hsize 1.5true in \baselineskip=12pt \parindent=0pt
 9     Your name, \hfil\break Your address, \hfil\break Etc.}}}
10
11 \def\date #1{\rightline{\vbox{\hsize 1.5true in\noindent #1}}\bigskip}
12
13 \def\address #1{\vbox{\baselineskip=12pt\halign{## \hfil\cr #1}}}
14
15 \def\sal #1{\noindent #1}
16
17 \def\endletter #1#2{\nobreak\medskip\rightline{\vbox{\hsize 1.5true in
18     \parindent=0pt #1\vskip 1.25 true cm #2}}}
19
20 \letterhead
21 \date{The date.}
22 \address{Name\cr Street\cr City\cr Postal code\cr Country.\cr}
23
24 \sal{Dear Reader,}
25
26 This is a letter without content. An earlier example of doing a letter
27 in \TeX\ had more in it, but I was told by well-meaning people that its
28 content distracted readers from its form.
29
30 And {\sl form\/} is what is important here.
31 \endletter{Sincerely,}{The Author.}
32 \vfil\eject
```

NOTES

6–18: These lines illustrate how you can define your own commands. The structure is always this: \def, followed by the name of the new command (including possible 'parameters'), followed by the 'replacement text' enclosed in braces. This replacement text is the text, or set of commands, that the new command summarizes. A simple example of a new command is one that merely reproduces text that you frequently repeat. Thus, if you are in the habit of writing long and passionate, but identical, letters to different people, you can say

\def\passion {*long passionate text*}

and then you only have to type '\passion' each time.

6–9: These lines define a 'letterhead' command that automatically draws a horizontal rule across the page, then places on the right of the page (via \rightline) a box (\vbox) of horizontal size 1.5 inches containing lines saying 'Your name', 'Your address', 'Etc.'. The interline spacing within the box is reset (using \baselineskip) to 12 points, and the paragraph indentation is set (by \parindent) to 0 points. Changes like this, made within a \vbox or an \hbox, will not leak out of the box and affect the placement of material outside. Boxes are discussed in Example XV and in the Appendix.

11: Like \letterhead, this creates a box of size 1.5

inches on the right of the page. \noindent suppresses paragraph indentation here. This command has a 'parameter', denoted by #1, which you must specify when you use the command. See line 21.

13: \address sets up the format for a table, using \halign. It automatically aligns material that it acts on. ## must be used here in place of the usual # in an \halign 'preamble' (see how \halign is used in Example VI).

15: \sal is set up to place your salutation correctly.

17, 18: This defines a two-parameter command. You may use up to nine parameters when defining commands. \nobreak discourages a page break at the \medskip just after.

20–31: These show how the commands defined above may be used. The definitions of such commands are usually placed in a separate file, which can be used as 'input' each time the commands are needed. For example, the author has a set of commands he uses for writing letters, stored in a file called *letter.tex*. Then, typing '\input letter' at the start of every letter allows him to use his \letterhead, \address, etc., commands.

21: The date here has to be entered by you. Under \year in the Appendix, you will find a new command that extracts the date automatically.

Example XI **67**

XI. A LETTER

Definitions; letters.

Your name,
Your address,
Etc.

The date.

Name
Street
City
Postal code
Country.

Dear Reader,

This is a letter without content. An earlier example of doing a letter in TeX had more in it, but I was told by well-meaning people that its content distracted readers from its form.

And *form* is what is important here.

Sincerely,

The Author.

```
1  \centerline{\bf XII. A MEMORANDUM}
2  \centerline{\sl More definitions; storing variables; loop commands; memoranda.}
3  \headline{\hfil\it Example XII\newpageno} \bigskip %'\newpageno' IS NOT STANDARD
4
5  \newcount\thusfar
6  \def\pattern #1#2{\thusfar=0
7      \loop #1\advance\thusfar by 1 \ifnum\thusfar<#2 \repeat}
8
9  \def\block #1{\vbox{\hsize 2.5 true cm\noindent \bf#1:}}
10
11 \def\memo TO:#1FROM:#2SUBJECT:#3DATE:#4\par{\centerline{\sl MEMO!}
12     \bigskip \hrule height1pt \medskip
13     \vbox{\parindent=75pt\parskip=1pt
14     \item{\block{TO}}#1
15     \item{\block{FROM}}#2
16     \item{\block{SUBJECT}}#3
17     \item{\block{DATE}}#4 }\medskip \hrule height1pt \bigskip}
18
19 \memo
20 TO: You.
21 FROM: Me.
22 SUBJECT: Writing elegant memoranda.
23 DATE: Today.
24
25 This shows you one way to do a memorandum. You type the main body as you
26 would any other text in \TeX: blank lines for new paragraphs,
27 {\tt\string\noindent} to suppress paragraph indentation, etc.
28
29 I trust this has been an edifying memo.
30 \bigskip
31 \centerline{\pattern{$\star$}{25}}
32 \vfil\eject
```

NOTES

5: It is possible to store information in internal registers of TeX. The registers are classified according to whether they contain pure (whole) numbers, quantities that have dimension (like sizes), the entire contents of boxes (both \vbox and \hbox), etc. Each register in a given class is labelled by a number. The registers that hold pure numbers are named \count, and are labelled \count0, \count1, and so on. Since some of these registers are already in use by TeX to store things like page numbers (\count0), TeX provides the command \newcount that allocates new, hitherto unused, registers to you when you need to store something. Here, \thusfar actually represents the number labelling the newly allocated register, but you don't ever need to use that number or even to know what it is: you just use the made-up name \thusfar in place of the number. The Appendix entry \newcount tells you more about register allocation.

6–7: \pattern produces a number (specified by #2) of copies of the symbols or text used for #1. It first sets the variable in the register \thusfar to zero, then uses TeX's \loop...\repeat command to repeatedly produce copies of #1. After each copy, the variable labelled by \thusfar is increased (via \advance) by 1, and the whole process is repeated if the variable is less than the value of #2. \ifnum is one of several conditional commands in TeX: it compares numbers.

9: \block makes a box of fixed horizontal size, to be used in \memo.

11–17: These lines define the combination of commands: \memo TO:...\par. They are set up so that they can be used simply, without the clutter of extra braces. \memo sets TeX up to look for the words 'TO:', 'FROM:', etc.; it then puts the text that follows these words in the right place. The effects of the command end at the first explicit paragraph-end. Everything must be put in exactly as listed in the command: capitalization, colons and all. Such 'high-level' commands can be very useful: they make it possible for you to write documents containing only a very few commands, with all the dirty little details of the formatting of your document hidden inside. What is actually printed out here is the text in \block, and what you enter for #1, etc. It is not necessary that the words in \block be the same as the ones in the command name, as they happen to be here.

19–24: This is how \memo is to be used. The words TO:, etc., must be entered exactly as they are here, but the material after each colon can be altered freely. The text of the memo starts after a blank line.

31: Shows how \pattern may be used.

Example XII   **69**

XII. A MEMORANDUM

More definitions; storing variables; loop commands; memoranda.

MEMO!

TO: You.

FROM: Me.

SUBJECT: Writing elegant memoranda.

DATE: Today.

This shows you one way to do a memorandum. You type the main body as you would any other text in TeX: blank lines for new paragraphs, \noindent to suppress paragraph indentation, etc.

I trust this has been an edifying memo.

★★★★★★★★★★★★★★★★★★★★★★★★

```
1   \centerline{\bf XIII. A CONVERSATION}
2   \centerline{\sl Conditional commands; a simple script.}
3   \headline{\hfil\it Example XIII\newpageno}  \baselineskip=14pt
4
5   \newcount\spk
6   \def\beginscript {\bgroup \parindent=0pt \spk=1 \sl \rightskip.4in
7        \def\par {\ifnum\spk=1 \endgraf \it \spk=2 \leftskip.4in \rightskip0in
8              \else \endgraf \sl \spk=1 \leftskip0in \rightskip.4in \fi}}
9
10  \def\endscript {\egroup}               \def\(#1){{\rm #1}}
11
12  \bigskip\noindent This conversation, between an American man and a Canadian
13  woman, was overheard on a flight on Iceland Air:\bigskip
14
15  \beginscript
16  \baselineskip=12pt \parskip=7.5pt
17  I don't know why they make you learn two languages up there---we manage well
18  with one here.
19
20  Isn't it just dreadful? It really isn't fair! What do English people have to
21  know French for? Anyway, they all learn it, but try to find anyone in Quebec
22  who speaks English!
23
24  \(Sympathetically.) Must be tough.\par
25  \(With a warm glance.) You seem interesting. Have you been to Iceland before?
26  \par    Yeah!\par    What's it like?\par
27  \(Thoughtfully.) The people are very nice there, very straightforward, very
28  honest\dots \par
29  \(Approvingly.) I like that, I like it when they're honest. But that's true all
30  over Northern Europe, isn't it? You see the difference in France. In the North
31  they are all really honest, in the South they rob you. As for Italy\dots \par
32  \(With a man-of-the-world air.) Yeah! You'll like the Icelanders. They used
33  to be quite simple folk, but they're getting really sophisticated---they even
34  have Kentucky Fried Chicken now\dots \par
35  \(With a now-that-we're-discussing-culture-I'm-on-home-ground look.) They say
36  the modern art is marvellous in Iceland. \par
37  \(Looking slightly awkward, a man on unfamiliar territory.) They're also
38  really into furniture design.\par
39  I can't wait to get there!\par    Yeah!\par
40  \endscript
41  \baselineskip=22 true pt  \vfil\eject
```

NOTES

5: \newcount is discussed on the previous page.

6–8: \beginscript does several things. It begins a group (with \bgroup, a command defined to be equal to {) in which TeX's normal paragraph formatting mechanism is altered. The group ends, restoring the original format, only with the \egroup (= }) invoked by the \endscript command. \bgroup and \egroup are used because they allow you to create groups that span definitions, even though the direct use of { and } will not permit it. (The reason has to do with the precise point at which TeX replaces a command by its definition.) The new paragraph format is achieved by redefining TeX's normal end-of-paragraph command, \par: typeface now switches back and forth between italics and slanted for successive paragraphs, and they are alternately left and right indented through \leftskip and \rightskip. The variable stored in the register labelled by \spk marks paragraphs alternately as '1' or '2'. The \ifnum... \else...\fi command combination picks one format when \spk represents a '1' and the other format otherwise. \fi must be used to terminate all conditional commands in TeX except those within \loop commands. \endgraf is a standard command defined to have the effect of the normal \par command. It is useful in cases, such as this, where \par is temporarily redefined.

10: \(#1) is a command with no text characters in its name. See line 24 for an example of its use.

19, 23: The blank line signal for the end of a paragraph has the effect here of causing format changes in paragraphs *with no visible commands used at all.*

24, 28, etc.: Paragraphs may also be ended with explicit \par commands.

26: New paragraphs don't need separate lines, though this isn't the best way to arrange an input file.

Example XIII   **71**

XIII. A CONVERSATION

Conditional commands; a simple script.

This conversation, between an American man and a Canadian woman, was overheard on a flight on Iceland Air:

I don't know why they make you learn two languages up there—we manage well with one here.

> *Isn't it just dreadful? It really isn't fair! What do English people have to know French for? Anyway, they all learn it, but try to find anyone in Quebec who speaks English!*

Sympathetically. *Must be tough.*

> With a warm glance. *You seem interesting. Have you been to Iceland before?*

Yeah!

> *What's it like?*

Thoughtfully. *The people are very nice there, very straightforward, very honest...*

> Approvingly. *I like that, I like it when they're honest. But that's true all over Northern Europe, isn't it? You see the difference in France. In the North they are all really honest, in the South they rob you. As for Italy...*

With a man-of-the-world air. Yeah! *You'll like the Icelanders. They used to be quite simple folk, but they're getting really sophisticated—they even have Kentucky Fried Chicken now...*

> With a now-that-we're-discussing-culture-I'm-on-home-ground look. *They say the modern art is marvellous in Iceland.*

Looking slightly awkward, a man on unfamiliar territory. *They're also really into furniture design.*

> *I can't wait to get there!*

Yeah!

```
1  \centerline{\bf XIV. FERMAT'S LAST THEOREM}
2  \centerline{\sl Programming in \TeX.}
3  \headline{\hfil\it Example XIV\newpageno} \medskip %'\newpageno' IS NOT STANDARD
4
5  \newcount\var \newcount\pw \newcount\tmp \newcount\cnt
6  \def\pow#1#2#3{\var=#1 \pw=#2 \tmp=\var \cnt=1
7        \loop \multiply\var by\tmp \advance\cnt by1 \ifnum\cnt<\pw \repeat
8        \global#3=\var}
9
10 \newcount\xf \newcount\xnf \newcount\yf \newcount\ynf \newcount\zf \newcount\znf
11 \def\n {\number}
12
13 \def\fermat#1#2#3{$\global\xf=#1 \global\yf=#2 \global\pw=#3
14        \pow{\xf}{\pw}{\xnf} \pow{\yf}{\pw}{\ynf}
15        \global\tmp=\ynf \global\advance\tmp by\xnf
16        {\n\xf}^{\n\pw}+{\n\yf}^{\n\pw}={\n\tmp}$.\hfil\break
17        \ifnum\xf>\yf \zf=\xf \else \zf=\yf \fi
18        \loop {\pow{\zf}{\pw}{\znf}} \ifnum\znf<\tmp \advance\zf by1 \repeat
19        \ifnum\znf=\tmp  The sum seems to be exactly ${\n\zf}^{\n\pw}$.
20          \ifnum\pw=2 {\it Yawn!} Tell me something I don't know, will you?
21          \else Incredible!  But, perhaps you'd better check my work.\fi
22        \else \advance\zf by-1
23        This lies between ${\n\zf}^{\n\pw}$\pow{\zf}{\pw}{\znf}($={\n\znf}$)
24        \advance\zf by1
25        and ${\n\zf}^{\n\pw}$\pow{\zf}{\pw}{\znf}($={\n\znf}$).\fi}%
26
27 \noindent Are there positive whole numbers $x$, $y$, $z$ and $n$ that satisfy
28 $x^n+y^n=z^n$ when $n>2$? It was claimed by Pierre Fermat, over three hundred
29 years ago, that he could prove there were not. His proof has never been found,
30 nor has anybody so far discovered another. To assess the validity of Fermat's
31 'theorem', it is instructive to look at a few examples:
32 \medskip
33 \item{\it 1.}\fermat{73}{71}{3}   \smallskip
34 \item{\it 2.}\fermat{2}{3}{13}    \smallskip
35 \item{\it 3.}\fermat{23}{37}{5}   \medskip
36 \noindent (''Fascinating,'' you murmur, ''profound even, no doubt, but what deep
37 \TeX\ truth does this illustrate? We're now at Example XIV, and I know what
38 input would create this output. It's pretty trivial---I could even scribble it
39 right here in the margin.'' Well, read the notes on the facing page,
40 examine the input box\dots and marvel at \TeX's capabilities.) \vfil\eject
```

NOTES

COMMENT

This example and the 'explanations' below are not easy to follow unless you know some programming or, at least, some mathematics. The example shows how TeX may be used to shape the content of a document, not just its form. Lines 5–25 define new commands, the main one being \fermat. Lines 33–35 show how \fermat may be used: You feed it three numbers representing x, y and n. It then internally *calculates* the value of $x^n + y^n$, finds the nearest nth powers to this sum, and presents the answer nicely typeset. All of which raises the fascinating possibility of your being able to live a life of leisure, with TeX generating papers and books for you from time to time.

5, 10: These registers will be needed for calculations. \newcount is explained on page 68.

6–8: \pow takes #1, raises it to the power #2 and makes #3 equal to the answer. \global is used to prefix assignments or definitions that you want to have persist outside the group in which they are introduced.

11: \number prints characters that represent numbers. It will be used in several places here to print the contents of registers, hence the abbreviation \n is introduced.

13–16: These lines obtain nth powers from \pow, then find the sum of these powers (and store it in \tmp). $ signs are not necessary for the calculations, but are necessary to typeset line 16. They perform the added function here of suppressing the extra blank spaces that are occasionally introduced in the output by complicated commands.

17: The larger of x and y is the starting value for z.

18: nth powers of successive values of z are calculated till the number in \tmp is equalled or exceeded.

23–25: The nth powers immediately below and above \tmp are calculated and presented.

Example XIV **73**

XIV. FERMAT'S LAST THEOREM

Programming in TeX.

Are there positive whole numbers x, y, z and n that satisfy $x^n + y^n = z^n$ when $n > 2$? It was claimed by Pierre Fermat, over three hundred years ago, that he could prove there were not. His proof has never been found, nor has anybody so far discovered another. To assess the validity of Fermat's 'theorem', it is instructive to look at a few examples:

1. $73^3 + 71^3 = 746928$.

   This lies between 90^3 $(= 729000)$ and 91^3 $(= 753571)$.

2. $2^{13} + 3^{13} = 1602515$.

   This lies between 3^{13} $(= 1594323)$ and 4^{13} $(= 67108864)$.

3. $23^5 + 37^5 = 75780300$.

   This lies between 37^5 $(= 69343957)$ and 38^5 $(= 79235168)$.

("Fascinating," you murmur, "profound even, no doubt, but what deep TeX truth does this illustrate? We're now at Example XIV, and I know what input would create this output. It's pretty trivial—I could even scribble it right here in the margin." Well, read the notes on the facing page, examine the input box... and marvel at TeX's capabilities.)

74

```
1  \centerline{\bf XV.\quad\hbox{\raise6pt\hbox{O}\kern-8.5pt\lower4pt
2  \hbox{N}\kern8pt\raise6pt\hbox{B}\raise3pt\hbox{O}X\lower3pt\hbox{I}%
3  \lower6pt\hbox{NG}}}
4  \centerline{\sl Arranging material in horizontal and vertical boxes.}
5  \headline{\hfil\it Example XV\newpageno}  \bigskip  \baselineskip=14pt
6  \hbox to\hsize{\leaders\hbox to 20pt{$\ast$\hfil}\hfill}
7  \hbox to\hsize{\leaders\hbox to 20pt{\hfil$\ast$\hfil}\hfill}
8  \hbox to\hsize{\leaders\hbox to 20pt{\hfil$\ast$}\hfill}
9  \vfil
10 \vbox{\hsize 4 true in During a superior boxing match (Ali-Frazier I, for
11 instance) we are deeply moved by the body's communion with itself by way of
12 another's intransigent flesh.\hfil\break
13 \hbox to\hsize{\hfill Joyce Carol Oates, {\it On Boxing}, Doubleday (1987).}}
14 \vfil
15 \moveright .5 true in\vbox{\hbox{\dots Ali was weary.}
16 \hbox{He had hit Foreman harder than he had ever hit anyone.}
17 \hbox{He had hit him often.} \hbox{Foreman's head must by now be
18 equal to a piece of vulcanized rubber.}
19 \hbox{\hfill Norman Mailer, {\it The Fight}, Little Brown (1975).}}
20 \vfil
21 \hbox{\vbox{\hsize 3.2 true in \baselineskip=14 true pt
22 Head trauma constituted 68 percent of the injuries, a category that included
23 concussion, brain hemorrhage, skull fracture and fracture of the facial bones.
24 Injuries to the upper extremity and trunk were the next most common.
25
26 R.W. Enzenauer et al., \sl Boxing-related injuries in the U.S.\ Army,
27 \it The Journal of the American Medical Assoc., \rm March 10, 1989.}
28 \kern .25 true in \vbox{\hsize 2.5 true in
29 I may curse the blood specks on my shirt\dots but I return again and again\dots
30 Whether that makes me a humanist or a voyeur, I'm not sure.\hfil\break
31 John Schulian,\ \ {\it Writers' Fighters and Other Sweet Scientists},\hfil\break
32 Andrews and McMeel (1983).}} \vfil
33 \hbox to\hsize{\leaders\hbox to 20pt{\hfil$\smile$\hfil$\frown$}\hfill}
34 \hbox to\hsize{\hfil
35 \vbox to.5in{\hsize .2in\leaders\vbox to 8pt{\vfil\noindent$\diamond$\par}
36 \vfill} \quad
37 \vbox to.5in{\hsize .2in\leaders\vbox to 8pt{\vfil\noindent$\diamond$\par\vfil}
38 \vfill} \quad
39 \vbox to.5in{\hsize .2in\leaders\vbox to 8pt{\noindent$\diamond$\par\vfil}
40 \vfill}\hfil}
41 \baselineskip=22 true pt \eject
```

NOTES

ABOUT BOXES

Boxes allow you complete control over positioning. \hsize and \vsize stand for horizontal and vertical sizes. Outside explicitly introduced boxes, they refer to the page size; inside, they refer to the box size. An \hbox normally has the horizontal size of its contents; similarly the vertical size of a \vbox. These sizes may be altered by saying 'to *new size*' just after the command. See lines 6–8 or 33–39. A horizontal size for a \vbox may be specified within the box. See line 10. The size may also be implicitly specified: a \vbox containing an \hbox will pick up the horizontal size of the \hbox. If no size is given, a \vbox will have the horizontal size of the page. Boxes may be moved up or down using \raise or \lower, and right or left by \moveright or \moveleft. A box can be moved vertically only when TeX is processing material *horizontally* (i.e., it is putting together a line), and it can be moved horizontally only during *vertical* processing.

1–3: \raise and \lower do just that here. \kern gives horizontal space in this context.

6–8: \hsize here is the horizontal size of the page. \leaders make repeating patterns. The pattern here is an * in a 20-point box, positioned differently depending on where \hfil is placed. The final \hfill fills the outer \hbox with the pattern.

13: Since this line is still within the \vbox opened on line 10, \hsize here is the one specified there, not the size of the page as was used (by default) in lines 6–8.

15: \moveright does exactly that to a box.

15–19: \hboxes in a \vbox are stacked above each other. \hfill on line 19 does nothing because the \hbox it is in has the horizontal size of its contents.

21–32: \vboxes in an \hbox are placed side by side. \kern gives horizontal space between the boxes here.

35–39: \leaders can make vertical patterns as well.

Example XV   **75**

XV. _O_N B_OX_I_{NG}

Arranging material in horizontal and vertical boxes.

* * * * * * * * * * * * * * * *
   * * * * * * * * * * * * * * * *
     * * * * * * * * * * * * * * * *

During a superior boxing match (Ali-Frazier I, for instance) we are deeply moved by the body's communion with itself by way of another's intransigent flesh.

Joyce Carol Oates, *On Boxing*, Doubleday (1987).

... Ali was weary.

He had hit Foreman harder than he had ever hit anyone.

He had hit him often.

Foreman's head must by now be equal to a piece of vulcanized rubber.

Norman Mailer, *The Fight*, Little Brown (1975).

Head trauma constituted 68 percent of the injuries, a category that included concussion, brain hemorrhage, skull fracture and fracture of the facial bones. Injuries to the upper extremity and trunk were the next most common.

R.W. Enzenauer et al., *Boxing-related injuries in the U.S. Army, The Journal of the American Medical Assoc.*, March 10, 1989.

I may curse the blood specks on my shirt... but I return again and again... Whether that makes me a humanist or a voyeur, I'm not sure.

John Schulian, *Writers' Fighters and Other Sweet Scientists*, Andrews and McMeel (1983).

```
 1 │ \def\frame #1#2#3#4{\vbox{\hrule height #1pt%        TOP RULE
 2 │  \hbox{\vrule width #1pt\kern #2pt%                  RULE AND SPACE ON LEFT
 3 │  \vbox{\kern #2pt%                                   SPACE AT TOP
 4 │  \vbox{\hsize #3\noindent #4}%                       MATERIAL THAT WILL BE BOXED
 5 │  \kern #2pt}%                                        SPACE AT BOTTOM
 6 │  \kern #2pt\vrule width #1pt}%                       SPACE AND RULE ON RIGHT
 7 │  \hrule height0pt depth #1pt}}%                      BOTTOM RULE
 8 │
 9 │ \def\fitframe #1#2#3{\vbox{\hrule height#1pt%        TOP RULE
10 │  \hbox{\vrule width#1pt\kern #2pt%                   RULE AND SPACE ON LEFT
11 │  \vbox{\kern #2pt\hbox{#3}\kern #2pt}%               TOP, MATERIAL, BOTTOM
12 │  \kern #2pt\vrule width#1pt}%                        SPACE AND RULE ON RIGHT
13 │  \hrule height0pt depth#1pt}}%                       BOTTOM RULE
14 │
15 │ \def\shframe #1#2#3#4{\vbox{\hrule height 0pt%       NO TOP SHADOW
16 │  \hbox{\vrule width #1pt\kern 0pt%                   LEFT SHADOW
17 │  \vbox{\kern-#1pt\frame{.3}{#2}{#3}{#4}%             SHADOW STARTS #1 PT FROM TOP
18 │  \kern-.3pt}%                                        MOVE UP RULE THICKNESS AT BOT.
19 │  \kern-#1pt\vrule width 0pt}%                        STOPS #1 PT FROM RT; NO RT SHAD
20 │  \hrule height #1pt}}%                               BOTTOM SHADOW
21 │
22 │ \def\s #1{\frame{.3}{2}{8pt}{\centerline{#1\vphantom{(}}}\ }
23 │
24 │ \centerline{\bf XVI. PLAYING AROUND}
25 │ \centerline{\sl Framing text; shading boxes; other simpleminded effects.}
26 │ \headline{\hfil\it Example XVI\newpageno} %'\newpageno' IS NOT STANDARD
27 │ \vfil
28 │ \centerline{\frame{.1}{10}{3in}{\noindent Framing text in boxes is often an
29 │ effective way of catching the attention of your readers. Of course, having
30 │ something significant to say {\sl within\/} these boxes usually helps in
31 │ retaining their attention.}}
32 │ \vfil
33 │ \centerline{\fitframe{2}{1}{\frame{.8}{6}{2.25in}{\noindent
34 │ Whatever you do, don't put stuff in framed boxes just for the heck of it.}}}
35 │ \vfil
36 │ \centerline{\fitframe{.3}{.5}{But it's hard to resist such a snug fit!}}
37 │ \vfil
38 │ \centerline{\shframe{3}{10}{130pt}{\centerline{And, finally, this should just}}}
39 │ \vskip 30 pt
40 │ \centerline{\shframe{12}{10}{120pt}{\centerline{LEAP OUT AT YOU.}}\quad}
41 │ \vfil\eject
```

NOTES

1–7: \frame creates a 'frame' (i.e., a ruled box of specified width) around text. **#1** is the rule thickness in points, **#2** the space between the rules and the enclosed text (points), **#3** the horizontal size of the box (in units to be specified) and **#4** the actual text. If the text you want framed is several paragraphs long, you will need to say '\long\def' above instead of \def. (As a precautionary measure, TeX does not normally permit more than one paragraph in place of a parameter in a command.) \kern leaves space, either horizontal or vertical depending on context. The % signs allow explanatory comments to be included. **9–13**: \fitframe adjusts its horizontal size to fit its contents. **#1** and **#2** are still the rule thickness and inner space, respectively; **#3** is the text. This text should not be longer than the horizontal size of the page, unless you like things spilling over into margins. **15–20**: \shframe makes a frame with a 'shadow' on the left and bottom. **#1** is the shadow thickness in points, with **#2**, **#3** and **#4** as in \frame. You may want to experiment with this command: replacing the 0pt dimensions in it with other values will give top and right shadows (you will also have to adjust the various \kern values). **22**: \s produces a single character box; it is just \frame with an 8-point horizontal size and set up to center its contents. The effect is illustrated on pages 79 and 83. **28–40**: Some ways to use these framing commands.

Example XVI **77**

XVI. PLAYING AROUND

Framing text; shading boxes; other simpleminded effects.

Framing text in boxes is often an effective way of catching the attention of your readers. Of course, having something significant to say *within* these boxes usually helps in retaining their attention.

Whatever you do, don't put stuff in framed boxes just for the heck of it.

But it's hard to resist such a snug fit!

And, finally, this should just

LEAP OUT AT YOU.

```
1   \newcount\tw              %top width in pt
2   \newcount\bw              %bottom width in pt
3   \newcount\h               %height in pt
4   \newcount\bs              %bottom shift in pt
5   \newcount\th              %line thickness in 1/64th of a pt
6   \newcount\gp              %line gap in 1/64th of a point
7   \newcount\rs              %running shift
8   \newcount\rw              %running width
9   \newcount\rh              %running height
10  \newcount\tmp             %for temporarily storing variables
11
12  \def\trap #1#2#3#4#5#6{\vbox{\offinterlineskip
13      \tw=#1 \bw=#2 \h=#3 \bs=#4 \th=#5 \gp=#6 \rh=0
14      \multiply\tw by 65536 \multiply\bw by 65536 \multiply\bs by65536
15      \multiply\th by1024 \multiply\gp by1024
16      \loop
17      \tmp=\bs \multiply\tmp by\rh \divide\tmp by\h
18      \rs=\tmp                                 %running shift calculated
19      \tmp=\bw \advance\tmp by-\tw \multiply\tmp by\rh
20      \divide\tmp by\h \advance\tmp by\tw \rw=\tmp    %running width calculated
21      \hbox{\kern\rs sp\vrule height0sp depth\th sp width\rw sp}%RULE DRAWN HERE
22      \vskip\gp sp                            %GAP LEFT HERE
23      \ifnum\rh<\h  \tmp=\rh \multiply\tmp by 65536
24        \advance\tmp by\th \advance\tmp by\gp \divide\tmp by65536 \rh=\tmp
25      \repeat}}
26
27  \def\rect #1#2#3#4{\trap{#1}{#1}{#2}{0}{#3}{#4}}
28
29  \line{\hfil}
30  \vfil
31  \centerline{\s{T}\s{O}\quad\s{C}\s{R}\s{O}\s{W}\s{N}\quad
32  \s{I}\s{T}\quad\s{A}\s{L}\s{L}\s{.}\s{.}\s{.}}
33  \vfil
34  \vbox{\offinterlineskip
35  \centerline{\trap{0}{60}{180}{30}{10}{60}%
36  \trap{2}{65}{100}{-25}{20}{60}\hskip20pt%
37  \trap{2}{65}{100}{-38}{20}{60}\hskip65pt%
38  \trap{0}{60}{180}{-90}{10}{60}}
39  \centerline{\rect{200}{15}{5}{100}}}
40  \vfil\vfil\eject
```

NOTES

1–10: These are variables that will be used in calculations below.

12–25: \trap builds a trapezoid out of horizontal rules. #1 and #2 are the widths at the top and the bottom, #3 the height and #4 the shift at the bottom (i.e., the horizontal gap between the top and bottom left corners). All are in points. #5 is the rule thickness and #6 the vertical gap between successive rules, both in 1/64th of a point—if you choose very small values for these parameters, you will cause TeX to 'overflow'. As each rule is drawn, the current height (measured from the top) is stored in \rh, and the current widths and shifts in \rw and \rs.

12, 34: \offinterlineskip switches off the interline spacing so that the figures drawn will sit directly on top of each other without gaps.

13: Each of the newly labelled registers is set equal to the appropriate input variable.

14–15: TeX rounds off variables to the nearest whole number, so it is advisable to use small units. The numbers chosen here make all variables effectively use units of a *scaled point*, 65536 of which equal a point.

17–18: The 'running shift' is calculated by multiplying the bottom shift by the current-height/height.

19–20: The width of the next rule to be drawn is calculated similarly.

21: The rule is now drawn, shifted (using \kern) by the current shift.

22: The gap between rules is left here.

23–25: If the current height is still not at the final height, the current height is advanced by the rule thickness plus the vertical gap, and the whole process is repeated.

27: This uses \trap to draw a rectangle of width #1 and height #2, using rules of thickness #3, with a gap between rules of #4.

31–32: Shows a use of \s, from the previous page.

35–39: Shows how \trap and \rect may be used.

Example XVI   **79**

T O   C R O W N   I T   A L L . . .

```
 1 | \centerline{\bf XVII. SCENES FROM A MAGAZINE}
 2 | \centerline{\sl Simple aspects of magazine design.}
 3 | \headline{\hfil\it Example XVII\newpageno}      \bigskip \hrule \bigskip
 4 |
 5 | \footline{\sl \ifnum\pageno=1 \hfil \else
 6 |   \ifodd\pageno Date \hfil \the\pageno \else \the\pageno \hfil \sl BRUTE\fi\fi}
 7 |
 8 | \newcount\colnumber \newbox\col \newdimen\tmpdim \newdimen\size
 9 | \newdimen\coljump \coljump=.2 true in                 %GAP BETWEEN COLUMNS
10 |
11 | \def\niceskip {\vskip\baselineskip}
12 | \def\nstrut {\vrule height\topskip depth0pt width0pt}  %TO PROP THINGS UP
13 |
14 | \def\beginart #1/#2{\vbox\bgroup#1 \colnumber=#2  \parskip=0pt
15 |       \advance\colnumber by-1 \tmpdim=\coljump \multiply\tmpdim by\colnumber
16 |       \size=\hsize  \advance\size by-\tmpdim
17 |       \advance\colnumber by1 \divide\size by\colnumber
18 |       \vbadness=10000 \hbadness=2000 \tolerance=2000
19 |       \setbox\col=\vbox\bgroup\hsize\size \noindent\nstrut}
20 |
21 | \def\endart {\global\size=\baselineskip \vfil \egroup
22 |       \multiply\size by\colnumber  \advance\size by-\baselineskip
23 |       \tmpdim=\ht\col  \advance\tmpdim by\size  \divide\tmpdim by\colnumber
24 |       \hbox{\splittopskip=\topskip \doittoit}\egroup}
25 |
26 | \def\doittoit{\ifnum\colnumber>0 \vsplit\col to \tmpdim
27 |       \global\advance\colnumber by-1
28 |       \ifnum\colnumber>0 \hskip\coljump \fi \doittoit \fi}
29 |
30 | \font\head=cminch scaled 833        \font\shead=cmdunh10 scaled\magstep2
31 | \font\blare=cmss10 scaled 2073      \font\title=cmssdc10 scaled 2488
32 |
33 | \centerline{\vbox{\line{\head B\hfil R\hfil U\hfil T\hfil E}
34 | \bigskip \hrule \medskip
35 | \line{\shead \ The\hfil Magazine\hfil for\hfil Sensitive\hfil Men\ }
36 | \smallskip \hrule}} \vfil
37 | \centerline{\title Special Anniversary Issue} \vfil
38 | \centerline{\title COMPUTERS} \vskip .3in
39 | \centerline{\title \&} \vskip .3in
40 | \centerline{\title COOKERY} \vfil
41 | \centerline{\blare BRUTE looks back over} \bigskip
42 | \centerline{\blare 15 years of recipes} \vfil\hrule\eject
```

NOTES

5–6: The current page number is stored by TEX in a register labelled `\pageno`. These lines set a `\footline`: if the page number is 1, the footline is blank; otherwise, odd and even page numbers are set on opposite sides.

8–9: These are whole number, box and dimension registers that will be used in the multiple-column commands `\beginart` and `\endart`. `\coljump` is the gap between columns: it is given a value right away.

11: Gives a vertical skip equal to the interline spacing.

12: `\topskip` is the space left by TEX between the top of a box and the baseline of the first line.

14–19: `\beginart` starts collecting material for an article that is to go into the number of columns specified by #2. Several quantities can be entered for #1: a new `\hsize`, `\coljump`, etc. See how `\beginart` is used on page 84. Lines 15–17 calculate the column width, allowing for gaps between columns. Line 18 resets the parameters of TEX that control spacing; these commands are discussed in the Appendix.

21–24: `\endart` finishes collecting material, then calculates the column height (stored in `\tmpdim`). The columns will go in an `\hbox`. `\splittopskip` is the space at the top of each column. The actual splitting into columns is done by `\doittoit`.

26–28: `\vsplit` splits off from the box of accumulated material, the top portion of height `\tmpdim`. For all but the last column, a horizontal space equal to `\coljump` is also left. This is done repeatedly, till `\colnumber` number of columns have been born. The repetition is achieved via recursion: as you can see, the definition of `\doittoit` involves itself.

30–31: Fonts to be used in various places.

Example XVII　　**81**

XVII. SCENES FROM A MAGAZINE

Simple aspects of magazine design.

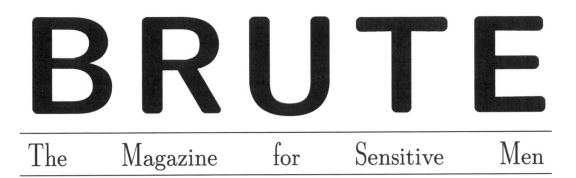

BRUTE

The	Magazine	for	Sensitive	Men

Special Anniversary Issue

COMPUTERS

&

COOKERY

BRUTE looks back over

15 years of recipes

82

```
1  \def\ff #1{\fitframe{.2}{.7}{#1}}
2
3  \hrule
4  \vskip 1.2 in
5  \centerline{\vbox{\hsize260pt
6  \centerline{\fitframe{5}{.7}{\ff{\ff{\ff{\ff{\ff{\frame{.2}{10}{150pt}%
7  {\vskip15pt \blare
8  \centerline{Computer Tips}
9  \medskip
10 \centerline{from}
11 \bigskip
12 \centerline{\title BRUTE}
13 \vskip15pt}}}}}}}
14 \medskip
15 \vskip1pt
16 \hbox{\frame{.5}{7}{245pt}{\line{\quad
17 \vbox{\hbox to1.5in{\leaders\hbox to 5pt{$\rangle$\hfill}\hfill}}\hfil
18 \vrule height2pt depth 0pt width40pt\hskip.3in}}}
19 \bigskip
20 \vskip1pt
21 \hbox{\frame{.5}{7}{245pt}{\sans
22 \centerline{\ \s{}\s{}\s{H}\s{O}\s{W}\s{}\s{T}\s{O}\s{}\s{}}
23 \vskip2pt
24 \centerline{\ \s{M}\s{A}\s{I}\s{N}\s{T}\s{A}\s{I}\s{N}%
25 \s{}\s{Y}\s{O}\s{U}\s{R}}
26 \vskip2pt
27 \centerline{\ \s{}\s{H}\s{A}\s{R}\s{D}\s{}%
28 \s{D}\s{R}\s{I}\s{V}\s{E}\s{}}
29 \vskip4pt
30 \centerline{\fitframe{.3}{2}{\ \rm Our Regular Columnist\ }}}}}}}
31 \vfil
32 \hrule\eject
```

NOTES

COMMENT

The framing commands used on this page were defined in Example XVI.

———————

1: An abbreviation for `\fitframe` to give rules of thickness .2 of a point and an inner space equal to .7 of a point.

5: The `\vbox` that opens here will be closed only on line 30: the entire figure on the facing page can be treated as a single unit.

6–13: These lines draw the 'monitor'.

6: Frames are fitted here repeatedly inside each other.

7, 12: `\blare` and `\title` are just the font names introduced on the previous page.

21–30: These lines draw the 'keyboard'.

Example XVII **83**

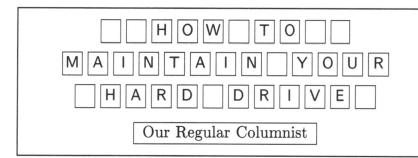

```
 1  \hrule\vskip1.2in
 2  \font\tinyrm=cmr7
 3  \leftline{\blare Saffron Ice Cream}
 4  \smallskip
 5  \hrule height1pt depth0pt width\hsize
 6  \smallskip
 7  \rightline{\sans Cooking Column}
 8  \bigskip
 9  \beginart \hsize=5.4 true in \coljump=.15 true in / {3}
10  \baselineskip=14 true pt \tinyrm
11  Saffron is a spice made by drying the style of the crocus, a flower in the iris
12  family. It has a wonderful fragrance and flavor for which there are no
13  substitutes. It is also one of the most expensive spices in the world, currently
14  selling at about one-quarter the price of gold. However, a little goes a long
15  way, so it is possible to occasionally indulge.
16
17  This recipe makes an utterly memorable ice cream. It has been known to make even
18  the most disinterested of eaters pause in mid-speech, their eyes widening in
19  surprise, when the first spoonful hits their tongues.\niceskip
20  \centerline{\bf Ingredients}
21  \item{1/3} cup light cream.
22  \item{1} generous pinch (say 1/2 gram) saffron threads.
23  \item{12} pods cardamom.
24  \item{1/2} gallon vanilla ice cream. \niceskip
25  \centerline{\bf Method}     \noindent
26  An hour before serving, warm the cream till it feels very slightly hot to the
27  touch, then add the saffron. Leave the cream on very low heat, just enough to
28  maintain a warm temperature, for an hour. If it looks as though the liquid
29  is evaporating away, add more cream. The cream will turn an intense golden
30  color. At the end of an hour, peel the cardamom seeds and crush finely, then add
31  to the cream. Stir and remove from heat.\par
32  A few minutes before serving, place the ice cream in a large bowl and pour and
33  scrape the saffron-cream mixture over it. Very quickly, using a hand-held mixer,
34  beat the saffron-cream into the ice cream. This takes muscle and care, but the
35  rewards for your efforts are now very near. It is usually easiest to work your
36  way in from the edges and, of course, it helps if the ice cream is softened
37  slightly beforehand.\par Eat at once.
38  \endart
39  \bigskip
40  \hrule height1pt depth0pt width\hsize
41  \vfil\hrule\eject
42  \footline{\hfil}
```

NOTES

It must be stressed that the \beginart...\endart combination shown here is suitable only for short articles that will fit onto single pages.

9: The commands before / are optional, but they show how the horizontal size of the full display and the gaps between columns may be reset. By the definition of this multiple-column command on page 80, the default size for the display is the full page size and the default gap between columns .2 inch. As you can see from the output, the new horizontal size is slightly less than that of the page.

The number after the / is the number of columns.

10: For three or more columns on a standard-size page (7 inches or less in horizontal size), you are likely to run into problems with 'overfull' boxes: i.e., TEX will find it hard to find good line breaks. You will then have to choose new values for \tolerance and \hbadness (just as a new \baselineskip has been chosen here). Both commands are discussed in the Appendix.

16, 31: Blank lines or \par may be used as usual here to end paragraphs.

42: Our magazine pages are over. \footline is reset.

Example XVII 85

Saffron Ice Cream

Cooking Column

Saffron is a spice made by drying the style of the crocus, a flower in the iris family. It has a wonderful fragrance and flavor for which there are no substitutes. It is also one of the most expensive spices in the world, currently selling at about one-quarter the price of gold. However, a little goes a long way, so it is possible to occasionally indulge.

This recipe makes an utterly memorable ice cream. It has been known to make even the most disinterested of eaters pause in mid-speech, their eyes widening in surprise, when the first spoonful hits their tongues.

Ingredients

1/3 cup light cream.

1 generous pinch (say 1/2 gram) saffron threads.

12 pods cardamom.

1/2 gallon vanilla ice cream.

Method

An hour before serving, warm the cream till it feels very slightly hot to the touch, then add the saffron. Leave the cream on very low heat, just enough to maintain a warm temperature, for an hour. If it looks as though the liquid is evaporating away, add more cream. The cream will turn an intense golden color. At the end of an hour, peel the cardamom seeds and crush finely, then add to the cream. Stir and remove from heat.

A few minutes before serving, place the ice cream in a large bowl and pour and scrape the saffron-cream mixture over it. Very quickly, using a hand-held mixer, beat the saffron-cream into the ice cream. This takes muscle and care, but the rewards for your efforts are now very near. It is usually easiest to work your way in from the edges and, of course, it helps if the ice cream is softened slightly beforehand.

Eat at once.

```
1  \rightline{\title Acknowledgements} %WARNING: SEE PAGE 1 FOR \title DEF.
2  \rightline{\sl Font switching; ragged right edges;}
3  \rightline{\sl suppressing hyphenation.}
4  \vskip 2.5 true in \vskip-2\baselineskip
5  \headline{\hfil}
6
7  \font\smrm=cmr9                    \font\smit=cmti9
8  \font\smsl=cmsl9                   \font\smbf=cmbx9
9  \def\medfont {\let\rm=\smrm \let\it=\smit \let\sl=\smsl \let\bf=\smbf
10      \baselineskip=12pt \rm}
11
12 \vbox{\hsize 5.6 true in \pretolerance=10000
13 \raggedright \raggedbottom \medfont
14 \noindent Luca Bombelli helped me learn \TeX, put up with the many na\"\i ve
15 questions I had, and made several extremely useful suggestions. Carl Brown,
16 Harvey Rarback and Jim Simone gave me much help with computers. George
17 Greenwade, Rainer Sch\"opf and Philip Taylor helped with \TeX\ archive
18 information. Aida El-Khadra told me a little about German hyphenation. Several
19 other people looked at this book at various stages and offered suggestions or
20 encouragement. They include Parag Amladi, Abhay Ashtekar, Barbara Beeton, Matt
21 Choptuik, Mike Creutz, Rosanne Di\thinspace Stefano, Josh Goldberg, Isabell
22 Harrity, Nahmin Horwitz, Bob Melter, Barbara Nichols, Frank Paige, Peter
23 Palffy-Muhoray, Tomas Rokicki and Joette Stefl-Mabry. In particular, Victor
24 Eijkhout and Catherine Wulforst carefully read the almost-final draft and made
25 very detailed criticisms. I'm grateful to them all. I'm also grateful to the
26 editors at Academic Press---Sari Kalin, Camille Pecoul, Natasha Sabath and
27 Jenifer Swetland---for the enthusiasm they have shown for this book.
28 \smallskip
29 I'm especially grateful to Donald Knuth for the many hours of pleasure I've had
30 working with \TeX, for his enthusiastic and encouraging response to the first
31 version of the book, and for several detailed and very helpful comments he made.
32 \smallskip
33 Of course, I alone am responsible for errors or other flaws that still remain.
34 \smallskip
35 The first version of the book was written in 1987, when I was a postdoctoral
36 fellow with the Relativity Group at Syracuse University, supported in part by
37 NSF grants PHY8318350 and PHY8310041. Since then I have been on the faculty of
38 Long Island University and a guest scientist with the High Energy Theory Group
39 at Brookhaven National Laboratory. I thank my colleagues at all these
40 institutions for their support.\smallskip}   \vfil\eject
```

NOTES

4: The \vskips are chosen to give an effective gap of 2.5 inches from the bottom of the main title line.

5: The headline, unnecessary here, is suppressed.

7–10: This is a simple illustration of how font size may be switched by a single command. Lines 7–10 define names for some 9-point Computer Modern fonts. \medfont then allows you to continue using the commands \rm, \it, \sl and \bf for roman, italic, slanted and bold type; it also chooses a different interline spacing, and it makes \rm the default style. Such commands are useful, for they allow you to switch font sizes in a document but yet continue using the same commands for italics, etc. The references on the next page use this feature. To return to the original font size, you should have an analogous command defined that makes \rm, \sl, etc., now refer to those styles in the original size. Otherwise, you will have to use braces to localize the effect of \medfont.

12: \pretolerance refers to the tolerance that TeX has for white space on a line, before it attempts hyphenation. TeX assigns values of a quantity called 'badness' to spaces that are too large, and it tries to arrange words so as not to let the badness exceed the value of \pretolerance. If it cannot, it will start looking for hyphenations. The highest value of badness it will assign is 10000, so this value of pretolerance effectively suppresses hyphenation.

13: The normal right justification and vertical justification (which causes the baselines of the bottom lines on every full page to line up) that TeX provides mean that it must stretch or shrink horizontal and vertical spaces slightly. The normal interword and inter-sentence spaces are therefore allowed to be elastic, as are the inter-paragraph spaces, the spaces given by \bigskip, \medskip, etc. \raggedright makes the horizontal spaces rigid, and \raggedbottom does that for vertical spaces. This, of course, switches off right and vertical justification.

Acknowledgements

Font switching; ragged right edges;

suppressing hyphenation.

Luca Bombelli helped me learn TeX, put up with the many naïve questions I had, and made several extremely useful suggestions. Carl Brown, Harvey Rarback and Jim Simone gave me much help with computers. George Greenwade, Rainer Schöpf and Philip Taylor helped with TeX archive information. Aida El-Khadra told me a little about German hyphenation. Several other people looked at this book at various stages and offered suggestions or encouragement. They include Parag Amladi, Abhay Ashtekar, Barbara Beeton, Matt Choptuik, Mike Creutz, Rosanne Di Stefano, Josh Goldberg, Isabell Harrity, Nahmin Horwitz, Bob Melter, Barbara Nichols, Frank Paige, Peter Palffy-Muhoray, Tomas Rokicki and Joette Stefl-Mabry. In particular, Victor Eijkhout and Catherine Wulforst carefully read the almost-final draft and made very detailed criticisms. I'm grateful to them all. I'm also grateful to the editors at Academic Press—Sari Kalin, Camille Pecoul, Natasha Sabath and Jenifer Swetland—for the enthusiasm they have shown for this book.

I'm especially grateful to Donald Knuth for the many hours of pleasure I've had working with TeX, for his enthusiastic and encouraging response to the first version of the book, and for several detailed and very helpful comments he made.

Of course, I alone am responsible for errors or other flaws that still remain.

The first version of the book was written in 1987, when I was a postdoctoral fellow with the Relativity Group at Syracuse University, supported in part by NSF grants PHY8318350 and PHY8310041. Since then I have been on the faculty of Long Island University and a guest scientist with the High Energy Theory Group at Brookhaven National Laboratory. I thank my colleagues at all these institutions for their support.

```
1  \line{\hfil\title References} %WARNING: SEE PAGE 1 FOR \title DEF
2  \line{\hfil\sl Automatic numbering; lists within lists.}
3  \headline{\hfil}
4  \vskip 2.5 true in \vskip-\baselineskip
5
6  \newcount\q  \q=0
7  \def\nref {\global\advance\q by1 \item{\bf\the\q.}}
8
9  {\medfont \frenchspacing
10 \nref D.E. Knuth, {\it The \TeX book}, Addison Wesley (1986).
11 \nref G. Orwell, {\sl Politics and the English Language},
12 reprinted as \#38 in Volume 4 of {\it The Collected Essays, Journalism
13 and Letters of George Orwell}, Penguin Books (1970).
14 \nref V.S. Naipaul, {\it A House for Mr.~Biswas}, Andr\'e Deutsch (1961);
15 American edition by Alfred A.~Knopf (1983). \copyright\
16 1961, 1969 by V.S.~Naipaul.
17 \nref B. Belitt, {\sl The Heraldry of Accommodation: A House
18 for Mr.~Naipaul}, {\it Salmagundi}, \#54, 23--42 (1981).
19 \nref R. Penrose, {\it Rev. Mod. Phys.} {\bf 37}, 215--220 (1965).
20 \nref S.W. Hawking and G.F.R. Ellis, {\it The Large Scale
21 Structure of Space-time}, Cambridge Univ. Press (1973).
22 \nref V. Moncrief and J. Isenberg,
23 \itemitem{\bf a.}{\it Comm. Math. Phys.} {\bf 89}, 387--413 (1983);
24 \itemitem{\bf b.}{\it J. Math. Phys.} {\bf 26}, 1024--1027 (1985).
25 \nref A. Borde, {\it Phys. Lett.} {\bf A102}, 224--226 (1984).
26 \nref D.E. Knuth, {\it Surreal Numbers}, Addison Wesley (1974).
27 \nref K. G\"odel,
28 \itemitem{\bf a.} {\sl A Remark About the Connection Between Relativity
29 Theory and Idealistic Philosophy}, in {\it Albert Einstein:
30 Philosopher-Scientist}, ed. by P.A. Schilpp, Open Court
31 Publishing Co. (1949);
32 \itemitem{\bf b.}{\sl An Example of a New Type of Cosmological Solution
33 of Einstein's Field Equations of Gravitation}, {\it Rev. Mod. Phys.} {\bf 21},
34 447--450 (1949).
35 \nref R. Penrose, {\it Phys. Rev. Lett.} {\bf 14}, 57--59 (1965).
36 \nref S.W. Hawking, {\it Phys. Rev. Lett.} {\bf 15}, 689--690 (1966).
37 \nref H.R. Lewis, {\it Phys. Rev. Lett.} {\bf 18}, 510--512 (1967).
38 \nref F.J. Tipler, {\it Phys. Rev.} {\bf D17}, 2521--2528 (1978).
39 \nref A. Borde, {\it Cl. and Quant. Grav.} {\bf 4}, 343--356 (1987).
40 \nref G.H. Hardy, {\it Ramanujan}, Chelsea Publishing Co. (1978).\par}
41 \bye
```

NOTES

6–7: The new numerical variable \q will keep track of the reference number. At each new reference entry, introduced by \nref, \q is increased by 1, and its current value is extracted and printed by the \the command. This allows you to change items in the list without having to change numbering each time.

9: \medfont is the font switching command from page 86. \frenchspacing makes all single spaces the same, wherever they occur. (Normally, TeX leaves slightly bigger spaces after a punctuation mark like a period.) This is useful in bibliographies and lists of references. The effect of \frenchspacing can either be confined within a group (i.e., within braces) as is done here, or switched off by saying \nonfrenchspacing later.

23, 24, etc.: \itemitem gives you a list within a list.

40: When certain paragraph parameters are reset locally (i.e., within a group), the final paragraph must be ended before the closing brace of the group. Otherwise, that paragraph will not honor the new settings. See the notes on pages 6 and 20. The explicit paragraph-ending command \par is used here to end the paragraph before the }; this preserves the new setting for \baselineskip up to the end.

References

Automatic numbering; lists within lists.

1. D.E. Knuth, *The TEXbook*, Addison Wesley (1986).

2. G. Orwell, *Politics and the English Language*, reprinted as #38 in Volume 4 of *The Collected Essays, Journalism and Letters of George Orwell*, Penguin Books (1970).

3. V.S. Naipaul, *A House for Mr. Biswas*, André Deutsch (1961); American edition by Alfred A. Knopf (1983). © 1961, 1969 by V.S. Naipaul.

4. B. Belitt, *The Heraldry of Accommodation: A House for Mr. Naipaul*, *Salmagundi*, #54, 23–42 (1981).

5. R. Penrose, *Rev. Mod. Phys.* **37**, 215–220 (1965).

6. S.W. Hawking and G.F.R. Ellis, *The Large Scale Structure of Space-time*, Cambridge Univ. Press (1973).

7. V. Moncrief and J. Isenberg,
   a. *Comm. Math. Phys.* **89**, 387–413 (1983);
   b. *J. Math. Phys.* **26**, 1024–1027 (1985).

8. A. Borde, *Phys. Lett.* **A102**, 224–226 (1984).

9. D.E. Knuth, *Surreal Numbers*, Addison Wesley (1974).

10. K. Gödel,
    a. *A Remark About the Connection Between Relativity Theory and Idealistic Philosophy*, in *Albert Einstein: Philosopher-Scientist*, ed. by P.A. Schilpp, Open Court Publishing Co. (1949);
    b. *An Example of a New Type of Cosmological Solution of Einstein's Field Equations of Gravitation*, *Rev. Mod. Phys.* **21**, 447–450 (1949).

11. R. Penrose, *Phys. Rev. Lett.* **14**, 57–59 (1965).

12. S.W. Hawking, *Phys. Rev. Lett.* **15**, 689–690 (1966).

13. H.R. Lewis, *Phys. Rev. Lett.* **18**, 510–512 (1967).

14. F.J. Tipler, *Phys. Rev.* **D17**, 2521–2528 (1978).

15. A. Borde, *Cl. and Quant. Grav.* **4**, 343–356 (1987).

16. G.H. Hardy, *Ramanujan*, Chelsea Publishing Co. (1978).

```
 1  \input tbeappndmac
 2  \startat{91}{1}
 3
 4  %NOTE: '\pn' below is the boldface font (cmbx12) used also for page numbers.
 5  {\let\par=\endgraf \leftskip-.5in \parskip3pt \parindent\indsize
 6  \baselineskip13.5pt \start \noindent
 7  This is an alphabetical Appendix. It lists topics as well as commands.
 8  \medskip
 9  \ti {\pn The commands} listed are of two types: {\htopic primitive} and
10  composite. Primitive commands are the basic building blocks of \TeX,
11  indecomposable into other \TeX\ commands. {\emph They are marked by an $\ast$
12  when listed in this Appendix}. Composite commands are ones defined in terms
13  of primitives. Those that are listed here are part of the widely distributed
14  package, {\emph Plain~\TeX}. The package is discussed later in this Appendix.
15  For the most part, Plain~\TeX\ commands will be treated just like primitives:
16  they will be explained purely in terms of the effects they have. In a few cases,
17  however, you will also be told exactly how the command is defined. This will
18  allow you to see how Plain~\TeX\ is set up internally, and to alter the
19  definitions to suit your own needs.
20  \medskip
21  \ti {\pn Finding things} in the Appendix is easy. For instance, mathematical
22  symbols are to be found under various sub-headings of {\htopic mathematics}
23  (like {\htopic mathematics:\ greek letters}), other special characters are
24  listed under {\htopic special characters}, and spacing commands are discussed
25  under {\htopic spacing} and {\htopic mathematics:\ spacing}.
26  Single-character commands are listed at the start, since the effects of such
27  commands are not \hbox{always obvious}. % To prevent an isolated word.
28  \medskip
29  \ti {\pn Input boxes} will not be shown for the rest of this Appendix.
30  When you need to see input,
31  say for $\spadesuit$, you will be shown snippets of the input
32  file, like so:
33  \beginliteral
34  @dots say for $\spadesuit$, you will be shown snippets of the input @dots
35  \endliteral
36  \noindent It should not take you too long to get used to this approach.
37  \medskip
38      Etc., etc.
```

NOTES

The input for the Appendix is repetitive, and it is not particularly useful to display it all. Therefore, this will be the last input box you will see for a while. The actual formatting commands, stored in a file called *tbeappndmac* (for 'TEX by Example Appendix Macros'), are interesting and are reproduced in the Epilogue. Some sample input is also displayed there. And in those places where something interesting does happen in the input, you will be given a glimpse of it, as shown on the facing page.

The commands used on this page are largely nonstandard. Their definitions are reproduced in the Epilogue.

Appendix

An index and a glossary.

This is an alphabetical Appendix. It lists topics as well as commands.

- **The commands** listed are of two types: primitive and composite. Primitive commands are the basic building blocks of TEX, indecomposable into other TEX commands. *They are marked by an * when listed in this Appendix.* Composite commands are ones defined in terms of primitives. Those that are listed here are part of the widely distributed package, *Plain TEX*. The package is discussed later in this Appendix. For the most part, Plain TEX commands will be treated just like primitives: they will be explained purely in terms of the effects they have. In a few cases, however, you will also be told exactly how the command is defined. This will allow you to see how Plain TEX is set up internally, and to alter the definitions to suit your own needs.

- **Finding things** in the Appendix is easy. For instance, mathematical symbols are to be found under various sub-headings of **mathematics** (like **mathematics: greek letters**), other special characters are listed under **special characters**, and spacing commands are discussed under **spacing** and **mathematics: spacing**. Single-character commands are listed at the start, since the effects of such commands are not always obvious.

- **Input boxes** will not be shown for the rest of this Appendix. When you need to see input, say for ♠, you will be shown snippets of the input file, like so:

  ```
  ... say for $\spadesuit$, you will be shown snippets of the input ...
  ```

It should not take you too long to get used to this approach.

- **Basic aspects** of TEX are explained in scattered places throughout the Appendix. Though an alphabetical arrangement is not ideal for systematic learning, it should still be possible for you to learn a little about TEX in an organized way. **Boxes** and **glue** explain the model underlying TEX; **paragraphs**, **pages** and associated entries describe, qualitatively, the mechanics of the program. These are all *informal* accounts: no attempt is being made to provide details. For those, you will have to consult Donald Knuth's *TEXbook*.

A list of command characters   6–7

$$\backslash \quad \{ \quad \} \quad \$ \quad \& \quad \hat{} \quad \_ \quad \% \quad \tilde{} \quad \#$$

Their roles are explained under **Command characters** in the Introduction. See also **category codes**. A few combinations of these characters play special roles:

$$ starts and ends the 'mathematics: display' mode.

&& is used to make a repetitive preamble for a table. See table 3 in Example VI.

is used in place of **#** when defining a command that contains an alignment. See the definition of **\address** in Example XI, or that of **\table** under **tables** below.

A list of ligatures

A ligature is a combination of two or more characters that is printed as a single character. The following combinations are regarded by TEX as ligatures in most fonts (the character they give is shown in parentheses):

$$`` \text{ (")}, \quad '' \text{ (")}, \quad -- \text{ (–)}, \quad --- \text{ (—)}, \quad ?` \text{ (¿)}, \quad !` \text{ (¡)},$$
$$\text{ff (ff)}, \quad \text{fi (fi)}, \quad \text{fl (fl)}, \quad \text{ffi (ffi)}, \quad \text{and} \quad \text{ffl (ffl)}.$$

A list of single character commands

$$\backslash', \quad \backslash`, \quad \backslash", \quad \backslash=, \quad \backslash., \quad \backslash\tilde{}, \quad \backslash\hat{}, \quad \backslash b, \quad \backslash c, \quad \backslash d, \quad \backslash H, \quad \backslash t, \quad \backslash u \text{ and } \backslash v$$

give **accents** (see the entry below). The commands

$$\backslash\#, \quad \backslash\$, \quad \backslash\%, \quad \backslash\&, \quad \$\backslash\{\$, \quad \$\backslash\}\$, \quad \$\backslash|\$ \text{ and } \$\backslash\_\$$$

produce

$$\#, \quad \$, \quad \%, \quad \&, \quad \{, \quad \}, \quad \| \text{ and } \_,$$

respectively. For the effects of

$$\backslash i, \quad \backslash j, \quad \backslash l, \quad \backslash L, \quad \backslash o, \quad \backslash O, \quad \backslash P \text{ and } \backslash S,$$

see **special characters**.

$$\backslash \quad (\textit{i.e.,} \backslash \textit{ followed by a space}), \quad \backslash/, \quad \$\backslash>\$, \quad \$\backslash,\$, \quad \$\backslash;\$ \text{ and } \$\backslash!\$$$

are spacing commands. See **spacing** and **mathematics: spacing**. Finally,

\+ starts new lines in alignments made with **\settabs**;

\- suggests hyphenation;

* suggests a line break at a multiplication. See **mathematics: line breaks**.

Note: \ , \/ and \- are primitive commands.

accents (text)   x–xi, 36–37, 58–59

è	\'e	é	\'e	ê	\^e	ë	\"e	ẽ	\~e
ē	\=e	ė	\.e	ĕ	\u e	ě	\v e	e̋	\H e
âe	\t ae	ę	\c e	ẹ	\d e	e	\b e		

These accents may be put on other letters as well. If the letters 'i' and 'j' are to be accented from above, they must be stripped of their dots. **Special characters (text)** shows how to do this. Also, see Example IV. Note that '\t ae' (from the table above) must not be typed as '\tae'; however, you may type '\t{ae}'. The second method is often preferable because it indicates the scope of the command.

\advance *   2, 68, 72, 78, 80, 88

Advances the values of variables stored by TEX. For example, the command is used internally by Plain TEX to automatically advance the values of page numbers each time a page is sent out into the world. See \output.

alignments   26–27, 40–51

See matrices and tables.

\allowbreak

Suggests possible line breaks to TEX at places that it would not pick on its own. For example, a formula will not be broken at a comma (since that is usually not a good place for a break) unless a break is explicitly allowed, as it is just here: (a, b, c, d, e, f). The input for this was:

```
... allowed, as it is just here:\quad $(a,\allowbreak b,\allowbreak c,
\allowbreak d,\allowbreak e,\allowbreak f)$. The input for ...
```

arguments

The argument of a command is, roughly, the text on which it acts; e.g., the argument of \centerline{Don't argue!} is Don't argue!. Not all commands take arguments and, wherever possible, it is preferable to set commands up without them. If a command accepts arguments, the program will read ahead to the end of the argument before carrying out the command. The process consumes time and memory. For something like \centerline, this is unavoidable: TEX has to look ahead and find out what is to be centered before it can typeset the line. But for something like, say, a typeface change, all you need is this: the new typeface must start being used at some point, and then continue being used till 'switched off'; there is no need for the program to read ahead to find out first where the switch-off point is. So, though it would be possible to define, say, a 'change-to-italics' command of the type \italic{...}, with an argument, such a command would be highly inefficient. The standard procedure (using {\it... }) is far better, and the basic idea there should be followed as far as possible (i.e., define separate 'switch-on' and 'switch-off' points—for \it the switch-off point is just the place where } occurs).

at   viii-ix

A keyword used to specify the size of a font.

\baselineskip *   xiv–1, 44–45, 50–51, 58–59, 66–67, 70–71, 74–75, 84–87

Represents the value of the gap between 'baselines'—roughly, the bottoms of lines of text, though characters like 'y' descend below the baseline—of successive lines. Plain TEX sets it to be 12pt. See page *xiv* and paragraphs.

\begingroup *

A grouping command that may be used in place of { to start a group in certain situations, but which is not always interchangeable with it. \begingroup must be paired with a matching \endgroup. See \bgroup and grouping for more details.

\bf   vi–vii, 2–3, 8–9, 20–21, 86–87

Gives you **bold roman type**, if you type '{\bf bold roman type}'.

\bgroup   70–71, 80

Represents an *implicit* left brace; it may be used in place of { in many situations. A **group** begun this way usually ends with \egroup, though it is possible to use } in some cases. (See \let for the Plain TEX definition of \bgroup.)

\bgroup and \egroup (as also \begingroup and \endgroup) allow you greater freedom in grouping than you are permitted with { and }. Suppose, for example, that you want to define a command that changes the output format of several pages of text. It is convenient to be able to start the changes with one command and then switch them off wherever you want with another. See **arguments** above. Such commands can be defined using \bgroup (or \begingroup) in the definition of the first command, and then ending the group by using \egroup (or \endgroup) in the definition of the 'switch-off' command. See Example XIII, the definition of \ignore under **comments**, or the definitions of \table and \caption under **tables**. { and } cannot be used singly in this way. See **grouping** for a few more details.

\bigbreak   24–28

Suggests a possible page break to TEX; if the suggestion isn't taken, a vertical gap equal to \bigskip is left instead.

\bigskip   vi–ix, xii–xiii, 8–9, 11–13

Leaves a vertical space: _____ . This is a 12 point space that can stretch or shrink, when needed. the Plain TEX definition of \bigskip is:

```
\bigskipamount=12pt plus 4pt minus 4pt
\def\bigskip{\vskip\bigskipamount}
```

If you do not like the space that \bigskip gives, all you have to do is change the definition at any point in your file. Subsequent uses of \bigskip will obey the new definition.

blank spaces   10–13, 32–33

• A single *blank space* can be left by typing '\ ' (i.e., \ followed by a space). For spaces of other lengths, see \obeyspaces and \hskip.

• A *blank line* can be obtained by typing '\hfil\break\line{}'. \hfil\break ends the current line, and \line{} makes the next line blank. If you are already at the start of a line *within a paragraph* (i.e., not starting a new paragraph), use \line{} to leave it blank. If you want the next available line left blank, without forcibly ending the current one, type '\vadjust{\hfil\break\line{}}' anywhere in the line below which you want the blank one. If you want the first line of

a new paragraph left blank, use either \hfil\break or \line{}. The first alternative will effectively absorb the paragraph indentation; i.e., the next line won't be indented. The second method will carry the indentation over to the line that immediately follows.

The input that gave the blank line above was:

```
... line below which you \vadjust{\hfil\break\line{}} want the blank
one. If you want the first line of a new paragraph left blank, ...
```

• A *blank page* is created by \vfil\eject\line{}\vfil\eject. This ends the current page right away and then leaves the next one blank. If you are already at the start of the page you want left blank, use \line{}\vfil\eject. If you merely want the next full page to be blank, without forcibly breaking the current one, use \pageinsert with just '\vfil' as the insert.

- For more about leaving spaces, see null and spacing.

boldface

See \bf.

\botmark *

See \mark.

\box *

A box register, where information can be stored. Boxes are discussed as a separate topic below. There are 256 box registers available: \box0, ..., \box255. (See the discussion of \count.) You can store something in a box register by typing, for example, '\setbox0=\hbox{Pandora's box}'. This information can be retrieved by either typing '\box0' or '\copy0': both print the box contents, but the first also erases the register. For example, 'Pandora's box, Pandora's box, Pandora's box, ' was obtained from these lines in the input file:

```
... register. \setbox0=\hbox{Pandora's box}For example, '\copy0,
\copy0, \box0, \box0' was obtained from these lines in ...
```

As you will have noticed, the second \box0 did nothing—the first had already emptied the box. You can store information in a \vbox, and retrieve it, in exactly the same way. \box0, ..., \box9 are always kept available for temporary storage (they are called 'scratch registers') and \box255 is reserved for use as a place where information about the current page is stored just before it is shipped out by TEX. See \newbox for information about allocating box registers.

If you use a lot of explicitly introduced boxes, you may end up with more complex structures (boxes-within-boxes-within-boxes...) on a page than you really need. To help you out, TEX allows you to 'unbox' the contents of a box: \unhbox and \unvbox behave like \box, except that they strip off the outer level of boxing; \unhcopy and \unvcopy behave similarly like \copy.

boxes   74–75

TEX organizes material in rectangular arrangements called boxes. There are two types: horizontal (\hbox) and vertical (\vbox). The two behave differently in the way they arrange material within and in how they fit together with other boxes. See Example XV for an illustration and \hbox, \vbox and \box for more details.

From single characters, to complex arrangements of text and formulas, all the way to entire pages, TEX thinks of entities that it deals with merely as rectangles of certain specified sizes. (Complex arrangements are just boxes, containing boxes, containing other boxes....) If you want to understand how the program works, you will have to study how such boxes are put together. A detailed explanation can be found in Knuth's TEXbook.

The space between boxes is considered by TEX to be occupied by an entity that it calls glue. The construct is discussed separately. Glue has elastic properties, allowing spaces between boxes to stretch or shrink as needed, within limits specified beforehand. Rectangular boxes and elastic glue make up the 'model' on which TEX is based.

Example XV illustrates the use of explicitly introduced boxes. One basic feature of boxing has been used at several places in this book: material in a box will not be split by TEX. If it is in an \hbox, it will not permit line breaks; if it is in a \vbox, it will not be broken vertically (for page breaks). For example, Tables 1–4 in Example VI were each put in \vboxes to prevent the material inside from being divided over two pages.

The horizontal size of a box is called its width. A point is chosen on the left edge of every box to serve as its 'reference point'. The horizontal line through this point is called the 'baseline' of the box. The baselines of boxes containing single characters are chosen to make the characters align properly and the baselines of larger boxes are determined from the baselines of their contents, following a set of precise rules. See \vbox and \vtop. The vertical sizes of a box above and below its baseline are called its height and depth respectively.

When boxes are put next to each other horizontally, as when TEX is putting together a line of text, they are aligned along their baselines. When boxes are being stacked vertically, their reference points are placed directly one above the other. A box is considered underfull if it is larger than the total size of its contents and overfull if it has too much crammed in it. These 'contents' can be other boxes as well as white space (i.e., glue) that is explicitly asked for.

\break   x–xiii, 18–19, 54–57

Breaks—i.e., ends—lines or pages, depending on the context. If TEX is in horizontal mode (very roughly, in the middle of a line), \break will break the line; if TEX is in vertical mode (roughly, between lines), it will break the page. In either case, unless the rest of the line or page is filled with white space by an explicit command (\hfil or \vfil), TEX will report an 'underfull' box. See modes to find out when TEX is in the 'middle of a line' and when it is 'between lines'.

$\buildrel$

See mathematics: special effects.

by

See keywords.

\bye   xii, 17, 58, 88

A composite command that explicitly takes care of several things before it ends the TEX session: it ends the current paragraph by inserting the paragraph-ending command \par, it fills the rest of the page with white space and it ensures that inserts (see \midinsert, \pageinsert and \topinsert) being held by the program will get printed. It is usually preferable to end a TEX file with \bye rather than directly with \end. However, if you happen to have redefined \par to do special things at the end of paragraphs—this is briefly discussed under \endgraf—\bye may give you too many of these special effects at the end (because of the explicit insertions of \par).

$\cal$ 14–15, 30–35

Produces $\mathcal{C}$alligraphic $\mathcal{S}$cript. Available only in the mathematics mode, and just for uppercase letters. $\cal X$ produces $\mathcal{X}$. The available letters are:

$$\mathcal{A} \quad \mathcal{B} \quad \mathcal{C} \quad \mathcal{D} \quad \mathcal{E} \quad \mathcal{F} \quad \mathcal{G} \quad \mathcal{H} \quad \mathcal{I} \quad \mathcal{J} \quad \mathcal{K} \quad \mathcal{L} \quad \mathcal{M}$$
$$\mathcal{N} \quad \mathcal{O} \quad \mathcal{P} \quad \mathcal{Q} \quad \mathcal{R} \quad \mathcal{S} \quad \mathcal{T} \quad \mathcal{U} \quad \mathcal{V} \quad \mathcal{W} \quad \mathcal{X} \quad \mathcal{Y} \quad \mathcal{Z}$$

If you use the command with lowercase letters, you get general weirdness; for example, $\cal x$ gives §. Therefore, if you are using calligraphic characters in a longer expression, you must group correctly (i.e., use { and } to mark the portion you want in this style).

$\cases$ 26–27

Produces displays like:

$$|x| = \begin{cases} +x & \text{for } x \geq 0; \\ -x & \text{for } x < 0. \end{cases}$$

See also Example II. The input used for the display above was:

```
$$|x|=\cases{+x&for $x \geq 0$;\cr
           -x&for $x < 0$.\cr}$$
```

\catcode *

See category codes.

category codes

When TEX processes a page, it responds differently to the different characters that it encounters: some characters are printed, others interpreted as commands to do other things. For example, a '$' is normally taken not as an instruction to print '$', but instead as a signal to switch on/off the mathematics mode. The response depends on the 'category code' of the character. There are 16 categories of characters, with codes ranging from 0 to 15. The categories, and the standard assignments of characters to each category, are:

0	*Escape*	\	8	*Subscript*	_
1	*Begin group*	{	9	*Ignored*	null
2	*End group*	}	10	*Space*	space
3	*Math mode on/off*	$	11	*Letter*	a, ..., Z
4	*Alignment tab*	&	12	*Other*	none of the others
5	*End of line*	return	13	*Active*	~
6	*Parameter*	#	14	*Comment*	%
7	*Superscript*	^	15	*Invalid*	delete

Category codes should not be confused with **character codes** (that topic is discussed separately): character codes identify the actual character, category codes identify the *role* the character is currently playing. Each character that is fed to TEX is seen by it internally as a pair of codes: character and category. The assignment of a category code is made early during the processing of a file; this makes the switching of category codes, needed for a few advanced applications, sometimes difficult to achieve.

The switching of category codes is illustrated in the Epilogue, in the definition of a command called **\literal**, and in the definition of the command **\ignore** under **comments** in this Appendix. Switching their category codes makes characters play roles different from their usual ones. For example, *any* character with assigned category code 11 will act like a 'letter'—and can then be used in a command name. The technique is commonly used as a precaution when designing packages of new commands: the character @, normally in category 12, is temporarily assigned to category 11 and used in the names of commands that are employed purely internally in the package (leading to such command names as **\n@me**).

Category codes are assigned to characters by using the command \catcode. For example, \catcode37=1 places the character corresponding to decimal character code 37 in category 1; i.e., the character will now play the role of the grouping symbol {. If character codes are not known, or if it is tedious to look them up, then a technique discussed at the end of the entry on character codes may be used to summon these codes automatically. In that technique, '\$ summons the character code of $, and so on. Thus, \catcode'\$=4 will make $ play the role of the alignment tab &. (& itself will continue to play the same role, unless its category is also changed.)

centering   vi–vii, 6–9, 20–21, 44–45

To center material *vertically* on a page, place the command \vfil above and below the material. You will probably also need to type '\eject' at the end of the page to ensure that other, more powerful, spacing commands don't interfere and push everything back up to the top. See also \null.

For *horizontal* centering, there are several methods. For centering text on a single line, use \centerline. For mathematical expressions, use \centerline and then $ to switch on/off the mathematics mode. Or, put double $ signs around the expression. The second approach centers the expression, displays it in a larger format, and puts space between it and the surrounding text. See, for example, Equations 1–3 in Example II. This 'display style' may also be used for text material by typing '$$\vbox{*material*}$$', as was done for Table 3 in Example VI.

\centerline   vi–vii, 6–9, 20–21, 44–45

Centers expressions; e.g., the input for this line was:

`\centerline{Centers expressions; e.g., the input for this line was:}`

When using \centerline in a paragraph, the preceding line must be explicitly broken (with, say, \hfil\break) first. See also \line. Commands like \centerline, which are based on \line, position material with respect to the chosen horizontal size, \hsize: they will ignore alterations to paragraph shape made by \narrower, \rightskip or \leftskip.

\char   *

See character codes.

character codes

TEX represents characters internally (i.e., to itself) using a numerical code. The code can be expressed in different ways: *decimal* notation, *octal* (base 8) or *hexadecimal* (base 16). It is possible for you to summon a character by directly referring to its code, using the command \char (discussed further below).

Code tables are shown in Appendix F of the *TEXbook*. (Or, look below for a decimal version.) In those tables, octal numbers are preceded by ' and hexadecimal ones by ". The code for a character in one of the tables may be obtained by looking at the row and column labels. For example, a row label of *'01x* and a column label of *'5* corresponds to a character code of *'015*, more concisely written as *'15*. If you are specifying characters through their codes, you must also specify the font that you want, for different characters can occupy the same position in code tables for different fonts. Thus, {\sl\char'15} produces *fl*, whereas {\tt\char'15} produces '. In either font this is equivalent to typing '\char13', since the octal number 15 equals the decimal number 13.

This facility is very useful in allowing you to print characters that are not present on your keyboard, or that are present but reserved for use as commands. For instance, the " symbol is being used in this Appendix as a command, and it is printed here by typing '{\tt\char'42}'.

You can generate a quick 'poor persons' character and code table for yourself by using the command defined below:

```
\def\chartable #1{\smallbreak\vbox{\noindent
    {\sl Characters in the {\it#1} font, with decimal codes\/}:
    \vskip0pt \raggedright \hbadness5000 \tolerance10000 \font\ft=#1 \ft
    \baselineskip=14pt \ifdim\baselineskip<3.25ex \baselineskip=3.25ex\fi
    \count255=0 \dimen0=10pt
\loop \setbox0=\hbox{\char\count255} % To find the widest character.
    \ifdim\wd0>\dimen0 \dimen0=\wd0 \fi \advance\count255 by1
    \ifnum\count255<128 \repeat
\count255=0 \advance\dimen0 by 25pt \noindent
\loop\hbox to\dimen0{\hbox to23pt{\hfil
                    \rm\the\count255:\ }\char\count255\hfil}
    \advance\count255 by1 \ifnum\count255<128 \quad \repeat
\smallbreak} \font\tenrm=cmr10 }
```

The command lists all the characters in a given font, alongside their character codes. (See fonts for a discussion of font names.) For example, \chartable{cmr10} gives:

Characters in the cmr10 font, with decimal codes:

0: Γ	1: Δ	2: Θ	3: Λ	4: Ξ	5: Π	6: Σ
7: Υ	8: Φ	9: Ψ	10: Ω	11: ff	12: fi	13: fl
14: ffi	15: ffl	16: ı	17: ȷ	18: `	19: ´	20: ˇ
21: ˘	22: ¯	23: ˚	24: ¸	25: ß	26: æ	27: œ
28: ø	29: Æ	30: Œ	31: Ø	32: ˜	33: !	34: ”
35: #	36: $	37: %	38: &	39: '	40: (	41:)
42: *	43: +	44: ,	45: -	46: .	47: /	48: 0
49: 1	50: 2	51: 3	52: 4	53: 5	54: 6	55: 7
56: 8	57: 9	58: :	59: ;	60: ¡	61: =	62: ¿
63: ?	64: @	65: A	66: B	67: C	68: D	69: E
70: F	71: G	72: H	73: I	74: J	75: K	76: L
77: M	78: N	79: O	80: P	81: Q	82: R	83: S
84: T	85: U	86: V	87: W	88: X	89: Y	90: Z
91: [	92: “	93:]	94: ^	95: ˙	96: '	97: a
98: b	99: c	100: d	101: e	102: f	103: g	104: h
105: i	106: j	107: k	108: l	109: m	110: n	111: o
112: p	113: q	114: r	115: s	116: t	117: u	118: v
119: w	120: x	121: y	122: z	123: –	124: —	125: ″
126: ˜	127: ¨					

If you don't want to look up code tables, there is an alternate approach that works for those characters that you can type: the symbol ' invokes the code of the character in question. For example, the decimal code for d is 100; \char100 is then exactly equivalent to \char'd. You may also use commands with single character names, like, for example, \%: the decimal code for % is 37; \char37 and \char'\% are then equivalent. This last feature is useful in invoking character codes of command characters.

\columns 44–45

Specifies the number of columns when making a table with \settabs; see Table 1 in Example VI and tabbing.

commands

The names of commands in TEX are chosen to suggest the effects that they will have. This makes them easy to remember and it makes what they do easy to spot when reading input text, as on the left-hand pages of the bulk of this book. The significance of some commands is not obvious, however—mainly those controlling spacing, or where single characters play command roles. Look at the lists at the start of the entries in this Appendix for a summary of some of these commands. The first page of the Appendix also tells you where information about certain classes of commands is to be found. For a list of new commands defined in this book, see new commands in this book.

comments   viii-ix, 6–7, 20–21, 44–45, 76–77

The standard comment character is %. TEX will ignore everything to the right of it and will skip to the next line. For multi-line comments, however, it is tedious to have to put the character at the start of every line. To handle such cases, a new command, \ignore, is defined here:

```
%NOTE: The 'scratch register' \count255 is used in the definition below.
\def\ignore {\begingroup \count255=0
     \loop \catcode\count255=14  % Make everything a comment character.
        \advance\count255 by1 \ifnum\count255<128
     \repeat \catcode'\!=0 }      % Make ! an escape character.
{\catcode'\!=0 !gdef!E{!endgroup}}% Define the 'stop ignoring' command.
```

[*Technical explanation (may be skipped)*: The command reserves one character for a special purpose and it changes the category code of all other characters to 14 (the comment category). When the command is invoked, TEX regards each line thereafter as a comment and skips it, unless the first character on the line happens to be the reserved one. The reserved character is !, a character unlikely to be the first one on a line, unless deliberately placed there for a special reason. It plays the role of \; a new command, !E, signals the end of the text to be ignored. This !E must be placed at the start of a line, otherwise TEX won't see it.]

Here is an example of how the command may be used:

```
\ignore
Everything from now on will be ignored by TeX until it sees a line that
STARTS with '!E'. That will then switch TeX back on. TeX will also not
entirely ignore other lines that begin with an ! so you should make sure
no lines begin this way. Till '!E' is seen, none of these do anything:
\vskip 50000in,  \end,  \bye,  etc.
You can go crazy with spellings and syntax, too, because \TEX is not
watching. For example, \centerline{trial}! Pretty daring, huh?
!E
```

The \ignore command is also useful in other contexts. When you are working on a long manuscript, you sometimes want TEX to process only a part of it, say, a complicated table. You can use \ignore to get TEX to skip as much material as necessary (it has been tested on as many as forty pages of text; it skipped them all very rapidly) and to process only what you want it to. It must be stressed that you can use ! as ordinary punctuation in sentences, even if you want the sentences ignored: it is only if it *starts* a line that it will be seen at all by TeX (when under the influence of \ignore) and interpreted specially. If, for any reason, your file contains lines that start this way, you must rearrange the lines or edit the definition of \ignore (to make another character 'special' for the purposes of this command) before using it.

\copy *

See \box.

\count * 68

TeX stores values of whole numbers in one of 256 registers, labelled \count0, ..., \count255. For example, the page number is usually stored in \count0 (which is given the alternate name \pageno). You can store values of your own, as shown from Example XII onward. \count255 is usually reserved for temporary use as a 'scratch register'. For example, \count255=30 stores 30 in \count255, and \the\count255 extracts the contents of the register, (i.e., the number 30). The input lines for this were:

```
... extracts the contents of the register, \count255=30
(i.e., the number \the\count255). The input lines for this ...
```

Storing a number in a register erases its previous contents, so you need to be careful about how you do this. You don't usually want to erase the previous contents of \count0, for example. The next nine \count registers are also usually reserved for special page-description purposes and they, too, should not be tampered with. See \newcount for a discussion of register allocation. However, storage is 'local' in that variables stored in a register within a group do not affect the register contents outside the group. (See grouping.) So, you do not need to be ultra-careful all the time. For example, the last few input lines were:

```
... you do not need to be ultra-careful all the time.
{\pageno=1000} % JUST A TEST TO SEE IF PAGE NUMBERING GETS MESSED UP.
For example, the last few input lines ...
```

Yet the page numbering is still fine.

\cr * 26–27, 38, 40–45, 48–51, 54–55, 66–67

'Carriage return': it signifies the end of a line in an alignment like a table or a matrix. There is also a related primitive command, \crcr: this acts exactly like \cr except when it just follows \cr or \noalign, whereupon it does nothing. The command is useful, for example, if you are defining a new command of your own that involves an alignment. You can build in \crcr to cover some places where people using the command may forget to put in a \cr.

dashes xiv–3

To get:	-	–	—	−
You type:	-	--	---	$-$

These 'dashes' have names: hyphen, en-dash, em-dash and minus, respectively.

\day *

TeX talks to your computer at the start of every job and asks what day it is; for example, today is day 26 of the month. The input for this was:

> ... `for example, today is day \number\day\ of the month.`

TEX can also ferret out the month and year (see `\month` and `\year`).

\def ∗   2, 66, 68, 70, 72, 76, 78, 80, 86

Allows you to define your own commands; there are many different ways that you can do this. See Example XI onward, the Epilogue, **definitions** and **new commands**.

definitions   2, 66, 68, 70, 72, 76, 78, 80, 86

TEX has **primitive commands**, `\def` and `\let`, that allow you to define new commands of your own in a very powerful way. After you use TEX for a while, you will begin to appreciate how much you can do with this facility. If there is a standard format you frequently use, for example, you can absorb all the detailed format instructions into a few commands or even into command characters that are defined at the start. For example, such formatting commands were written to help ease the pain of putting this Appendix together; the commands are shown in the Epilogue.

delimiters   42–43, 54–55, 60–63

Symbols such as brackets, parentheses, etc., that are used (typically in mathematics) to separate parts of expressions from other parts. See **mathematics: delimiters**.

depth   12–13, 48–49, 76–85

Every **box** that TEX makes is considered to have a 'baseline' (see **boxes**). 'Depth' refers to the vertical size of the box below this baseline. See `\dp`. The word is also used as a **keyword** when specifying the depth of **rules**.

derivatives

See Examples V and VII.

diagrams

Blank spaces may be left for pictures and diagrams, as shown in Example III. It isn't easy to draw diagrams from within TEX (though fancy **fonts** sometimes make it possible), but a command called `\special` allows you to 'import' diagrams from other (typically graphical) programs. The exact way in which this may be done varies from system to system, so you will have to consult a local expert to find out how to do it on yours.

\dimen ∗

Just like `\count`, but these **registers** store variables that have **units**; e.g., variables representing size (like `\hsize`) or paragraph indentation. `\dimen0`, ..., `\dimen9` and `\dimen255` are available for 'scratch' use. See `\newdimen`.

dimensions

See **units**.

displayed mathematics

See **mathematics: displays**.

\$\displaylines\$ 60–63

Allows you to display a list of centered equations. See Example IX. `\displaylines` is sometimes the preferred way to display an equation that is to be split over many lines. See **mathematics: line breaks**.

$\displaystyle$ * 62–63

Invokes the spacing rules, typeface styles, etc., of the mathematics display mode (used automatically when expressions are entered between double $ signs). It may be explicitly asked for even when expressions are not being displayed. Also see mathematics: displays.

\divide * 78–79, 80–81

Allows you to divide variables stored in TeX's registers by integers.

\dp *

Gives the depth of boxes. For example, once a page is put together, the material that is to go on it is stored by TeX in \box255; when the page is shipped out, the box is left empty. The depth of this box may be extracted by \dp255 and used in calculations, if needed. The value may be printed in the output by typing '\the\dp255'. Currently the depth of \box255 is 0.0pt, reflecting its present emptiness. See also \ht.

dvi

From 'DeVice Independent'. When TeX processes a file—called, say, *filename.tex*—it transfers coded instructions to a new file, which it names *filename.dvi*. This file contains descriptions of each page, specifying the fonts to be used, the positions of all characters, etc., in a manner independent of your printer. It is the *dvi* file that is read by the 'driver' of your printing or viewing device and converted into print or into a screen preview.

Though the creation of an intermediate file may at first seem an unnecessary complication, it is actually very useful. Once made, the same *dvi* file can be read by a variety of devices (hence the name *device independent*): the final document will look largely the same, whatever the device. Thus, a page previewed on the screen, laser-printed, or printed by a professional typesetting machine will, in each instance, have exactly the same contents, located at essentially the same positions. All these devices produce *digital* images (i.e., images composed of separate dots), and such differences as there are in the final result arise from differences in their resolutions (i.e., how finely they can draw these dots and how accurately they can place them).

At the moment (Aug 1991), standard resolutions are around 70 dots per inch for most computer screens, 300–600 dots per inch for laser-printers and 1200–2600 dots per inch for typesetters. Comparison of laser-printed output with typeset output shows the clear differences between the two, especially when the typeface is small: 10 point type (or smaller) looks distinctly fuzzy when laser-printed, whereas it is quite sharp when typeset. (That is why preprints and other laser-printed documents are usually set in 12-point type, or are magnified by \magstep1.) To produce a book such as this, files are processed by TeX and previewed on the screen, sample printouts are made on laser printers (or dot matrix) and, when everything seems satisfactory, the *dvi* file is sent to a professional typesetting machine.

Dvi files can be transmitted electronically, but you have to be careful that the transmission method does not distort the contents of the file. The original 'source' file, the *tex* one, usually transfers better. However, *dvi* files can be exchanged on tapes or disks, generally without problems.

\egroup 70–71, 80

Generally used to end a group begun with \bgroup.

\eject   vi, viii, 8

Ejects a page. See **page breaks**.

\else   *   70, 72

Used in conjunction with \if... in conditional commands.

em, ex

Font-dependent units of measure, useful when you want sizes that will automatically tailor themselves to the sizes of the font style currently being used. They are both printers' terms. Historically, an *em* was defined to be the width of the letter *M*, but in TEX it is an arbitrary font-dependent unit. For example, the gap between the square brackets in both [   ] and [   ] is exactly 1em, but the second one represents the \bf value. The spaces were left by typing '[{\hskip1em}]' and '[{\bf\hskip1em}]'. See also \quad. An *ex* is the 'x-height' of the current font.

\end   *   vi

Marks the end of the file as far as TEX is concerned. In most situations, \bye is actually a better way to end your file.

\endgraf   70–71

Defined in Plain TEX to be the same as \par, through \let\endgraf=\par. It is very useful in situations where \par itself has been redefined, as it has been in this Appendix. The redefinition is shown in the Epilogue. Another example of a redefinition of \par occurs in the definition of \beginscript in Example XIII.

\endgroup   *

Ends a group begun with \begingroup.

enlargements

See **fonts** and **magnifying**.

\enskip

Gives this[ ]much space; it is defined in Plain TEX by

    \def\enskip{\hskip.5em\relax}

\enspace

Gives this[ ]much space; it is defined in Plain TEX by

    \def\enspace{\kern.5em }

The space is 'unbreakable' (it does not allow a line break), as opposed to the one left by \enskip.

$\eqalign$ 40–43

Aligns equations, as in Example V.

$\eqalignno$ 38–41, 56–57

Aligns equations and places equation numbers; see Examples V and VII.

$\eqno$ * 26–29, 40–43

> Numbers equations on the right; see Equations 1–3 in Example II, or Equation 4 in Example V.

equation alignments 38

> See Examples V, VII and IX, $\eqalign$, $\eqalignno$ and $\leqalignno$.

equation numbers

> See Examples II, V, VII and IX, $\eqno$, $\leqno$, $\eqalignno$ and $\leqalignno$.

errors

> When processing a file, TEX will respond to errors with an error message. It will also carry out, in a few cases, some minimal damage control. This will not change your original file, but it will allow TEX to recover from the error to some extent and to continue processing the rest of the file. The error message will look like something along these lines:
>
> ! *Error message.* This is followed by
>
> *a few, sometimes confusing-looking lines.* (Commands that you gave may be replaced by their definitions in terms of primitive commands—some of which you may never have seen before—or TEX may try to show you how it tried to correct matters on its own.) You will also be shown the line number, and the line where the error was found. At the end of all this you will see a
>
> ?
>
> TEX then awaits your response.

> **A. Responding to error messages.**
>
> You may use lowercase and uppercase letters interchangeably when responding. In the responses listed below, <CR> stands for 'press the **return** key' (called **enter** on some keyboards).
>
> h<CR> will provide you with a little more information about the error.
>
> e<CR> (or x<CR>) will stop TEX from further processing, and will allow you to return to your file to edit it. For serious errors, this may be your best option.
>
> i<CR> will allow you to insert something so that TEX can recover and proceed; the insertion is usually not permanent and you will eventually need to re-edit your original file to make a permanent correction there.
>
> <CR> allows you to proceed, after TEX has engaged in its own damage control. For errors that are not too serious, you can make a note of each error as it is found, then use <CR> to go on. You can edit the file at the end, making all the corrections in one go.
>
> ?<CR> will list all of these options, plus a few others.

> The next two pages tell you a little about what common error messages mean.

B. Common classes of error messages.

1. Underfull and overfull boxes.

These are not true errors, in that they do not cause TeX to stop. But they can affect the way your output looks. And the messages they trigger can be bewildering, particularly if you are new to TeX. The messages refer to whether TeX was able to fill the page with text and other material in a manner that it considers pleasing. If there is too much material trying to go into too small a space, TeX will report an 'overfull' box, and if there is too little material in too large a space, it will announce an 'underfull' box.

Overfull boxes can look quite bad, especially because the program draws attention to them by printing thick black lines where they occur. They can be taken care of by rearranging the input. For example, you will get such a message if you are trying to display an equation that is too long to fit properly on one line. You will then have to break the equation at some point, so that it can go on two lines.

'Underfull box' messages have to do with how much white space TeX can endure on a line or on a page before speaking out. (This refers to space that was not explicitly asked for by spacing commands like, for example, those discussed under `blank spaces`.) See `\hbadness` and `\vbadness` to find out how to change TeX's endurance limit. See also `\break`. Though the messages sound alarming—the amount of 'underfullness' is expressed in terms of a unit quaintly named 'badness'—such 'errors' often do not affect the way the output looks and it may be possible to ignore them. In some cases, you may have to put in an `\hfil` or a `\vfil` to ask explicitly for blank space, or to rearrange where it occurs. Plain TeX is set up to make the tops and bottoms of full pages line up; if you are using a rigid vertical spacing—especially with a large `\baselineskip`—you may get 'Underfull `\vbox`' messages. Making the vertical spacing slightly elastic will help (but don't overdo it); see `\parskip`.

2. Missing \$ signs.

Places where \$ signs are missing are usually easy to find. TeX will try to help you (and itself) out by sometimes temporarily inserting such a sign in places where one seems needed. Occasionally, though, such a message might puzzle you because it may seem that you do not need a \$ sign right there, or that you already have one; typically, this will be in a place where TeX has internally used the mathematics `mode` to define some command.

For example, `\underbar`, used to underline text, is defined within Plain TeX using `\underline`, the corresponding mathematics command. Therefore, using `\underbar` in the mathematics `mode` will trigger an error message. Even in such cases, slightly puzzled though you may perhaps be, tracking down the source of the error is usually not difficult.

3. Missing { and }; runaway arguments.

Finding where { or } are missing can be a nuisance, especially over large tracts of text. One technique to avoid making such mistakes in the first place is to type *both* symbols right away when opening a group. Then you do not have to worry about remembering to close groups that you had previously opened. For example, you can center something by first typing '`\centerline{}`', and then entering between the two braces the material that you want centered. Similarly, when changing typeface, say, to italics, first type '`{\it }`' and then place the material to be italicized within the braces.

Common places where the final } tends to be forgotten are when typeface is changed, or when complicated new commands are being defined, since in these cases the group can end several lines below where it was opened. The sources of such errors are tricky to spot, for you may only get an error message much further on, or even (in the case of typeface-switching) at the very end of the file: if TEX reaches the end of a file while still within a group (i.e., having encountered more { symbols than } ones), it will say so then. It will tell you the 'level' as well—the number of groups that are still open.

To prevent some errors like this from getting out of hand, TEX does not allow certain commands to act on more than one paragraph. If the program reaches the end of the paragraph but not the end of the material on which the command acts, it will stop and tell you that the paragraph ended before the command was complete. For example, \centerline will decline to act on more than one paragraph.

4. Missing numbers.

TEX will complain if it does not find a number in places where it expects a quantity to be specified (e.g., after an \hskip or a \vskip), and it will treat the missing number as zero. Thus, an \hskip with no number following will be treated as \hskip0pt. Such errors are very easy to fix. But there is a twist: TEX will sometimes complain about the absence of a number even when one appears out of place. This occurs if, right after issuing a complete command, you inadvertently use a word that TEX can interpret as a keyword for that command.

For example, if you want the word 'plus' typeset just after typing '\hskip1pt', then '\hskip1pt plus' will not work: TEX will take plus *in this context* as representing a continuation of the command and thus as referring to the stretchability of the horizontal space (see the separate entry for plus). In such cases, you need to first tell TEX to \relax before you can go on: in the example above, you would type '\hskip1pt\relax plus'. To make matters worse, TEX will get confused even if it spots a keyword in the very first fragment of the text that follows; for example, 'This is so\hskip1pt plush' will also trigger a 'missing number' error message. Again, the solution is a soothing touch of \relax in the same place as before. A separate entry for keywords in this Appendix lists them all.

5. Misspellings.

Depending on the context, TEX will respond to misspellings in different ways. An incorrectly spelled unit (say, ot instead of pt) will elicit an 'illegal unit' response; an incorrectly spelled command will usually elicit an 'undefined' message. The second of these misspellings may be handled, for the time being, by typing 'i\command <CR>', where command stands for the correctly spelled command. (The change usually does not carry over to your file: you will have to edit it separately.) A common misspelling is not separating a command from the text immediately after.

6. A command in the wrong place at the wrong time.

Certain commands cannot be used in certain places. For example, mathematics mode commands cannot be used outside this mode, most paragraph-ending commands (see paragraphs) cannot be used inside an \hbox, etc. Such improper usage will usually trigger an explicit error message listing the offending command and the current mode that TEX is in. Of these messages, the ones that are most likely to confuse you involve \raise and \lower, or \moveleft and \moveright. The first pair only works in horizontal mode, the second in vertical.

7. Unavailable fonts.

You may have either misspelled the external name of a font that you want, or it may truly not be available on your system. You will have to make the necessary change in your file.

\every... ∗

A class of commands, covering these: \everycr, \everydisplay, \everyhbox, \everyjob, \everymath, \everypar and \everyvbox. Picking one to illustrate how they all work, \everymath inserts something every time the mathematics mode is switched on. For example,
"Mathematics forever! $1 + 1 = 2$" and "Mathematics forever! $\int \alpha^2 d\alpha$."
were produced by typing (in the input):

```
... mathematics mode is switched on. For example,\hfil\break
{\everymath={\hbox{\rm Mathematics forever!\ }}
``$1+1=2$'' and  ``$\int\alpha^2d\alpha$.''}\hfil\break
were produced by ...
```

Braces were used to 'localize' the effect of \everymath; to check that we're back to normal, let's try a formula again: "$\int \alpha^2 d\alpha$."

The others in this class of commands may be used in the same way to insert something after every \cr, at the start of every mathematics display, at the start of every \hbox, at the start of the job, at the start of every paragraph and at the start of every \vbox, respectively. Incidentally, TEX provides no explicit 'every page' command. To insert material onto every page, you can use \headline to put things at the top and \footline to put things at the bottom. \headline normally accommodates only a single line of material, but there are ways around that: the text of the headline at the top of every Appendix page, the page numbers and the topics (some of which are multi-line) are all placed using \headline (but the horizontal rule is not). The Epilogue shows you the commands that were used to do this. You can get even fancier 'every page' effects by playing with the \output routine.

\fi ∗ 70–73, 80–81

Ends conditional commands; see \ifdim.

\filbreak

Suggests a page break to TEX; see **page breaks**.

\firstmark ∗

See \mark.

\folio

A command that prints the number stored in \pageno. If the stored **page number** is negative, it gets converted to a roman numeral by \folio. The Plain TEX definition of this command is

```
\def\folio{\ifnum\pageno<0 \romannumeral-\pageno
    \else\number\pageno \fi}
```

\font ∗ viii–ix, xiv–1, 64–65, 80–81

Defines commands that call up **fonts**. See Example X.

fonts viii–ix, xiv–1, 8–9, 14–15, 64–65, 80–81

A font of type is a complete assortment of type of one style and size. Within a font there may be variations: for example, roman fonts usually come in *slanted*, *italic* or **bold** versions. These variations in a font are sometimes considered separate fonts on their own.

Every good typesetting system needs good fonts as helpmates. Along with TEX, Donald Knuth has also composed METAFONT, a font creation program that can be used to generate fonts. With this program, and with the assistance of several people (Hermann Zapf, Matthew Carter, Richard Southall, N. N. Billawala, Charles Bigelow and Kris Holmes), he has developed a family of fonts, the *Computer Modern* family, to go with TEX.

Sixteen of the Computer Modern fonts are 'loaded' automatically with Plain TEX and can be invoked using standard, predefined names. They are listed at the very end of this entry on fonts. Other Computer Modern fonts are also commonly available, but you need to gain access to them by using the `\font` command. This command links the external name of the font (i.e., the name of the file in which information about the sizes of characters in the font is kept) to a name chosen by you. You can then use this name to invoke the font whenever you need it. Example X shows how `\font` is to be used, as do the sample input lines reproduced below.

Commonly available Computer Modern fonts are listed underneath. The fonts that are already loaded are marked with an ∗. The font names in the left-hand column are the external names: 'cm' there stands for 'Computer Modern' and the numbers represent the font size, specified in points (1 inch = 72.27 points).

∗ cmr10:	Roman; 10 point.	
∗ cmsl10:	*Slanted; 10 point.*	
∗ cmti10:	*Text italic; 10 point.*	
cmu10:	Unslanted italic; 10 point.	
∗ cmmi10:	*Math‹italic,10point▷*	
cmmib10:	***Math‹bolditalic,10point▷***	
∗ cmsy10:	M⊣⊔〈⇔∫†⇕⌊⌋∫∅∞′ ⌣ ⟩〉\⊔∠	
∗ cmbx10:	**Bold extended; 10 point.**	
cmb10:	**Bold (unextended); 10 point.**	
cmbxsl10:	***Bold extended, slanted; 10 point.***	
cmbxti10:	***Bold extended, italic; 10 point.***	
∗ cmtt10:	`Typewriter; 10 point.`	
cmitt10:	`Italic typewriter; 10 point.`	
cmcsc10:	SMALL CAPITALS; 10 POINT.	
cmdunh10:	Dunhill; 10 point.	
cmff10:	Funny; 10 point.	
cmfib8:	Fibonacci; 8 point.	
cmss10:	Sans serif; 10 point.	
cmssbx10:	**Sans serif, bold extended; 10 point.**	
cmssdc10:	**Sans serif, demibold condensed; 10 point.**	
cmssi10:	*Sans serif, italic; 10 point.*	
cmssq8:	Sans serif, 'quotation'; 8 point.	
cmssqi8:	*Sans serif, 'quotation' italic; 8 point.*	

Here are a few sample lines of the input that was used to produce this list:

```
\medskip
{\baselineskip=13pt \parindent1.6in \parskip1pt
\item{$\ast$ cmr10:}\quad Roman; 10 point.
\item{$\ast$ cmsl10:}\quad {\sl Slanted; 10 point.}
```

```
\item{$\ast$ cmti10:}\quad {\it Text italic; 10 point.}
\item{cmu10:}\quad \font\temp=cmu10 {\temp Unslanted italic; 10 point.}
\item{$\ast$ cmmi10:}\quad \font\temp=cmmi10 {\temp Math, italic;
10 point.}
\item{cmmib10:}\quad \font\temp=cmmib10 {\temp Math, bold italic;
10 point.}
\item{$\ast$ cmsy10:}\quad \font\temp=cmsy10 {\temp Math, symbols;
10 point.}
...
\item{cmssqi8:}\quad \font\temp=cmssqi8 {\temp Sans serif, 'quotation'
italic; 8 point.}\smallskip}
```

In this input, a temporary name, \temp, is assigned in turn to each of the fonts (apart from some of the standard ones) and that name is used to summon the font.

Of the standard fonts (marked with an ∗), the fourth is the regular 'math italic' font and is switched on/off automatically when TeX sees $ signs. The next one is a math symbol font, also automatically invoked between $ signs. The $\cal$ command, for example, brings forth characters from it (only uppercase letters have 'regular' representations in this font). The other standard fonts on the list may be invoked by the usual \rm, \sl, \it, \bf and \tt commands. \rm is the default typeface of Plain TeX. More will be said about these fonts at the end of the entry. You will have noticed that different fonts follow different spacing rules and that some may represent standard characters in a decidedly unusual way (math fonts, for example).

The styles shown come with most TeX distributions; the version on your system may have fewer or more styles available and you will have to check with a local system expert to find out what you have. (You will also have a font called *cmex10* with large mathematical symbols and are likely to have available the 'inch' font used in Example XVII.) When you try to summon a font, TeX looks for information about it in a file with a name of the type '*external-name.tfm*', where *tfm* stands for TeX *font metric*; if it cannot find the file, it will tell you so. You may also have access to fonts outside the Computer Modern family, and you may further have access to fonts in non-English alphabets, or to ones that do not correspond to alphabetical characters at all (as in the math symbol fonts). For example, here is the 'alphabet' in a font called *circle10*:

The input for this was

```
\font\temp=circle10
\centerline{\obeyspaces\temp
a b c d e f g h i j k l m n o
p q r s t u v w x y z}
\bigskip
```

Such fonts can be used to draw pictures; others called 'halftone' fonts have been used to reproduce photographs.

Many fonts come in a range of sizes: e.g., the *cmr* fonts usually come in sizes of 5, 6, 7, 8, 9, 10, 12 and 17 points, of which the 5- and 7-point sizes (in addition to 10-point) are directly available (see below). The 5- and 7-point sizes are also directly available in some other styles; in fact, the 'script style' size in math italics is just 7-point size.

You can magnify sizes using the keyword `scaled`, or you can specify a size by using `at`; this is discussed in Example X and under magnifying below. Your printer may not be able to handle all sizes or all magnifications, so you may have to ask somebody or experiment a bit. You will usually find out what sizes you can use only after the dvi file has been created and when the actual `print` command is given: if a font is unavailable at a certain size you will be told so at this stage.

Though fonts may be magnified, they are really meant to be used at the size at which they were designed. Here is an example of the difference between 17-point roman type and 10-point roman type magnified to 17 (actually, 17.28) points:

17-point type.   10-point magnified type.

Finally, here is a list of all fonts that are loaded with TEX; their descriptive external names are listed, as well as the Plain TEX commands that invoke them:

cmr10	\tenrm	cmr7	\sevenrm	cmr5	\fiverm
cmmi10	\teni	cmmi7	\seveni	cmmi5	\fivei
cmsy10	\tensy	cmsy7	\sevensy	cmsy5	\fivesy
cmbx10	\tenbf	cmbx7	\sevenbf	cmbx5	\fivebf
cmsl10	\tensl	cmtt10	\tentt	cmti10	\tenit
cmex10	\tenex				

It is conventional to reserve the standard names \rm, \sl, \it, \bf, etc., for roman, slanted, etc., typeface at *whatever the current size is*. Since the default size is 10 points, \tenrm and \rm, \tensl and \sl, etc., usually mean the same thing. However, if you switch entirely to, say, 7-point size, it is convenient now for \rm to mean \sevenrm (and so on) so that you can continue using commands like \rm, \sl, etc. This is already built into some aspects of TEX; for example,

$$(\text{formula})^{\text{power}}$$

was obtained from

`$$({\rm formula})^{\rm power}$$`

As you see, \rm gave different sizes of type when used in different places. The question of switching font size so as to continue to enjoy the use of \rm, etc., is also discussed in the Notes for the Acknowledgements.

\footline 4, 80–81, 84–85

Produces footlines. Plain TEX automatically provides a footline with the page number in it (see below). This may be reset by using \footline, just as headlines are set with \headline. When specifying \footline (or \headline), it is a good idea to specify explicitly what typeface you want; otherwise, TEX will use whatever it happened to be using when it paused from its normal page-building activities to set the footline. See the Notes on page 4 (they are on headlines, but the comments are equally applicable to footlines).

The Plain TEX setting for \footline is:

`\footline={\hss\tenrm\folio\hss}`

\hss and \folio are discussed separately; \tenrm is the command for 10-point roman typeface. See the end of the entry under fonts.

\footnote   24–27, 34–35, 44–45

Produces footnotes: see Examples II, IV and VI. See also \vfootnote. The examples show you the default footnote style of Plain TeX. You can easily make changes. For example, if you want a smaller typeface, you can define a font-switching command to a smaller size (as shown in the Acknowledgements and in the Epilogue) and use this size in the text of footnotes. You can also change the rule that divides the footnote from the page. The default is specified by a command called \footnoterule whose Plain TeX definition is:

    \def\footnoterule{\kern-3pt \hrule width 2 true in \kern2.6pt}

By copying this definition into your file, then editing it, you can make changes to the appearance of the rule. Finally, one way to change the indentation of a footnote is to reset the value of \parindent just before using \footnote (and then restoring it after).

fractions   28–29, 38–43, 52–55, 60–63

See Example II and mathematics: special effects.

\frenchspacing   88–89

Makes all single spaces equal in size, even those after punctuation. The feature is useful when typesetting bibliographies or other text containing many abbreviations. You can return to regular spacing by typing '\nonfrenchspacing' or by confining the effect of \frenchspacing within a group (i.e. between { and }).

\global *   72–73, 80–81, 88–89

Allows you to assign values to variables, define commands, etc., 'globally' (i.e., to make assignments that transcend the particular group you are currently occupying). See Example XIV.

glue

A colorless, odorless, textureless substance that permeates every page that TeX typesets. The construct is used by TeX to keep track of white spaces on a page, and of how much each one is allowed to stretch or shrink. You may lay down glue directly using \vglue and \hglue, or \vskip and \hskip. The glue placed by the 'skip' commands is removed by the program in certain situations (\hskip is ignored at the start of a line within a paragraph, \vskip at the top of a page), but glue placed by \hglue or \vglue never disappears. See separate entries for these commands.

The stretchability or shrinkability of glue is specified by using the keywords plus and minus. See \bigskip, \medskip, smallskip or \parskip for examples.

\goodbreak

A suggestion to TeX, less drastic than \break, about a good place to 'break' a page (i.e., to end it and start a new one). See page breaks.

graphics

See diagrams.

grouping

You have seen examples of the concept throughout this book: portions of text are collected in groups, usually by placing { at the start and } at the end, and the effects of commands issued within are then generally confined to the group. If you want an effect to persist outside a group, prefixing the command \global usually does the trick.

In addition to { and }, TeX makes available other grouping mechanisms. There is a pair of **primitive commands**, \begingroup and \endgroup, and there are the commands \bgroup and \egroup, defined in Plain TeX to act like { and }, respectively. The commands are not always interchangeable: \begingroup and \endgroup cannot be used to delimit **arguments** of commands (i.e., to mark portions of text on which a command acts). For example, \centerline\begingroup *stuff* \endgroup is not allowed.

The entry under \bgroup gives you a little more information about the uses of such commands.

\halign * 42, 44–45, 48–50, 66–67

Aligns material for tables, etc. It is the base command under other horizontal alignment commands like \settabs. See Example VI.

\hangafter * 58–59

Is used in conjunction with \hangindent to specify the number of lines after which hanging indentation begins (when \hangafter is positive) or the number of lines that are to be indented (when \hangafter is negative). See Example VIII.

\hangindent * 58–59

Specifies the amount of hanging indentation, as shown in Example VIII.

\hbadness * 80

Sets the amount of horizontal 'badness' (roughly, the amount of white space that has not been explicitly asked for) that TeX will tolerate before it *reports* an underfull \hbox. When typesetting, TeX will scan entire paragraphs and will attempt to place material without too much white space. The amount of white space permissible is determined by a parameter called \tolerance. Once the material is placed, TeX will report every \hbox whose badness exceeds the chosen value of \hbadness. The default value in Plain TeX is 1000, on a scale between 0 and 10000. It must be stressed that this parameter does not affect the way TeX places material; it just determines which boxes TeX will draw to your attention.

\hbox * 2, 38–41, 54–57, 60–63, 74–83

Places material in a horizontal box; see **boxes**. You may specify the horizontal size of an \hbox (i.e., its **width**) by using the **keyword to**. For example,

'Two   inches'

was produced by this input:

```
... example,\smallskip
\hbox to 2in{'Two\hfil inches'} was produced ...
```

If a size is not specified, the \hbox has the width of its contents. That width can be changed by specifying its **spread** (i.e., how much the width can differ from the natural width). For example,

'Nice fit'   'Nice   fit'
was produced by:

```
\smallskip
\line{\hbox{'Nice fit'}\qquad\hbox spread 10pt{'Nice fit'}\hfil}
was produced ...
```

An `\hbox` normally places material along a single line. To make many lines appear, you have to place the text in a `\vbox` and then put that in the `\hbox`. For example,
Two
Lines
was produced by:

```
\smallskip
\hbox{\vbox{Two\hfil\break Lines}}
was produced ...
```

`\headline`   2, 4, 20–21, 24–25, 34–37

Produces headlines. See the Notes on page 4 and also `\footline`.

height   vi–vii, 12–13, 34–37, 48–49, 66–69, 76–85

Refers to the height of **boxes** or **rules** above their 'baseline'. See **boxes** and `\ht`. It is also a **keyword** used to specify the height of **rules**.

`\hfil` *   viii–xi, 12–13, 18–21, 44–45, 48–49, 54–55, 60–61, 74–75

Fills a line with white space. See **fil**, under **keywords**, for more information.

`\hfill` *   12–13, 44, 50–51, 60–63, 74–75, 82–83

Like `\hfil`, only stronger. Typically used to override other spacing commands. See `\fil` and **l**, under **keywords**, for more information. For example,

These two lines
were produced by:

```
\line{\hfil These two lines \hfil}
\line{\hfil were produced by: \hfill}
```

`\hfilneg` *

Cancels the effect of `\hfil`.

For example, the input

for these two lines was:

```
\line{\hfil For example, the input \hfil}
\line{\hfil for these two lines was: \hfil\hfilneg}
```

`\hfuzz` *

A parameter that is used to determine how much the material in a horizontal box is allowed to stick out before TeX reports an overfull box. In Plain TeX, `\hfuzz=0.1pt`.

`\hglue`

Horizontal **glue**. May be used directly, rather like `\hskip`, to paste in white space.
The command works even at the start of a line; for example, the last two input lines were:

```
to paste in white space.\hfil\break
{\hglue 1cm}The command works even at the start of a line;
```

As you see, glue placed by \hglue is not removed (unlike glue placed by \hskip—see below). See also \relax.

\hoffset * viii–ix, xiv–1

An 'output' instruction to the printer (or other display device) that determines the horizontal placement of a page. The start of the input for the Introduction shows you how to set this placement, and the Appendix formatting commands listed in the Epilogue show you how \hoffset can be controlled in a very powerful way.

\hphantom 62–63

\hphantom{*stuff*} calculates the width of *stuff* as it normally would, but sets the height and depth to zero. It does not print this *stuff*, leaving instead a space of the correct width. For example, here is a space   of width exactly equal to that of the word 'phantom'. The facility is useful when one wants to trick TeX. See also \phantom and \vphantom.

\hrule * vi–vii, 12–13, 34–37, 48–49, 58–59, 66–69, 76–77, 80–85

Draws a horizontal 'rule' (i.e., a ruled line). See rule.

\hsize * viii–ix, xiv–1, 66–69, 74–77, 80–87

Sets the horizontal size of pages and of boxes on pages. See page 1 and Example XV. The default value of \hsize in Plain TeX is 6.5 inches. Different values of \hsize may be chosen for boxes on a page, and these values will not affect the page \hsize. When specifying \hsize in a magnified document, you may need to use the keyword true. See units.

\hskip * 11, 78–79, 80, 82–83

Places glue that makes a horizontal space of specified size. For example, TeX will now jump exactly one   inch.
This command has no effect at the start of a line; as you can see from the input:

```
... \TeX\ will now jump exactly one{\hskip 1in}inch.\hfil\break
{\hskip 1cm}This command has no effect at the start of a line; as ...
```

In other words, TeX will remove glue placed by \hskip at places where it thinks you would not really want a space. For example, in a list like   a) first item, b) second item,   c) third item, you do not usually want the gap between items to show up at the start or the end of lines. The input for this paragraph was:

```
... \TeX\ will remove glue placed by "\hskip" at places where
it thinks you would not really want a space. For example, in a list like
\hskip.5in a)~first item,\hskip.5in b)~second item,\hskip.5in c)~third
item, you do not usually want the gap between items to show up at ...
```

Compare this with how \hglue works. See also \null and \relax.

\hss *

From *horizontal stretch or shrink*. It fills lines with white space (glue, really) that can stretch arbitrarily (as with \hfil) but can also shrink arbitrarily. See fil, under keywords.

\ht ∗ 80

Gives the height of boxes made by TEX. For example, the material that is to go on the current page is stored by TEX in \box255 (see \dp). The height of this box may be obtained using \ht. Currently the box is empty (the previous page has been shipped out, and the new one is still being built) and so its height, obtained by typing '\the\ht255', is 0.0pt. (The command \the extracts the value of \ht255 and prints it.)

hyphenation 22–23, 36–37, 86–87

TEX hyphenates rather nicely on its own. If you really do not want a word hyphenated, put it in an \hbox. If you want to suggest a possible hyphenation, put in a \- at the appropriate spot. This is called a 'discretionary hyphen'. The lines above contain two such hyphens at places that the program would not have picked on its own, as the input that was used for these lines shows:

```
\TeX\ hyphenates rather nicely on its own. If you really do not want a
word hyp\-henated, put it in an "\hbox". If you want to suggest a
possible hyphenation, put in a "\-" at the appr\-opriate ...
```

You will have noticed that the program ignored one suggestion but took the other. If you wish to suggest hyphenations of frequently occurring words, it is tedious to have to do so by placing discretionary hyphens each time. It is possible, instead, to make global suggestions using the primitive command \hyphenation{}; for example,

```
\hyphenation{ro-tt-en sug-ges-ti-ons}
```

The words on this list must be separated by a space; TEX will then consider the suggested hyphenations each time it encounters the words. There is yet another hyphenation device, provided by a command called \discretionary. It not only allows you to suggest where a word might be hyphenated, but also how to spell the fragments of the word before and after the hyphen and how to spell the full word if it is not hyphenated. This is useful in languages where hyphenation can change the spellings of words, or in suggesting hyphenation in the middle of a ligature. For example, I am told that the German word *backen* hyphenates as bak-ken. This can be indicated to TEX by typing

```
ba\discretionary{k-}{k}{ck}en
```

when the word is used. If the word is used frequently, you would be best off defining a new command that has that particular \discretionary pattern built into it.

Versions of TEX from 1990 onwards (version 3.0 and on) can simultaneously handle hyphenation patterns from different languages.

\ifcase ∗

One of a variety of conditional commands that TEX understands. This one allows you to handle situations with many different possibilities, or 'cases'. See \month for an example of its use.

\ifdim ∗

Allows you to compare quantities with dimension (like sizes, for example). The structure of the full command is
\ifdim *condition   instructions when condition is true*
  \else *instructions when condition is false* \fi
Four classes of conditional commands are shown in this book, but TEX also makes several others available; a full discussion is given in Chapter 20 of the *TEXbook*.

\ifnum ∗ 68–73, 78–81

Like \ifdim, but is used to compare pure (whole) numbers.

\ifodd ∗ 80–81

Checks for whether a variable represents an odd number. See the command for page numbering in Example XVII, or the specifications of \headline and \output in the Epilogue.

\ignorespaces ∗

Makes TEX ignore the consecutive blank spaces that immediately follow. This is sometimes useful when defining your own commands; it helps to ensure that certain blank spaces do not inadvertently appear.

ignoring text

See comments.

in vi–vii, xiv–1

See keywords.

\indent ∗ 30–31, 54–57

Forces paragraph indentation. May be used to indent lines within a paragraph that would not otherwise be indented (the first line after a displayed formula, for example) or to add extra indentation to the first line of a paragraph (\indent\indent gives double indentation).

indentation

See \indent and paragraphs.

indices 24–29, 36–44, 52–57

See Examples II and V and also mathematics: spacing below. Indices do not necessarily have to be numbers or letters, and they do not have to appear on the right of an expression. For example,

$$_2A^7 \qquad\qquad \cdots \qquad\qquad k_{[\mu}C_{\nu]\alpha\beta[\rho}k_{\sigma]}k^\alpha k^\beta.$$

The input for this was

```
$$_2A^7
\qquad\qquad  %SPACE BETWEEN FORMULAS
^{\ldots\spadesuit\flat}_{\ldots\diamondsuit\top}
\Re^{\natural\heartsuit\ldots}_{\sharp\clubsuit\ldots}
\qquad\qquad  %SPACE BETWEEN FORMULAS
k_{[\mu]C_{\nu]\alpha\beta[\rho}k_{\sigma]}k^{\alpha}k^{\beta}.$$
```

If your _ or ^ keys are broken, \sb and \sp may be used instead for subscripts and superscripts, respectively.

\input ∗ 60–61, 66

Inputs material from other files into a document. A typical use is to place all your format commands in one file (called, say, *format*) and then to type '\input format' at the start of documents that you want typeset. See the input box for the start of this Appendix.

inserts

> See Examples III and VI.

integrals

> See Example VII.

`\it`   vi–ix, xiv–1, 8–9, 20–21, 86–87

> Produces *italics*, if you type '`{\it italics}`'.

italics

> See `\it`.

`\item`   x–xiii, 6–7, 32–33, 36–37, 52–53, 68–69, 72–73, 84–85, 88–89

> Used to make itemized lists. See the input for
>
> 1. the Contents pages, or
> 2. Example IV, or
> 3. any other list in this book.
>
> For example, the input for the last few lines was:
>
> ```
> {\parindent20pt \noindent Used to make itemized lists. See the
> input for \item{1.} the Contents pages, or \item{2.} Example IV,
> or \item{3.} any other list in this book.\par} For example, ...
> ```
>
> The list is indented by the current value of `\parindent` (i.e., the current paragraph indentation); the indentation may be changed by changing the value of that parameter. See the first input line above.

`\itemitem`   30–31, 88–89

> Used to make
>
> • lists within lists; see the input for
>   ⋆ the References, or
>   ⋆ any other list-within-list in this book;
> • single lists twice as indented as can be achieved with `\item`.
>
> The input for this list was:
>
> ```
> {\parindent20pt \noindent Used to make
> \item{$\bullet$} lists within lists; see the input for
> \itemitem{$\star$} the References, or
> \itemitem{$\star$} any other list-within-list in this book;
> \item{$\bullet$} single lists twice as indented as can be
> achieved with "\item". \par}
> ```

itemized lists

> See `\item`, `\itemitem`, Contents, References and Example IV.

`$\joinrel$`

> See mathematics: special effects.

`\jot`

> A parameter typically used to change the spacing of multi-line displays. Its value in Plain TeX is 3pt. It may be reset to 300 points, for example, by typing '`\jot=300pt`'. See `\openup`.

justification 86–87

Text is automatically left- and right-justified in TEX; it is also justified vertically. (In other words, you get straight right and left margins and the bottoms and tops of pages line up.) See `\raggedright` and `\raggedbottom` to find out how to switch these features off. The Epilogue contains a new `\raggedleft` command.

\kern * 74–79

Leaves either a horizontal or a vertical space, depending on the context. If TEX is in horizontal **mode**, the command leaves a horizontal space, and if it is in vertical **mode**, a vertical space. See **modes**. TEX will not break a line at a horizontal space created by a `\kern` command (as opposed to a space left by, say, `\hskip`).

kerning

The practice of moving certain pairs of characters closer together so that they will fit together snugly without too much distracting space in-between. For example, compare the kerned pair **VA** with the unkerned one **V A**. TEX generally kerns very nicely, but if you are unhappy with what it does, `\kern` allows you to impose your own ideas of what is attractive. For example, the input for 'VA' and 'RA' was:

     '{\bf V\kern-3pt A}' and 'R\kern-2.1pt A'

keywords

Words that act as continuations (or modifiers) of certain commands, *when used in conjunction with them*. Here is a complete list:

- `bp`, `cc`, `cm`, `dd`, `in`, `mm`, `pc`, `pt`, `sp`: see **units**.
- `em`, `ex`: see the separate entry covering both, and also **units**.
- `at`, `scaled`: used with `\font` to specify font sizes; see Example X and **fonts**.
- `by`: used with `\multiply`, `\divide` or `\advance` to multiply, divide or 'advance' contents of **registers**.
- `depth`, `height`, `width`: used to specify the sizes of ruled lines; see **rule**.
- `fil`: special unit used to specify infinitely stretchable or shrinkable **glue**. For example, `\hfil` is effectively the same as '`\hskip0pt plus1fil`', `\hss` the same as '`\hskip0pt plus1fil minus1fil`', and `\hfilneg` effectively the same as '`\hskip0pt plus-1fil`'. For simple applications you are unlikely to need to use `fil` directly. See, however, the discussion of `\parfillskip`.
- `l`: tagged on after `fil` (to make `fill`, or even `filll`) to yield stronger 'fill with white space' commands; for example, `\hfill` is essentially equivalent to '`\hskip0pt plus1fill`'.
- `minus`, `plus`: used to specify stretchability or shrinkability of spaces. See **glue**.
- `mu`: the math unit of glue. A special unit is useful because of the different typeface sizes that are routinely used in the same formula. The unit adjusts itself automatically by being tied to the size of an **em**: `18mu = 1em`. It is used to specify sizes of horizontal spaces in formulas through the command `\mskip`. For example, the 'negative thin space' command in mathematics, `\!`, is defined in Plain TEX by '`\mskip -3mu`'. The other spacing commands, `\,`, `\>` and `\;`, are of size '`3mu`', '`4mu plus2mu minus4mu`' and '`5mu plus5mu`', respectively.
- `spread`, `to`: used to specify sizes of **boxes**; see `\hbox`, `\vbox` and Example XV.
- `true`: used to specify magnification-independent sizes; see page *xiv* and **units**.

\last... ∗

A class of commands, of which \lastbox, \lastskip and \lastkern are examples. They refer, respectively, to the last box (\hbox or \vbox) made, to the last 'skip', and to the last 'kern'. For example, 3.33333pt plus 2.08331pt minus 0.88889pt is the current value of \lastskip; it represents an interword gap. The input for this was:

```
... 'kern'. For example, \the\lastskip\ is the current value ...
```

\lastbox is used in the making of the new \table command, shown under **tables**.

LaTeX

A widely used package of commands built out of the primitive commands of TeX that makes it very easy to carry out certain standard typesetting tasks like, for example, double-column output. LaTeX commands are not always compatible with those of Plain TeX, so you have to be careful if you are switching between the two.

\leaders ∗   74–75, 82–83

Allows you to make repeating patterns. See Example XV.

$\left$ ∗   40–43, 60–63

Creates left delimiters (i.e., brackets, parentheses, etc.) that will have the correct size for a large formula. See Example IX. \left is to be used in displayed equations, and always in conjunction with \right: TeX will expect \left and \right to occur in pairs in each equation, and for \left to precede \right. The actual symbols used need not occur in balanced pairs: \left(may be paired with \right], for example, or even with \right[if you want an unusual effect. If you want a single delimiter, type '\left.' or '\right.' for the missing one.

\leftline   84–85

Places material flush left on a line.

For example, the input for the line above was:

```
\leftline{Places material flush left on a line.}
```

This isn't normally very impressive since material is usually set flush left anyway, but it is useful in certain situations to have available an explicit command of this type. See also \line.

\leftskip ∗   20–23, 70–71

Moves the left text margin in or out. See Example 1. The value of \leftskip used in setting a paragraph is the one in force just at the point that the paragraph ends. See **paragraphs**.

$\leqalignno$ 54–55

Aligns equations and places equation numbers to the left. See Example VII.

$\leqno$ ∗   52–53

Works like \eqno, but it places equation numbers to the left. See Example VII.

`\let` ∗ 86–87

Sets a command equal to some other command, or even to a single character. For example, the definition of `\bgroup` in Plain TEX is '`\let\bgroup={`'. `\let` works a little differently from `\def`: if you type '`\let\a=\b`', then `\a` will take on the meaning that `\b` had *at the time that* `\let` *was encountered*, even if `\b` is itself later redefined. On the other hand, '`\def\a{\b}`' makes `\a` take on the *current* meaning of `\b`, every time it is used; i.e., `\a` will change meaning if `\b` does. See also `\endgraf`.

ligatures

A list is given near the start of the entries in this Appendix. You can prevent ligatures by fooling TEX; for example, '`{f}i`' gives 'fi'.

`$\limits$` ∗ 52–55, 60–61

See mathematics: operations.

`\line` viii–ix, 12–13, 20–21, 34–37

Places material on a single line whose size is the current value of `\hsize`. Unless the material is going to fill the line, you will also need to use `\hfil` to place things correctly and to prevent an 'underfull box' error message. Commands like `\centerline`, `\leftline` and `\rightline` are all defined in Plain TEX using `\line`; if any of these commands is being used in the middle of a paragraph, the line immediately preceding must first be explicitly ended (using `\hfil\break`, say).
For example, the last couple of input lines were:

```
explicitly ended (using "\hfil\break", say).\hfil\break
\line{For example, the last couple of input lines were:\hfil}
```

If you are using `\line`, or any command based on it (like `\centerline`), as the *first line of a new paragraph*, the paragraph indentation will carry through to the next line (it can be suppressed, if needed, by `\noindent`). More precisely, TEX does not regard `\line` as beginning a new paragraph.

line breaks x–xi, 2, 8–9, 22, 26, 34

Caused by typing '`\hfil\break`'. See also `\allowbreak`. Expressions like 'yes/ no' will not be broken at the '/' if typed as '`yes/no`', but a break is permitted if '`yes\slash no`' is used instead. Line breaks are also permitted to occur at spaces left by `\ ` (i.e., a `\` followed by a single space), `\quad`, `\qquad` or `\hskip`. Finally, you can use discretionary hyphens to suggest line breaks (see hyphenation).

To *prevent* line breaks, you can use one of several techniques: (1) `\hbox`. Material in an `\hbox` will not suffer line breaks; for example, commands that are reproduced verbatim in the body of this Appendix (or in the Notes under the input boxes) are each placed in an `\hbox` to prevent a line break in the middle. (2) *Ties.* Words may be tied together using the command character ˜. This gives a single space between the words at which the line will not be broken. Ties are useful in several places: when referring to names of entities (you would type '`Theorem˜3`' or '`Section˜B`', for example), or when referring to variables in a sentence (for example, `height˜$h$`), or when listing cases in a paragraph (part of the input for this one is shown below as an example). In general, a tie should be used whenever a line break between words would be awkward. (3) `\nobreak`. Used in horizontal **mode** (very roughly, on a line, not between lines), this command prevents line breaks immediately after. (4) \kern. Line breaks are not permitted at spaces left by this command or at spaces left by commands like \enspace, \thinspace and \negthinspace which are based on it.

Here is part of the input used for the paragraph above:

```
... to prevent a line break in the middle.
(2)~{\sl Ties}. Words may be tied together using the command ...
```

See also mathematics: line breaks.

lines

For ruled lines, like ――――――――, see rule. For information on lines of text, look up what you want under separate entries in this Appendix. (For example, line breaks, line spacing, etc.)

\lineskip *

Specifies the gap to be left between two lines if the value of \baselineskip that you are using brings them too close. See \lineskiplimit to see what 'too close' means. Plain TeX sets the value of \lineskip to be 1pt. See also line spacing.

\lineskiplimit *

The parameter that determines how close two adjacent lines must be for extra space (see \lineskip) to be inserted. The Plain TeX value is 0pt. See line spacing.

line spacing

Controlled by setting \baselineskip. The default value in Plain TeX is 12pt. In addition to this, there are two other parameters that control interline spacing. \lineskiplimit is related to how close the top of one line can get to the bottom of the one above. Lines that are closer than the chosen value of \lineskiplimit are then separated by the value of \lineskip (the commands are discussed in separate entries above). See \offinterlineskip to find out how to suppress normal interline spacing. See also \openup.

lists

See \item, \itemitem, Contents, References and Example IV.

\llap   36–37

Allows material to overlap other material to the left. In particular, the 'overlap' could be with the left margin. For example, a\llap/ produces ⌀. See also \rlap and Example IV.

\loop   68–69, 72–73, 78–79

Used in conjunction with \repeat to carry out repetitive tasks. The structure of the command is '\loop A \if... B \repeat', which will cause TeX to do A and then check the condition in \if...; if the condition is true, TeX will do B and then repeat the process; if it is false, TeX stops looping. The \if... can be any legitimate conditional command of TeX (see, for example, \ifdim), but without the matching \fi (it is built into \repeat). TeX's \loop command is defined in a delicately recursive—i.e., self-referential—way, and you have to be careful when using loops within loops (you should use { and } to keep inner and outer loops separated).

\looseness ∗

A parameter that forces TeX to try to make paragraphs longer or shorter (in terms of the number of lines) than it otherwise would if left to its own devices. For example, **\looseness=2** makes TeX attempt to set the paragraph two lines longer than it would on its own, and **\looseness=-1** one line shorter. 'Attempt' because TeX will not exceed the amount of white space allowed to it by the **\tolerance** parameters. Why monkey around with TeX? There are several applications where one might want to make the total number of lines come out a certain way. For example, one usually wants to avoid isolated lines at the bottoms or tops of pages (so-called 'orphans' and 'widows') when typesetting books and magazines, and the **\looseness** command can be used to get rid of these if a trial run reveals their presence. The command can also be used in conjunction with the **\prevgraf** command, explained below, in some applications. This paragraph has **\looseness=1**; without that specification it would only be 13 lines long. (And that's the honest truth.)

The input for the first and last lines of the preceding paragraph was:

```
\looseness=1 A parameter that forces \TeX\ to try to make paragraphs
...
lines long. (And that's the honest~truth.)
```

The tie between the last two words (~) was placed there to block TeX from taking the easy way out: increasing the number of lines by moving just the last word to a new line. But, as you can see, the program has had the last laugh.

\lower ∗ 60–61, 74–75

Lowers boxes. See **\raise** for a little more information.

\lowercase ∗

Puts stuff in lowercase; e.g., the input for this was:

```
P\lowercase{UTS STUFF IN LOWERCASE; E.G., THE INPUT FOR THIS WAS:}
```

macros

Computer jargon for new commands, defined by you in terms of previously existing commands. See **definitions**.

\magnification viii–ix, xiv–1

Magnifies an entire document. Printing devices can often only handle certain sizes of typeface, so TeX provides several standard sizes through its **\magstep** command. (See the input for page 1.) Such a command must be issued right at the beginning, *before TeX has begun to set material without magnification.* See **units** for a discussion of how to specify sizes in a magnified document.

magnifying viii–ix, xiv–1, 64–65, 80–81

For entire documents see **\magnification**. For material within a document see **fonts** and **\magstep**. Normal (i.e., unmagnified) size is usually represented by the number 1000. Then, a font scaled to 500 is half-size and one scaled to 3000 is three times its normal size. So, if you type '**\font\huge=cmr10 scaled 5000**', you are asking for the 10-point Computer Modern roman font at five times its usual size (and are assigning the name **\huge** to it).

Printing devices cannot always handle all sizes; one set of sizes that is usually available is 1000 multiplied by powers of 1.2; for example, 1200, 1440, etc. TeX represents magnifications up to 4 digits only (see the discussion of \magstep). This can lead to slight problems if you are magnifying fonts within a magnified document. For example, a document at \magstep4 is scaled by 2074 (but the 'correct' value is $1000 \times 1.2^4 = 2073.6$). A font magnified to \magstep1 within the document might lead your printing device to believe that you want to scale by 2489 ($2074 \times 1.2 = 2488.8$), whereas it usually only has 2488 available. In such cases, you may have to use **at** in the \font command to specify an exact size that you know is available. See Example X and the definition of \title on input page *viii*.

\magstep   viii–ix, xiv–1, 64–65, 80–81

Specifies magnification in fixed steps. Plain TeX comes with the following built-in magnification sizes (on a scale where 'normal', or \magstep0, is 1000):

\magstephalf:	1095	\magstep1:	1200
\magstep2:	1440	\magstep3:	1728
\magstep4:	2074	\magstep5:	2488

Each size is obtained by multiplying 1000 by the appropriate power of 1.2. Thus \magstep1 represents a 20% magnification. These sizes are used to magnify entire documents (using \magnification) or to magnify fonts. See magnifying.

margins

Plain TeX provides pages with 1-inch top and left margins. The default page size (i.e., the size of the material on the page) is 6.5×8.9 inches, so you also get an inch of margin on the right and roughly an inch at the bottom, assuming you are using 8.5×11-inch paper. (The bottom must also accommodate a footline.) Margins may effectively be reset using the commands \hsize, \vsize, \hoffset and \voffset. The first two change the size of the material printed on a page, the last two control positioning. Between these commands, you can set any margins you like. For example, a 1.5-inch left margin and a 3-inch right margin on 8.5×11 paper would result from '\hsize 4in' and '\hoffset .5in'. You can also temporarily change margins in a document by using \leftskip and \rightskip.

\mark *

Placed in documents to mark text that can then be referred to *after* pages are set. For example, for each entry in this Appendix the entry heading is 'marked' using this command. (Look at the Appendix format commands listed in the Epilogue.) Once pages are set, the commands \topmark, \firstmark and \botmark extract marked text from the page. \topmark extracts the last marked text encountered just *before* the page, \firstmark the first marked text *on* the page and \botmark the last marked text on the page. (So, one page's \botmark will be the next one's \topmark.) The little subject headings at the top of the outer margins of the pages in this Appendix are each either the \firstmark for their respective pages (left-hand ones) or the \botmark (right-hand pages).

mathematics   24–33, 38–43, 52–57, 60–63

All special symbols commonly available in the mathematics mode are listed over the next several entries. A few 'special effects' are also given, and the adjustment of spacing in mathematical formulas is discussed. Other aspects of typesetting mathematical expressions are listed under separate headings. (For example, fractions, equation alignments, matrices, roots.) To use the mathematics mode, all input must be typed between $ signs. (Only a couple of symbols are also available outside the mathematics mode; they are shown in the tables without $ signs.) Equations that are to be displayed on a separate line must be typed between double $ signs. This 'display style' automatically centers equations, presents them in a larger format and adds extra space above and below.

mathematics: accents   52–57

$\hat o$	`$\hat o$`	$\check o$	`$\check o$`	$\tilde o$	`$\tilde o$`	$\acute o$	`$\acute o$`
$\grave o$	`$\grave o$`	$\dot o$	`$\dot o$`	$\ddot o$	`$\ddot o$`	$\breve o$	`$\breve o$`
$\bar o$	`$\bar o$`	$\vec o$	`$\vec o$`				

As with accents on text, if i or j are to be accented they must first be 'undotted'. `$\imath$` and `$\jmath$` give $\imath$ and $\jmath$, respectively. 'Wide accents' are also available that can change size to match the expression underneath:

$\overline{o}$	`$\overline o$`	$\overline{abcde}$	`$\overline{abcde}$`
$\underline{o}$	`$\underline o$`	$\underline{abcde}$	`$\underline{abcde}$`
$\widehat{ab}$	`$\widehat{ab}$`	$\widehat{abcde}$	`$\widehat{abcde}$`
$\widetilde{ab}$	`$\widetilde{ab}$`	$\widetilde{abcde}$	`$\widetilde{abcde}$`

Whereas \overline and \underline provide lines that can grow to accommodate arbitrarily large expressions, the other two wide accents have a maximum size that can only comfortably accommodate three characters. It is also possible to accent accented expressions; however, one has to watch out for the positions of the accents. This is discussed under **mathematics: spacing** below. Also see various **\over...** and **\under...** commands, listed separately.

mathematics: delimiters   42–43, 54–55, 60–63

These are symbols like parentheses, brackets, curly braces, etc., that indicate where expressions begin and end.

(	(	)	)	[	[	]	]
{	`$\{$`	}	`$\}$`	|	`$\|$`	‖	`$\|$`
⌊	`$\lfloor$`	⌋	`$\rfloor$`	⌈	`$\lceil$`	⌉	`$\rceil$`
\	`$\backslash$`	/	/	⟨	`$\langle$`	⟩	`$\rangle$`

{ and } may also be obtained from `$\lbrace$` and `$\rbrace$` respectively, [and] from `$\lbrack$` and `$\rbrack$`, and | and ‖ from `$\vert$` and `$\Vert$`. The vertical arrow symbols listed under **mathematics: relations** may also be used as delimiters. All these delimiters will automatically become larger when they enclose large expressions if they are prefixed by **\left** (for opening delimiters) and **\right** (for closing delimiters). See Example IX, and separate entries for **\right** and, especially, **\left** in this Appendix. Except for the ones on the last line, they can all become arbitrarily large.

If you are not satisfied with the sizes of delimiters that are automatically provided, you can ask for them in several specific larger sizes. This is done by prefacing the appropriate command by \big, \Big, \bigg, or \Bigg. The effects of these are illustrated by the sequence where the first line is in 'normal size'. Apart from giving you control over delimiter size, these commands may be used singly, whereas \left and \right must occur in balanced pairs in an equation. It is also possible to specify whether a big delimiter is at the left of an expression, the right, or in the middle, by typing '\bigl', '\bigr', '\bigm', etc. This is important for fine spacing in formulas because TeX leaves slightly different spaces around opening, closing and middle delimiters. Here are the \Bigg sizes of all delimiters:

Finally, there are a few extra delimiters, some of which come only in large sizes; the minimum sizes of these are:

The commands that produce these are \arrowvert, \Arrowvert and \bracevert (for the first three pairs, respectively); \lgroup and \rgroup; \lmoustache and \rmoustache. They are made up of parts of other symbols, and are to be used prefixed by \left or \right or by \big, etc. For example, the input for the last part of the preceding display was:

```
...
\left\lgroup{\quad}\right\rgroup\qquad
\left\lmoustache{\quad}\right\rmoustache$$
```

mathematics: displays   24–31, 38–43, 52–57, 60–63

A 'displayed formula' is one that is shown on a separate line from text. Displays in TeX are automatically centered, and extra space is left above and below the formula. The spacing of the components of a displayed formula is slightly different from that of formulas in text (see mathematics: spacing) and some typefaces used are larger. The style is called 'display style': it can be invoked even in formulas that are not displayed, by using the command \displaystyle.

The space left above and below displayed equations is augmented by any additional vertical space you may have asked for just before, or just after, the display. For example, you will get extra space if you have used \smallskip, \medskip, etc., or even if you have just left a blank line (this will give you extra inter-paragraph space). Depending on the nature of your display, you may or may not want this extra space. If you really want to tinker with spacing, there are four parameters that govern the amount of space above and below displays; their values can be reset. The parameters along with their Plain TeX values are:

```
\abovedisplayskip=12pt plus 3pt minus 9pt
\abovedisplayshortskip=0pt plus 3pt
\belowdisplayskip=12pt plus 3pt minus 9pt
\belowdisplayshortskip=7pt plus 3pt minus 4pt
```

The first and third of these represent the spaces left above and below displays, respectively. The second and fourth represent the spaces left instead, when the line immediately preceding the display is short. In all of these, plus and minus refer to the stretchability and shrinkability of the space.

mathematics: greek letters   38–43, 54–57

α	`$\alpha$`	β	`$\beta$`	γ	`$\gamma$`	δ	`$\delta$`
ϵ	`$\epsilon$`	ε	`$\varepsilon$`	ζ	`$\zeta$`	η	`$\eta$`
θ	`$\theta$`	ϑ	`$\vartheta$`	ι	`$\iota$`	κ	`$\kappa$`
λ	`$\lambda$`	μ	`$\mu$`	ν	`$\nu$`	ξ	`$\xi$`
o	`$o$`	π	`$\pi$`	ϖ	`$\varpi$`	ρ	`$\rho$`
ϱ	`$\varrho$`	σ	`$\sigma$`	ς	`$\varsigma$`	τ	`$\tau$`
υ	`$\upsilon$`	ϕ	`$\phi$`	φ	`$\varphi$`	χ	`$\chi$`
ψ	`$\psi$`	ω	`$\omega$`				
Γ	`$\Gamma$`	Δ	`$\Delta$`	Λ	`$\Lambda$`	Θ	`$\Theta$`
Ξ	`$\Xi$`	Π	`$\Pi$`	Υ	`$\Upsilon$`	Σ	`$\Sigma$`
Φ	`$\Phi$`	Ψ	`$\Psi$`	Ω	`$\Omega$`		

Slanted capitals may be obtained by prefacing the commands by `\mit`. For example, `$\mit\Gamma$` gives $\mathit{\Gamma}$.

mathematics: line breaks   14

Formulas in text, sandwiched between single $ signs, will be broken by TeX only at a few places: after a relation symbol like $=$ or $<$, or (as a less preferred choice) after an operation symbol like $+$ or $-$. In all these cases, the break occurs only if the symbol is not buried within an explicit group (i.e., it is not between { and }). Thus, line breaks may be prohibited by 'hiding' parts of the formula, or all of it, between { and }—though you must be careful that you are not also interfering with the normal spacing rules that TeX follows for mathematics (see **mathematics: spacing**). Breaks are made permissible at places that TeX would not choose on its own, by using `\allowbreak`.

In a formula with implicit multiplications, line breaks may be suggested by using `\*` in places where multiplications are implied. Look, for example, at $x = (a - b) \times (c - d)(u - v)$. The input for this was:

```
... at $x=(a-b)\*(c-d)\*(u-v)$. The input ...
```

As you will have noticed, TeX ignores `\*` unless it is at a good place for a line break; at such a place it is replaced by '$\times$'.

Displayed formulas, typed between double $ signs, are never broken by TeX: you have to explicitly break them yourself. In some situations, it is better to display an explicitly broken equation using `\displaylines` (see Example IX) rather than pairs of $$ signs for each line of the equation (the second approach may leave too much space between the lines).

mathematics: operations   24–33, 52–57, 60–63

$+$	`$+$`	$\ddagger$	`$\ddagger$`	$\dagger$	`$\dagger$`	$\odot$	`$\odot$`
$-$	`$-$`	$\setminus$	`$\setminus$`	$\cdot$	`$\cdot$`	$\oplus$	`$\oplus$`
$/$	`$/$`	$\times$	`$\times$`	$\star$	`$\star$`	$\ominus$	`$\ominus$`
$.$	`$.$`	$\cap$	`$\cap$`	$\cup$	`$\cup$`	$\otimes$	`$\otimes$`
$\pm$	`$\pm$`	$\sqcap$	`$\sqcap$`	$\sqcup$	`$\sqcup$`	$\oslash$	`$\oslash$`
$\mp$	`$\mp$`	$\triangleleft$	`$\triangleleft$`	$\bullet$	`$\bullet$`	$\bigcirc$	`$\bigcirc$`
$\wr$	`$\wr$`	$\triangleright$	`$\triangleright$`	$\uplus$	`$\uplus$`	$\circ$	`$\circ$`
$\div$	`$\div$`	$\bigtriangleup$	`$\bigtriangleup$`	$\vee$	`$\vee$`	$\diamond$	`$\diamond$`
$\ast$	`$\ast$`	$\bigtriangledown$	`$\bigtriangledown$`	$\wedge$	`$\wedge$`	$\amalg$	`$\amalg$`

The command $\setminus$ produces a '\', and $\backslash$ (listed under mathematics: symbols below) also produces a '\'. But the spacings are different: e.g., $A\setminus B$ gives $A\setminus B$ whereas $A\backslash B$ gives $A\backslash B$. There are alternate names for $\wedge$ and $\vee$: $\land$ and $\lor$. Similarly, $\lnot$ is an alternate for $\neg$ (listed under mathematics: symbols). Some operators come in large sizes. The larger member of each pair shown below is used automatically for displayed equations.

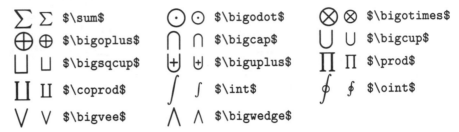

$\sum$ $\sum$ $\sum$	$\odot$ $\odot$ $\bigodot$	$\otimes$ $\otimes$ $\bigotimes$
$\bigoplus$ $\bigoplus$ $\bigoplus$	$\bigcap$ $\bigcap$ $\bigcap$	$\bigcup$ $\bigcup$ $\bigcup$
$\bigsqcup$ $\bigsqcup$ $\bigsqcup$	$\biguplus$ $\biguplus$ $\biguplus$	$\prod$ $\prod$ $\prod$
$\coprod$ $\coprod$ $\coprod$	$\int$ $\int$ $\int$	$\oint$ $\oint$ $\oint$
$\bigvee$ $\bigvee$ $\bigvee$	$\bigwedge$ $\bigwedge$ $\bigwedge$	

There is also a small integral sign, $\int$, produced by $\smallint$. Limits may be introduced on integrals, sums, products, etc. These are entered as superscripts and subscripts. In some cases, the limits will automatically appear above and below the symbol; in others, they will appear displaced to the right. These positions can be changed using the commands \limits (to move limits to the top and bottom) and \nolimits (to move limits to the side). See Examples VII and IX.

mathematics: punctuation   24–33

Standard punctuation characters can be used in the mathematics mode, with one exception. If you type '$a:b$', you get '$a : b$' (the spacing is more appropriate for a *relation*, which is how TeX interprets ':' in this mode). You must use \colon if you want a colon as punctuation; for example, '$a\colon b$' gives '$a : b$'. When typing a formula in text (i.e., one that is not to be displayed on a separate line), you should usually put punctuation outside the $ signs. For example, to get '$a = x$, y, or z.', type '$a=x$, y, or z.' instead of '$a=x, y,$ or $z.$'. The spacing will be more uniform the first way and it will offer TeX more line break possibilities. If you want to discourage some of these possibilities, use a tie. (For example, type 'or~z.'; see line breaks for a discussion of ties.)

In displayed equations (between double $ signs), put the punctuation in as part of the equation unless you are using text in the equation. In that case, the text and associated punctuation should all go in an \hbox. See Equation 13 in Example IX.

mathematics: relations   24–33, 38–43, 52–57, 60–63

$<$ $<$	$>$ $>$	$=$ =
$\perp$ $\perp$	$\leq$ $\leq$	$\geq$ $\geq$
$\equiv$ $\equiv$	$\doteq$ $\doteq$	$\prec$ $\prec$
$\preceq$ $\preceq$	$\succ$ $\succ$	$\succeq$ $\succeq$
$\sim$ $\sim$	$\simeq$ $\simeq$	$\ll$ $\ll$
$\gg$ $\gg$	$\subset$ $\subset$	$\subseteq$ $\subseteq$
$\supset$ $\supset$	$\supseteq$ $\supseteq$	$\sqsubseteq$ $\sqsubseteq$
$\sqsupseteq$ $\sqsupseteq$	$\asymp$ $\asymp$	$\approx$ $\approx$
$\cong$ $\cong$	$\bowtie$ $\bowtie$	$\models$ $\models$
$\vdash$ $\vdash$	$\dashv$ $\dashv$	$\smile$ $\smile$
$\frown$ $\frown$	$\mid$ $\mid$	$\parallel$ $\parallel$
$\in$ $\in$	$\ni$ $\ni$	$\propto$ $\propto$

These relations can be negated by prefixing the commands by \not; for example, $\not\perp$ gives ⊥̸. This does not always give pleasing results: $\not\parallel$ gives ∦. In some cases, TeX comes equipped with an alternative: $\notin$ gives ∉, $\neq$ or $\ne$ give ≠ (though in this Appendix \ne has been redefined to typeset new entries). In other cases, one has to make adjustments oneself; here is one crude way: $\not\kern1.4pt\parallel$ gives ∦. There are some alternate names here as well: $\le$ and $\ge$ have the same effect as $\leq$ and $\geq$; $\owns$ is equivalent to $\ni$.

Other relation symbols that are available are:

←	$\leftarrow$	⟵	$\longleftarrow$
→	$\rightarrow$	⟶	$\longrightarrow$
⇐	$\Leftarrow$	⟸	$\Longleftarrow$
⇒	$\Rightarrow$	⟹	$\Longrightarrow$
↑	$\uparrow$	↓	$\downarrow$
⇑	$\Uparrow$	⇓	$\Downarrow$
↔	$\leftrightarrow$	⟷	$\longleftrightarrow$
⇔	$\Leftrightarrow$	⟺	$\Longleftrightarrow$
↕	$\updownarrow$	⇕	$\Updownarrow$
↦	$\mapsto$	⟼	$\longmapsto$
↩	$\hookleftarrow$	↪	$\hookrightarrow$
↗	$\nearrow$	↘	$\searrow$
↙	$\swarrow$	↖	$\nwarrow$
↼	$\leftharpoonup$	⇀	$\rightharpoonup$
↽	$\leftharpoondown$	⇁	$\rightharpoondown$
⇌	$\rightleftharpoons$		

All the vertical arrows also come in larger sizes; these sizes are obtained by the same commands that are used for large delimiters. Alternate names here are $\to$ and $\gets$ for $\rightarrow$ and $\leftarrow$, respectively. $\iff$ produces ⟺ just as $\Longleftrightarrow$ does, but with more space on either side.

Finally, here are two symbols that do *not* come with Plain TeX but are useful nevertheless:

\lapproxeq gives ⪅   and   \gapproxeq gives ⪆.

These can only be used if you have access to the definitions (shown under mathematics: special effects).

mathematics: roman type for special functions   38–43

Functions like 'sin', 'cos' and 'log', as well as a few other expressions, are usually set in roman type, even in formulas. This can be done in TeX by using:

```
\arccos  \arcsin  \arctan  \arg      \cos     \cosh   \cot   \coth
\csc     \deg     \det     \dim      \exp     \gcd    \hom   \inf
\ker     \lg      \lim     \liminf   \limsup  \ln     \log   \max
\min     \Pr      \sec     \sin      \sinh    \sup    \tan   \tanh
```

It is possible to put expressions above and below some of these, when displaying equations. For example,

$$\lim_{x\to\infty} \qquad \overset{\heartsuit}{\max}$$

The commands that achieve this are the ones normally used for superscripts and subscripts; the expressions that will have such indices placed above or below are

\det, \gcd, \inf, \lim, \liminf, \limsup, \max, \min, \Pr and \sup. For the others, TeX will use the normal placements for indices:

$$\sin^2 x + \cos^{-2} x \neq 1 \quad \text{in general.}$$

The input for this was:

```
$$\sin^2x + \cos^{-2}x \neq 1 \quad {\rm in\ general.}$$
```

There are two varieties of 'mod' to cover the two ways it is often used: between variables, or at the end of a formula. They are produced by `$\bmod$` and `$\pmod$`, respectively; e.g., `$(a\bmod b)$` gives $(a \bmod b)$, and `$\pmod{n}$` gives $\pmod{n}$.

mathematics: spacing   14–15, 38–43, 60–63

TeX spaces characters according to whether it thinks they represent operations, relations, punctuation, left or right delimiters, etc. By using the spacing commands

$$\backslash!, \qquad \backslash,, \qquad \backslash>, \qquad \backslash;, \qquad \text{\quad} \quad \text{and} \quad \text{\qquad},$$

whose effects are shown in the Introduction (the first gives a 'negative space', the others positive spaces of increasing lengths), it is possible to rearrange this spacing as desired. The definitions of the first four of these commands are given under keywords; \quad and \qquad are defined in individual entries.

It is also possible to fool TeX by using grouping symbols; for example, '`$a,b$`' gives 'a, b', whereas '`$a{,}b$`' gives 'a,b'; or, '`$a:b$`' gives '$a : b$', but '`$a{:}b$`' gives '$a{:}b$'. Other ways to control horizontal spacing are shown in the input for Equation 8 in Example IX, or discussed under `\mskip`.

Equations 5 and 10 in Example IX show how vertical spacing can be controlled. The method in some of these equations is to use variants of the `\phantom` command. In particular, `\vphantom` in conjunction with `\smash` (see Equation 10 in Example IX) provides a powerful way to position symbols where you want them. `\phantom` may also be used to position indices. For example, $R_{abc}{}^d$ is created by `$R_{abc}^{\phantom{abc}d}$`, and $R^{ab}{}_{cd}$ is created by `$R_{\phantom{ab}cd}^{ab}$`. These effects can also be obtained somewhat more easily by fooling TeX; for example, the input for

$$R^{ab}{}_{cd}, \quad R^{abc}{}_d \quad \text{and} \quad R^a{}_b{}^c{}_d.$$

was:

```
$$R^{ab}{}_{cd},\quad R^{abc}{}_d\quad{\rm and}\quad R^a{}_b{}^c{}_d.$$
```

Observe that the vertical positioning of indices in this 'display style' is slightly different from that used in the 'text style' expressions above the displayed line. Vertical positioning of indices (or of any material, even outside the mathematics mode) can be controlled using `\raise` and `\lower` (see Equation 5 in Example IX and also positioning text on a page). The positioning of accents on accents also requires some adjustments. These may be made using the `\skew` command. The amount of 'skew' can be controlled by specifying a number; for example, the input for $\hat{\hat I}$, $\hat{\hat I}$, $\hat{\hat I}$ and $\hat{\hat I}$ was:

```
... the input for $\hat{\hat I}$, $\skew3\hat{\hat I}$,
$\skew5\hat{\hat I}$ and $\skew9\hat{\hat I}$ ...
```

See also `\rlap`, `\llap`, mathematics: punctuation and `\mathsurround` for a little more information about spacing.

mathematics: special effects

It is possible to put symbols on other symbols. For example,

$$\overset{\mu,\nu}{\longmapsto} \quad \text{\$\{\textbackslash buildrel\textbackslash mu,\textbackslash nu\textbackslash over\textbackslash longmapsto\}\$}$$

$$\overset{\text{def}}{\propto} \quad \text{\$\{\textbackslash buildrel\textbackslash rm def\textbackslash over\textbackslash propto\}\$}$$

$$\overset{\circ}{g}_{\mu\nu} \quad \text{\$\{\textbackslash buildrel\textbackslash circ\textbackslash over g\}\_\{\textbackslash mu\textbackslash nu\}\$}$$

Another command, `$\joinrel$`, allows you to join relation symbols. This is how several of the relation symbols available in TeX are put together. For example, the symbol $\longleftrightarrow$ is produced by the command `$\longleftrightarrow$`, defined by

    \def\longleftrightarrow{\leftarrow\joinrel\rightarrow}

In other words, the symbol is created by joining $\leftarrow$ and $\rightarrow$. Other effects are:

$$\overset{a}{\underset{b}{}} \quad \text{\$\{a\textbackslash atop b\}\$} \qquad \frac{a}{b} \quad \text{\$\{a\textbackslash above2pt b\}\$}$$

$$\left\{\begin{matrix}a\\b\end{matrix}\right\} \quad \text{\$\{a\textbackslash brace b\}\$} \qquad \binom{a}{b} \quad \text{\$\{a\textbackslash choose b\}\$} \qquad \left[\begin{matrix}a\\b\end{matrix}\right] \quad \text{\$\{a\textbackslash brack b\}\$}$$

The first of these effects is useful, for example, if there are double (or more) limits on integrals, sums, etc. The second is useful in expressions where there might be fractions on top of other fractions (it provides a 'fraction bar' whose thickness can be set to n points by typing '\above*n*pt'). The remaining three have many uses; for example, they may be used to include two-row matrices in the body of some text (i.e., without using the display style). For more unusual arrays of this nature, there is a mouthful of a command, \abovewithdelims, that allows you to explicitly specify the left and right delimiters as well as the thickness of the fraction bar. For example, if you make the following definition:

    \def\oddity{\abovewithdelims\rbrace\lbrace1pt}

you will get $\left\}\begin{matrix}a\\b\end{matrix}\right\{$ when you type '`${a\oddity b}$`'.

Finally, here are some useful new commands (the main one is \stacksymbols):

```
\def\stacksymbols #1#2#3#4{\def\theguybelow{#2}
    \def\verticalposition{\lower#3pt}
    \def\spacingwithinsymbol{\baselineskip0pt\lineskip#4pt}
    \mathrel{\mathpalette\intermediary#1}}
\def\intermediary#1#2{\verticalposition\vbox{\spacingwithinsymbol
    \everycr={}\tabskip0pt
    \halign{$\mathsurround0pt#1\hfil##\hfil$\crcr#2\crcr
            \theguybelow\crcr}}}
```

```
\def\lapproxeq{\stacksymbols{<}{\sim}{2.5}{.2}}
\def\gapproxeq{\stacksymbols{>}{\sim}{3}{.5}}
```

The last two lines define the new symbols $\lesssim$ and $\gtrsim$, introduced above under mathematics: relations. The definitions are based on the new command \stacksymbols; this is set up so that the symbols will automatically become smaller if used in indices. **\stacksymbols** allows you to construct many composite symbols, and it allows you to fine-tune spacing to your satisfaction. For example,

$$a \qquad \underset{\sim}{g} \qquad b$$

was obtained from this input:

```
$$a\qquad
\stacksymbols{g}{\tilde{}}{8}{1}\qquad
\stacksymbols{g}{\tilde{}}{-1}{4}\qquad
b$$
```

The first two arguments in \stacksymbols are the two symbols that are to go one over the other. The next argument controls the overall vertical position, and the last the spacing within the composite symbol.

In the definition of \stacksymbols, two TEX commands were used that are not discussed or defined elsewhere in this book. \mathrel is used when making new relation-symbols so that TEX will know how to arrange spacing when the new symbol occurs in a formula. \mathpalette (which acts on two arguments) ensures that the new symbols will grow or shrink correctly when they are displayed, when they occur as indices, etc.

mathematics: symbols   32–33, 38–43, 52–57, 60–63

ℵ	$\aleph$	∀	$\forall$	∃	$\exists$
′	$\prime$	ℏ	$\hbar$	∅	$\emptyset$
∇	∇	¬	$\neg$	√	$\surd$
ı	$\imath$	ȷ	$\jmath$	ℓ	ℓ
♭	$\flat$	♯	$\sharp$	♮	$\natural$
⊤	$\top$	⊥	$\bot$	\	$\backslash$
ℜ	$\Re$	ℑ	$\Im$	∂	∂
∞	∞	∠	$\angle$	△	$\triangle$
♣	$\clubsuit$	◇	$\diamondsuit$	♡	$\heartsuit$
♠	$\spadesuit$	…	$\ldots$	⋯	$\cdots$
℘	$\wp$	·	$\cdotp$	.	$\ldotp$
⋮	$\vdots$	⋰	$\ddots$		

mathematics: typeface styles and sizes   40–41, 60–63

The standard typeface for mathematical expressions is called *math italic*. There are also typefaces for mathematical symbols. The typefaces come in different sizes: 'text style' for ordinary expressions that are in the middle of text; 'display style' for expressions that are displayed on a separate line; and 'script style' and 'scriptscript style' for indices. TEX picks styles for the different terms in an expression on its own, but you can also issue instructions to override these choices by typing '\textstyle', '\scriptstyle', etc. See Equation 1 in Example V. You also have available to you a 'calligraphic' typeface (see \cal). Packages more advanced than Plain TEX, especially ones geared to the needs of mathematicians (like $\mathcal{AMS}$-TEX, the package adopted by the American Mathematical Society), usually offer styles beyond these.

Incidentally, the input that produces the $\mathcal{AMS}$-TEX logo is:

```
$\cal A\kern-.1667em\lower.5ex\hbox{$\cal M$}\kern-.075em S$-\TeX\
```

$\mathstrut$

Assigns a standard vertical size to formulas. For example, the input for

$$\sqrt{a} + \sqrt{b} \quad \text{and} \quad \sqrt{a} + \sqrt{b}.$$

was:

```
$$\sqrt{a} + \sqrt{b} \qquad \hbox{and} \qquad
\sqrt{\mathstrut a} + \sqrt{\mathstrut b}.$$
```

The Plain TEX definition of the command is '\vphantom('.

\mathsurround *

A parameter that determines how much space TEX will leave before and after a formula. In Plain TEX the value is 0pt. For example, here are the effects of two different values for \mathsurround:

2 points: $a < b$ and $b < c \Rightarrow a < c$.

5 points: $a < b$ and $b < c \Rightarrow a < c$.

The input for the two was:

```
{\mathsurround=2pt 2 points: $a<b$ and $b<c$ $\Rightarrow$ $a<c$.}
\hfil\break
{\mathsurround=5pt 5 points: $a<b$ and $b<c$ $\Rightarrow$ $a<c$.}
```

matrices   40–41

If you want parentheses around the matrix, use \pmatrix. Otherwise, \matrix allows you to specify your own delimiters. See Example V. TEX also provides a command called \bordermatrix which produces entities like

$$\begin{matrix} & \triangle & \heartsuit & \wp \\ \Im & \begin{pmatrix} a & b & c \\ \ell & d & e & f \\ \aleph & 1 & \mu & -73 \end{pmatrix} \end{matrix}$$

if given

```
$$\bordermatrix{&\triangle&\heartsuit&\wp\cr
\Im&a&b&c\cr \ell&d&e&f\cr \aleph&1&\mu&-73\cr}$$
```

as input. In addition, it is possible to produce matrices with 'invisible' left or right delimiters by typing '\left.' or '\right.' when using the \matrix command.

\medbreak

Suggests a possible page break to TEX; if the suggestion isn't taken, a vertical gap equal to \medskip is left instead.

\medskip   x–xiii, 10–13, 66–67

Leaves a vertical space: ───────── . The standard size of this space is called \medskipamount, set to equal 6pt plus2pt minus2pt; i.e., a 6 point space that can stretch or shrink when needed. \medskip is defined by \vskip\medskipamount. (See \bigskip.)

METAFONT

A font-creating program, composed by Donald Knuth.

\midinsert   46–49

Tries to insert material where it finds it, otherwise takes it to the top of the next available page. See Example VI.

minus 11, 50

Specifies the shrinkability of glue; e.g., the command '\hskip 10pt minus 4pt' will leave a space between 6 and 10 points in size. See plus and keywords.

modes

As TeX processes a file, it is, at any given point, in one of six possible modes. The mode it is in will determine how it responds to certain commands (like \break). The modes are:

- *Horizontal*: When stringing things together horizontally, towards building a paragraph. Once TeX starts putting together material for a paragraph (loosely referred to as 'TeX is on a line' at several places in this book), it stays in horizontal mode till the paragraph ends. See paragraphs for lists of things that start TeX's paragraph-building activities, or end them.

- *Restricted horizontal*: When stringing things together horizontally, towards building an \hbox.

- *Vertical*: When putting things together vertically, towards building a page (loosely referred to elsewhere in this book as being 'between lines'). TeX is in this mode when between paragraphs.

- *Internal vertical*: When putting things together vertically, towards building a \vbox.

- *Math*: When putting together a formula to be placed in a paragraph.

- *Display math*: When putting together a formula that will be placed on a new line; after the formula is built, the interrupted paragraph resumes.

\month *

At the start of a job, TeX checks your computer for what month it is; you can use \month to extract this information. For example, the input for: "Darn it, if it ain't month 8 already!" was:

``Darn it, if it ain't month \number\month\ already!''

Now, numbers are fine for days of the year and for the year itself, but it isn't usual to run around saying "My birthday is early in month 9; try to start stashing away money for a present by month 6, will you?" To help you conduct more normal discourse, you will be shown a new command below that converts numbers to names by brute force.

This will allow you to make such well-informed comments as, "It's August; how very wet it is in Bombay at this time of the year." The input for this was:

```
\def\monthname {\ifcase\month\or January\or February\or March\or
    April\or May\or June\or July\or August\or September\or October\or
    November\or December\fi}
\def\Bombayclimate {\ifcase\month\or very cool\or cool\or pleasant\or
    warm\or hot\or damp\or wet\or very wet\or nice\or very warm\or
    nice\or nippy\fi}
\ind This will allow you to make such well-informed comments as,
``It's \monthname; how \Bombayclimate\ it is in Bombay at this
time of the year.'' The input for this ...
%NOTE: '\ind' is a private command, used to indent paragraphs.
```

\moveleft * 74–75

Moves boxes to the left. Works only when TEX is in a vertical **mode** (very roughly, when it is between lines, not in the middle of some horizontal line). See **modes**.

\moveright * 74–75

Moves boxes to the right. See **\moveleft**.

$\mskip$ *

The mathematics mode analogue of **\hskip**. The space to be skipped must be specified in terms of the math unit called **mu** (see **keywords**). Though **\hskip** also works in formulas, it cannot be used with **mu**; thus, **\mskip** is often preferable (because **mu** automatically adjusts itself to the size of the style being used in that part of the formula).

\multiply * 2, 72–73, 78–79, 80–81

Multiplies variables by whole numbers. See Example XIV.

\multispan 44–45, 48–49

Used to span multiple columns in a **table**; see the title of Table 2 or the material at the bottom of Table 3 in Example VI.

\narrower vi–vii, 6–7, 8, 20–21, 30–31

Displays text in a format narrowed by the current paragraph indentation (i.e., the current value of **\parindent**). The command is defined in Plain TEX using **\rightskip** and **\leftskip**. See **paragraphs** for a discussion of where such a command should be issued.

\negthinspace 10–11

Squeezes stuff together likeso, when you type '**like\negthinspace so**'. It is defined in Plain TEX by:

```
\def\negthinspace{\kern-.16667em }
```

\newbox 80

Allocates **\box** registers exactly as **\newcount** allocates **\count** registers. The command is useful for the same reasons that **\newcount** is. Once a register is allocated, however, **\box** commands work a little differently from **\count** commands. For example, *stuff* was produced by this input:

```
For example,
\newbox\justtesting \setbox\justtesting=\hbox{\it stuff\/}%
\box\justtesting\ was produced by ...
```

See **\box** for some related information.

new commands in this book

Several new commands are defined and used in this book. Many are abbreviations and are used purely locally (i.e., for just a few subsequent lines); others are typeface names or commands specific to the format of this book. Apart from the name \title (used for the large typeface in which section titles appear in scattered places throughout the book) and the command \newpageno (which places boldface page numbers in the margin), no new commands are used till Example X. This allows you to copy input and have it work exactly as it does here.

For the rest of the book, you have to be a little careful when copying input. In each of Examples X–XVII, new commands used in that example are mostly defined at the start of the input for the example, so you should look there before you copy input. If the input includes one of these new commands, you will also have to copy the definition. Those input pages, this Appendix, and the Epilogue were all formatted using a large number of specially designed commands. The commands are shown in the Epilogue. If you want to copy any of the definitions, you should make sure that you copy everything that will make a new command given there work correctly.

A few general-purpose commands have also been defined here and there in the book. They are listed below:

\letterhead, \date, \address, \sal and \endletter: 66.

\memo: 68.

\pattern: 68.

\beginscript and \endscript: 70.

\pow and \fermat: 72.

\frame, \fitframe, \shframe and \s: 76.

\trap and \rect: 78.

\beginart and \endart: 80.

\chartable: see character codes.

\ignore: see comments.

\monthname: see \month.

\stacksymbols, \lapproxeq and \gapproxeq: see mathematics: special effects.

\table, \caption and associated commands: see tables.

\now and \today: see \year.

\raggedleft, \beginliteral and \endliteral: see the Appendix format file in the Epilogue.

\newcount   68–73, 78–81, 88–89

TEX labels its internal registers by non-negative whole numbers: for example, the \count registers are labelled \count0, \count1, ..., \count255. Since it is hard to keep track of which register stores which variable, or to remember which registers are already in use, TEX offers an easier alternative. You can name registers using the \newcount command: TEX will automatically allocate one that is not being used. You can then refer to this register by name, and TEX will keep track internally of what register number it corresponds to. For example, \newcount\var allocates a \count register which can henceforth be referred to purely by the name \var. See \count.

It is a good idea to use \newcount (as well as the other \new... commands) in moderation. If you only need temporary storage, you should use one of the 'scratch' **registers**. If you are within a **group** and, again, need only to store something temporarily, you can use a register labelled by any number at all. Both of these will ensure that you are not storing large amounts of information unnecessarily. You should use \newcount to allocate yourself a register in those cases where you will need to use the register at many places through the document.

\newdimen 80

Like \newcount, but this allocates registers for quantities with dimension (i.e., **units**) such as ones representing size. See \dimen.

\noalign * 40–41, 48–49, 54–57, 60–63

Allows you to insert nonaligned material into an alignment.

\nobreak 66–67

Prevents line breaks when TEX is processing material horizontally and discourages page breaks when it is doing so vertically. See **modes**.

\noindent * vi–xiii, 6–9, 58–59, 66–67

Starts a paragraph without indentation.

$\nolimits$ * 52, 60–61

See mathematics: operations.

\nopagenumbers 2

Suppresses **page numbers**.

\null

Abbreviation for \hbox{}. Useful to fool TEX into thinking that a line or a page has begun. It will then honor spacing commands that it may otherwise ignore at the start of certain lines and pages. For example, \null\hskip will leave space in situations where \hskip by itself will not. Similarly, \null\vskip or \null\vfil will leave space at the top of a new page.

\number * 72–73

Extracts the numerical value of variables; see \day, \month and \year.

\obeylines

This command makes TEX obey the line arrangement
in the input literally; i.e., every input line (that
is not too long) will result in a separate output line.
In effect, each line is regarded as a paragraph by itself.
  (For example, the input for all this was:)

```
{\obeylines
This command makes \TeX\ obey the line arrangement
in the input literally; i.e., every input line (that
is not too long) will result in a separate output line.
In effect, each line is regarded as a paragraph by itself.
\qquad (For example, the input for all this was:)
\smallskip}
```

\obeyspaces

Makes   TeX   not   ignore   successive   spaces. The input for this was, partially

```
{\obeyspaces    Makes    \TeX\   not    ignore
    successive    spaces}.    The input    for ...
```

\offinterlineskip   48–49, 78–79

Removes the gap between baselines of successive lines. The effect is more than that of just typing '\baselineskip 0pt'. TeX has a parameter, \lineskip, that prevents lines from getting too close together. This parameter has the value 1pt in Plain TeX (i.e., lines that get too close will be forcibly separated by a point even if \baselineskip has been set to 0pt). But \offinterlineskip will switch this off as well. This is necessary when making tables, or other arrangements, that have vertical rules that must span several horizontal lines. There is also the command \nointerlineskip which suppresses the gap between lines just once, at the point where it is used (it must, of course, be used in an appropriate place).

\oldstyle

{\oldstyle 0 1 2 3 4 5 6 7 8 9} will produce 0123456789.

\omit * 48–49

Used in alignments to allow entries to ignore specifications in the preamble. See **tables** and Example VI.

\openup

'Opens up' vertical spacing; \openup2pt, for example, will add 2pt to all of TeX's line spacing parameters. Plain TeX also provides a 'unit' called \jot in terms of which \openup may be specified; one \jot equals 3pt. Multi-line equation displays in Plain TeX have a built-in default of 1\jot for \openup. You can reset \jot (see the separate entry for it) to change the line spacing for all such displays. For example, the input for

$$x = y$$
$$y \approx z$$

was:

```
$$\openup-\jot  % SPACING REDUCED BY A 'JOT'
\displaylines{x=y\cr y\approx z\cr}$$
```

\or *

Used with \ifcase. See \month for an example of the use of both commands.

\output *

Your last chance to mess around with pages and do fancy things before TeX ships stuff off to the dvi file. For example, it allows you to add repeated material to every page or to draw a 'frame' (a ruled box) around the entire page. The standard output routine of Plain TeX does several things: It places a headline at the top of a \vbox representing the current page, and a footline at its bottom. In-between, it puts another \vbox that has in it the actual page contents. It also advances the page number and ships the page out. Examples of output routines are shown in the Epilogue. Look at them if you want to see how to design your own.

A page break may be inhibited by placing '\nobreak' at a point where TEX will be in vertical mode, and it may be caused by placing '\break' (again, in vertical mode) or \eject (in either horizontal or vertical mode, but not inside a box). See modes for a discussion of when TEX is in what mode. When forcing a page break with \break or \eject, you must remember to type '\vfil' first—unless you've become fond of 'underfull \vbox' messages. These forced page breaks will also end the current paragraph. If you want a page break at the end of the current line, *with the paragraph continuing on the next page*, type '\vadjust{\vfil\eject}'.

You can suggest break points to TEX by typing '\smallbreak', '\medbreak', '\bigbreak', '\filbreak' or '\goodbreak'. In the first three cases, if TEX does not break the page at that point, it will leave a vertical space of the corresponding size (i.e., 'small', 'med', or 'big'). TEX will break a page at a \filbreak (in that case this command has the effect of \vfil\break) unless it encounters another \filbreak before the point at which it would normally have broken the page. \goodbreak merely suggests a good place to break the page: if the suggestion is not taken, nothing special is done. \bigbreak is used at a few places in this book, and the formatting commands for this Appendix (shown in the Epilogue) involve a redefinition of \par that uses essentially the exact Plain TEX definition of \goodbreak.

\pagegoal *

As TEX stacks material vertically, it keeps track of the total vertical size in a counter called \pagetotal. It aims to make the size as close to its goal, as represented by \pagegoal, as possible. \pagegoal is initially set equal to \vsize, but you can play tricks with it if you want fancy effects (and know what you are doing). For example, the value of \pagegoal TEX is working with here is 621.52243pt and the value of \vsize is 621.52243pt. These values are obtained by typing '\the\pagegoal' and '\the\vsize' respectively.

\pageinsert   30–33

Inserts a page's worth of stuff (for example, diagrams, tables, or a blank page) onto the next available full page. See Example III.

\pageno   vi–xiii, 2, 80–81

The name of the **register** where Plain TEX stores the current page number. The register is actually \count0 (see \count) but it is more convenient to refer to it by the given name \pageno. See page 60 (setting page numbers) or pages *vi* and *viii*. (setting page numbers in roman numerals).

page numbers   vi–xiii, 2, 80–81

• *Basic information.* Page numbers are provided automatically by Plain TEX, centered at the bottom of the page. Page numbering may be switched off by typing '\nopagenumbers'; starting values may be set by resetting \pageno, as was done at the start of Example IX. Page numbers in roman numerals may be obtained by using a negative starting value for \pageno: see pages *vi* and *viii*.

• *Details.* First, see \pageno. The automatic page numbering that Plain TEX provides is achieved internally by it through a command called \folio. The command extracts the value of the current page number from \pageno; if the value is negative, \folio converts it to a roman numeral (using \romannumeral). Then, the default \footline is set in Plain TEX to contain \folio, centered and in 10-point roman type (see \folio and \footline). \nopagenumbers works by internally resetting the footline this way: '\footline={\hfil}'. It is possible to achieve other effects by explicitly defining \footline (or \headline, if you want page numbers at the top) to do what you want. See page 2. Conditional commands (involving \ifnum) are useful in setting page numbers in different positions on different pages, or in suppressing page numbers for a few pages, or in setting particular types of headlines or footlines on particular pages. See the definitions of \footline at the start of Example XVII and those of \headline in the Epilogue.

pages

See \pagegoal and \pagetotal for a very brief account of how TEX makes a page. There are various subtleties (how it handles inserts, for example) that are not discussed here. Other aspects of page-making, like **page breaks**, **page size**, positioning **pages**, etc., are discussed under separate entries.

page size

See \hsize and \vsize.

`\pagetotal` *

Represents the total vertical size of the accumulated material for the current page. The value right now is 618.43333pt. (Since TEX reads past one page's worth of material before setting a page, the value in this case happens to represent the size of material that ended up on the previous page.) Once the value passes `\pagegoal`, TEX knows it is time to give birth to a new page.

To check that `\pagetotal` has changed after the last paragraph was set: the value is now 78.15277pt (extracted by typing '`\the\pagetotal`' in the input).

`\par` *   viii–ix, 12–13, 18–19, 58–59, 68–71, 74–75, 84–85

Ends a paragraph. The command is explicitly inserted by TEX at the end of every paragraph when it reads your document (before it processes it any further) even if you had used some other paragraph-ending mechanism (like a blank line in the input). This makes redefinitions of `\par` a very powerful way of getting TEX to do extra things at the end of every paragraph. See `\endgraf` and Example XIII.

paragraphs   13, 18–19, 20–23, 58–59

Making simple paragraphs is simple. Page 13 tells you all that you need to know. If you need greater control over your paragraphs, the summary given below provides more information. All the commands mentioned here are also discussed in their own entries.

• *Inducing indentation.* The first line of a paragraph is automatically indented by a standard amount. That amount may be changed by resetting `\parindent`. Other lines in the paragraph may be indented by using `\indent`. More complicated indentations may be obtained by using `\hangindent` and `\hangafter`.

• *Suppressing indentation.* Use `\noindent`.

• *Setting spacing.* `\parskip` may be used to reset the spacing between paragraphs, `\baselineskip` to reset the interline spacing within a paragraph.

• *Paragraph shapes/sizes.* See `\leftskip`, `\looseness`, `\narrower`, `\parshape`, `\prevgraf` and `\rightskip`. See also `\hangindent` and `\hangafter`.

• *Controlling the end of a paragraph.* See `\parfillskip`.

• *Learning a little bit about how TEX makes paragraphs.* Look at `\pretolerance`, `\tolerance`, `\hbadness` and `\hfuzz` for very brief accounts of some of the issues involved. Once a paragraph begins, TEX reads everything that follows as if it were all one long line (i.e., TEX is in horizontal **mode**) till the paragraph ends (see below). It is only then that it tries to chop up this line into smaller ones of the correct length, using the specified values of `\hfuzz`, `\pretolerance` and `\tolerance` (and also taking into account other factors, like penalties imposed if successive lines end with hyphens). Since TEX scans entire input paragraphs before it chooses output spacing, a change at the very end of a paragraph can affect the arrangement of text at the beginning.

• *When to set parameters that shape a paragraph.* Indentation is set when TEX begins scanning the paragraph; the size will therefore be determined by whatever value `\parindent` has just at that point. If you change `\parindent` in the middle of a paragraph, it will not affect that one, but it will alter the ones after. The settings for `\hangindent`, `\hangafter`, `\parshape` and `\looseness` that are used in shaping a paragraph are the ones in force at the point the paragraph ends. If they are changed in mid-paragraph, TEX will use the later values. They are automatically reset to their default values (`\hangindent=0pt`, `\hangafter=1`, `\parshape=0`,

\looseness=0) after the paragraph is typeset. Similarly, the values of \narrower, \leftskip, \rightskip, \baselineskip and \parfillskip that are used are also the ones at the end. However, these parameters are not automatically reset: you must do that yourself, or use grouping braces to localize the effects of the new settings. When using braces—for all these parameters, except \parindent—*it is important that the paragraph explicitly end before the closing brace.* Otherwise, TEX will be outside the group in which the new settings were in effect by the time it knows the paragraph is over, and it will use the old settings.

• *Common things that start a new paragraph.* When TEX is not already building a paragraph (say, when it is at the start of a file, or when it has just completed another paragraph), the occurrence of any of these will cause TEX to start putting together material for a new one: \indent and \noindent; any 'non-command' character (see the list of command characters at the start of this Appendix); a command like \char that causes characters to be printed; $ (this causes TEX to start a new paragraph and to enter the mathematics mode); commands that make accents; horizontal spacing commands like \quad, \hskip, \hfil, etc.; \valign; \vrule; \item and \itemitem. It is worth observing that the command \kern does not cause TEX to start a new paragraph: when encountered between paragraphs, it is interpreted as a *vertical* spacing command; only within an already-begun paragraph does TEX regard it as specifying horizontal spacing. Also, neither \hbox nor commands based on it (like \line and its dependents—see below) are regarded by TEX as starting a new paragraph.

• *Common things that briefly interrupt a paragraph.* \centerline, \leftline, \rightline and, in general, \line; displayed mathematics (typed between double $ signs). Once each of these have done their thing, the paragraph will automatically resume on the next line. However, you must keep in mind that the various \line commands should be used only after explicitly terminating the current line of the paragraph (using, say, \hfil\break).

• *Common things that end a paragraph.* A blank input line; an explicit \par or \endgraf command; a vertical spacing command like \vskip, \vfil, \smallskip, etc.; \item and \itemitem (these end the current paragraph and start a new one); \hrule; \halign; page break commands like \eject, \smallbreak, \goodbreak, etc.; \bye; \end.

\parfillskip   ∗   18–19

TEX scans entire input paragraphs before typesetting them. This allows you to control not only how a paragraph begins (i.e., set indentation) but also how it ends. You do this by setting a value for \parfillskip. The default is '0pt plus 1fil'; i.e., no extra space is asked for at the end of the paragraph, but glue is provided to fill as much of the last line as necessary with white space. For example, \parfillskip has been reset just for this paragraph to make it end two inches from the right margin. The input for this paragraph was, partially:

```
{\parfillskip 2in \TeX\ scans entire input paragraphs before
...
The input for this paragraph was, partially:\par}
```

\parindent   ∗   viii–ix, 6–7, 22–23, 66–71

Sets the value of the paragraph indentation. The default value in Plain TEX is 20pt. A negative value makes the first line stick out rather than in: the paragraph is 'outdented'. See paragraphs for more information.

\parshape ∗ 22–23

Licks paragraphs into shape. See the oddly shaped paragraph in Example I.

\parskip ∗ viii–ix, xiv–1, 68–71, 80

Sets the gap between paragraphs. In Plain TEX its value is 'Opt plus 1pt', where the **plus** allows it to stretch if needed. The stretchability can be increased if you want, and shrinkability can also be assigned, using **minus**. See **\bigskip**, **\medskip** and **\smallskip** for other examples of elastic vertical spacing.

\phantom 40–41, 62–63

 calculates the height, depth and width of *stuff* as it normally would, but does not print this *stuff*; it leaves instead a space of the correct dimensions. See **\hphantom** and **\vphantom**.

Plain TEX

A package of commands built out of the primitive commands of TEX. The package is so universally available, wherever TEX is, that when people say 'TEX' they almost always mean 'Plain TEX'. Any command listed in this Appendix that is not marked by an ∗ is a Plain TEX command and is, therefore, just an abbreviation for a collection of primitive ones. Appendix B of Donald Knuth's *TEXbook* contains the definitions, in terms of primitives, of essentially all Plain TEX commands.

The default format that you get with TEX is really a format provided by Plain TEX. It is suitable for the production of pre-prints and technical reports. For other kinds of documents the format must be altered, or an entirely different package used.

plus xiv–1, 11, 50

Specifies the stretchability of **glue**; e.g., the command '\hskip 10pt plus 5pt' will leave between 10 and 15 points of space, and even more if needed. (Glue is allowed to stretch beyond the specified limits—but not to shrink beyond specifications.) See **minus** and **keywords**.

point

A unit commonly used to specify quantities like paragraph indentation or interline spacing. One inch equals 72.27 points. A point is specified using the **keyword pt**.

positioning pages

See **\hoffset** and **\voffset**.

positioning text on a page

See Examples I, VIII, XV. The **\raise** and **\lower** commands, shown in the input for Equation 5 in Example IX and in Example XV, may be used to raise and lower boxes of material (see **boxes**). There are similar commands for horizontal adjustments of box positions: **\moveleft** and **\moveright**. See also specific entries throughout this Appendix for specific topics (like, say, **centering** or **paragraphs**).

\pretolerance * 86–87

The tolerance for white space that TEX has *before* it attempts hyphenation. (TEX will first try to set a paragraph without hyphenation, and only if it finds no pleasing arrangement will it then hyphenate.) The value may be set between -1 (will immediately consider hyphenations) and 10000 (never hyphenate—unless there are words that are longer than the line length). The default value in Plain TEX is 100. See the input for the Acknowledgements.

\prevgraf *

Keeps track of the number of lines in the most recently formed paragraph. The parameter is automatically reset to zero each time a paragraph begins. In the command that produces the double-columned Notes on the input pages of the main part of this book, for example, \prevgraf is used to keep track of the total number of lines: if the total is even, the notes are split into two columns one way; if odd, another way. The Epilogue shows you how this is done. As another example, you can set the value of \looseness based on what has happened in previous paragraphs to give some desired outcome at the end of a page or a document.

Incidentally, \prevgraf had the value 8 just before this paragraph began. The input for this was, partially:

```
{\count255=\prevgraf \ind Incidentally, "\prevgraf" had the value
\the\count255\ just before this paragraph began.} The input ...
% NOTE: '\ind' is a private paragraph-indenting command.
```

primitive commands

The basic commands of TEX out of which other commands are built. The most common such 'other commands' are ones in a package called Plain TEX. The package is discussed separately. This book discusses both the primitive, indecomposable commands of TEX as well as the composite commands of Plain TEX. To distinguish between the two in this Appendix, the primitive commands are identified by an * when they are listed (but not when they are discussed).

pt viii–ix, xiv–1, 9, 11–13

See point and keywords.

punctuation

This is mostly straightforward. However, quotation marks can be a little delicate. For example, 'yes', "yes", '"yes"' and "'no'" were obtained from

```
'yes', ''yes'', {'}''yes''' and ''\thinspace'no'\thinspace''
```

The last of these needed extra space inserted explicitly (whereas the one before did not) because TEX leaves more space before a " and after a " than it does before a ' or after a '. (\lq and \rq may be used if your keyboard does not have left and right quote symbols.) Also available are ¡ and ¿. See ligatures and Example IV.

\qquad 10–11, 14–15

Leaves this[   ]much space (produced by typing 'this[\qquad]much'). The command is defined in Plain TEX by:

```
\def\qquad{\hskip2em\relax}
```

See \quad.

\quad   10–11, 14–15

Leaves this[ ]much space (produced by typing 'this`[\quad]`much'). The command is defined in Plain TEX by:

    \def\quad{\hskip1em\relax}

Both em and \relax are discussed separately.

\raggedbottom   86–87

Plain TEX normally makes the bottom baselines of all full pages line up (so that, for example, facing pages will match). This means that the vertical spacing within the page has to be a little flexible. Such flexibility is built into \parskip as well as into other vertical spacing commands like \bigskip, etc. \raggedbottom reverses this, making the vertical spacing on a page somewhat rigid at the price of having 'ragged bottoms'. The feature can be switched off by typing \normalbottom. See also \raggedright.

\raggedright   86–87

Switches off the normal right-justification of text by making the interword spaces rigid (normally they are allowed to stretch and shrink a bit). See the Acknowledgements for an example.

\raise   *   60–61, 74–75

Raises boxes. Both \raise and \lower may be used only when TEX is processing material *on* a line (more precisely, when it is in a horizontal mode), not when it is between lines (i.e., not in vertical mode). See the title of Example XV.

registers   68

TEX can store a variety of types of information in 'registers'. There are specific classes of registers available for the storage of specific types of information. This book illustrates three of these, though there are others. Registers used to store pure whole numbers are called \count registers, those used to store quantities with dimension are called \dimen registers and those that store material to be (possibly) typeset are called \box registers. Each of these is discussed separately.

\relax   *

A command that essentially means 'do nothing'. One place where it is needed is after commands that could be followed by words that TEX might interpret as continuations of the command. For example, if you want to typeset the word 'height' just after the command \hrule, you have to type '\hrule\relax', otherwise TEX will interpret **height** as signifying the height of the \hrule and will then look for a number right after. If it doesn't see one, it will complain about a 'missing number'. You have to be similarly careful after all 'skip' commands (the problem words there are **plus** and **minus**). See **errors** and **keywords**.

\repeat   68–69, 72–73, 78–79

Used in conjunction with \loop to carry out repetitive tasks.

$\right$ *   40–43, 60–63

Makes a right **delimiter** of the correct size in a displayed mathematical expression. It can be used only in conjunction with $\left$; see that entry for a fuller discussion.

\rightline   viii-1, 66–67, 84–87

>   Puts everything on the line flush right; e.g., the input for this line was:

> ```
> \rightline{Puts everything on the line flush right; e.g., the input
> for this line was:}
> ```

See also **\line**.

\rightskip *   20–23, 70–71

> Moves the right text margin in or out. See Example I. The value of **\rightskip** used in setting a paragraph is the one in force just at the point that the paragraph ends. See **paragraphs**.

\rlap   2, 36–37

> Used to overlap material on the right (for instance, to place stuff in the right margin). For example, '¥' is produced by '\rlap{---}Y'. See Example IV and the **\headline** definitions for this Appendix, shown in the Epilogue.

\rm   8–9, 22–25, 40–41, 44–45, 52–55, 62–65, 70–71, 86–87

> Gives roman type (the default style in Plain TEX).

\romannumeral *

> Converts a number to roman numerals. For example, the current page number is CXLVI in these numerals. The input for this was:

> ```
> ... page number is \uppercase\expandafter{\romannumeral\pageno} in
> these numerals. The input ...
> ```

> **\expandafter**, above, works a trick that makes **\uppercase** act on the 'expanded' **\romannumeral** command (i.e., *after* the page number has been converted to a roman numeral). If lowercase numerals are satisfactory, **\romannumeral\pageno** is sufficient.

roots   24–25, 28–29, 62–63

> These may be obtained using **\root** and **\sqrt**. See Examples II and IX.

rule

> A printer's term for a line. Rules may be 'horizontal' (**\hrule**) or 'vertical' (**\vrule**). Both kinds have height, depth and width. For an **\hrule**, the default values are: *horizontal rules: height .4 pt, depth 0 pt, width of current conditions.*
> These specifications can be explicitly altered. For example,

---

|

were drawn by typing:

```
These specifications can be explicitly altered. For example,\medskip
\hrule
\bigskip
\hrule width3cm height1pt
\bigskip
\hrule width.5pt height.5cm
\bigskip
```

Such rules can only be drawn between lines of material. Vertical rules may also be asked for. They can be drawn in the middle of a line: | or | or | or ———— or ▪. The input for these was:

```
... be asked for. They can be drawn in the middle of a line:
\vrule\ or
\vrule height.4cm width.5pt depth0pt\ or
\vrule height0pt width.7pt depth.3cm\ or
\vrule height.5pt width1cm depth0pt\ or
\vrule height10pt width4pt depth-6pt. The input ...
```

The default specifications here are:

vertical rules: *height and depth of current conditions, width .4 pt.*

> It is also possible to 'frame' material. Commands that do this for you are shown in Example XVI.

See also \relax.

scaled xiv–1, 64–65, 80–81

See keywords.

$\scriptscriptstyle$ * 14–15, 62

The default style (font size usually 5 point) for indices of indices. Can be explicitly asked for if you want.

$\scriptstyle$ * 14–15, 40–41, 60–61

The default style (font size usually 7 point) for indices. Can be explicitly asked for if you want.

\setbox * 80

Stores material in box registers. See \box and \newbox for examples.

\settabs 42, 44–45, 50–51

Makes simple alignments. See Tables 1 and 4 in Example VI and tabbing.

\shipout *

The command that actually ships a page out into the dvi world. See the specifications of \output in the Epilogue.

size

See fonts, magnifying and units.

$\skew$

Makes adjustments of accents of accents. See mathematics: spacing.

\sl viii–ix, xiv–1, 8–9, 20–21, 86–87

Gives *slanted roman type*, if you type '{\sl slanted roman type}'.

\smallbreak 34–37

Suggests a possible page break to TEX; if the suggestion isn't taken, a vertical gap equal to \smallskip is left instead.

\smallskip 6–7, 11–13, 20–21, 48–49, 54–55

Leaves a vertical space: ============= . The standard size of this space is called \smallskipamount, defined to equal 3pt plus1pt minus1pt; i.e., a 3 point space that can stretch or shrink, if needed. Then, \smallskip is defined by \vskip\smallskipamount. (See \bigskip.)

\smash 62–63

\smash{*stuff*} will print *stuff* but will assign it zero height and depth in internal calculations. \smash is the opposite of \vphantom and is often used in conjunction with it to fool TEX. For example, \smash used by itself here causes the 'overline' to be set *very* low (since TEX now thinks the expression has zero height): $\overline{\int_0^1 dx = 1}$. The input for this was:

```
... has zero height): $\overline{\smash{\int_0^1dx=1}}$. The input ...
```

spacing 8–15

• *Horizontal text spacing.* Use \negthinspace, \thinspace, \ (i.e., a \ followed by a single input space), \quad and \qquad to adjust horizontal spacing. The effects of these are shown in the Introduction, and they are each discussed separately in this Appendix. A slight amount of extra space is sometimes needed at the end of *italic* or *slanted* type to ensure that the text does not lean too much into the space of the following character. This is done with an *italic correction*: \/. For example, you would type '{\it italic correction\/}'. Horizontal spaces of other sizes may be left by typing '\hskip *x*', where *x* must be given in units that TEX recognizes. A horizontal space at which you do not wish to allow a line break may be left using \kern. \hfil and \hfill may be used to fill parts of lines with white space.

• *Vertical spacing.* The setting for \baselineskip controls interline spacing. Use \smallskip, \medskip and \bigskip for vertical spaces of increasing size. All these commands are discussed separately. Vertical spaces of other sizes may be left by typing '\vskip *x*', where *x* must be given in units that TEX recognizes. \vfil and \vfill may be used to fill parts of pages with white space.

• *Generalities.* Some of these spacing commands may not work at the start of a line or a page (i.e., they work only *between* portions of text). There are good reasons for this: for example, if you are putting together a long vertical list of entries, each separated by a \bigskip, you usually want the space only between successive entries on the same page and not at the top of a page if a new entry happens to begin there. If you do want a space, you can fool TEX into thinking that the line or the page has begun by typing '\hbox{}' or, equivalently, '\null'. An alternative is to use \hglue or \vglue.

• See also blank spaces, \kern, line spacing, mathematics: spacing, \obeyspaces, overlaps, paragraphs and positioning text on a page.

\span *

Plays two roles in the making of tables. When it occurs in the *preamble*, it causes a command that may come after to be 'expanded' (i.e., replaced by its definition). When it occurs in an entry, it effectively joins adjacent columns. The command \multispan has \span built into it, for example. See tables.

`\special` *

Instructs the printer to do special things, like 'importing' pictures from other programs. See diagrams.

special characters (text)   6–19, 24–25, 40–41

œ	\oe	æ	\ae	å	\aa	ø	\o	ł	\l
Œ	\OE	Æ	\AE	Å	\AA	Ø	\O	Ł	\L
†	\dag	‡	\ddag	§	\S	¶	\P	ß	\ss
ı	\i	ȷ	\j	...	\dots	©	\copyright		

There is also a £ symbol, obtained from {\it\$}.

special effects

It is possible to fill a horizontal space entirely with certain types of material:

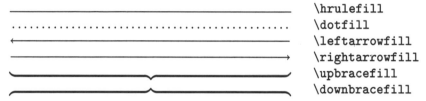

```
\hrulefill
\dotfill
\leftarrowfill
\rightarrowfill
\upbracefill
\downbracefill
```

`\dotfill` was used in the Contents. Other space-filling patterns can be obtained using `\leaders`.

spread

See keywords, `\hbox` and `\vbox`.

`\string` *   6–7, 10–13, 16–19, 68–69

Represents the command that follows it as the sequence of characters that make up its name. This is an easy way to print commands. For example, {\tt\string\end} gives \end, and {\tt\string{} gives {. The \tt is important: without it (for reasons having to do with what **character codes** correspond to what characters in different fonts), the \ in front of commands may be replaced by another character.

`\strut`   48–49

An invisible box of height 8.5 pt and depth 3.5 pt. Used to hold apart lines that might be too close together, or to ensure that lines are regularly spaced (for example, in a ruled table: see Table 3 in Example VI).

subscripts and superscripts   24–29, 36–44, 52–57

See indices and mathematics: spacing.

tabbing

It is	extremely easy	to set up	tabs across
a page	and to	place material	at different locations.

For example, the input for the last two lines was:

```
{\settabs 4\columns
\+ It is & extremely easy & to set up & tabs across \cr
\+ a page & and to & place material & at different locations.\cr}
```

Table 4 in Example VI shows you tabbing with variable widths. See also `\halign`.

tables   42–51

Example VI shows you how to build tables from scratch. The methods shown there are powerful, but that very power can make them inconvenient for routine tasks. The next few lines display the definitions of a set of commands that make the construction of ruled tables significantly simpler. The definitions themselves may seem to you to be rather horrible, especially if you are new to TEX. However, all you have to do is to copy these lines and then use the definitions in the simple ways shown after.

```
%********* DEFINITIONS FOR TABLE COMMANDS ******************************
\newdimen\tempdim                % For temporary storage.
\newdimen\othick    \othick=.4pt % To set the outer rule thickness.
\newdimen\ithick    \ithick=.4pt % To set the inner rule thickness.
\newdimen\spacing   \spacing=9pt % To set the interline spacing.
\newdimen\abovehr   \abovehr=6pt % Space above horizontal rules.
\newdimen\belowhr   \belowhr=8pt % Space below horizontal rules.
\newdimen\nexttovr \nexttovr=8pt % Space next to vertical rules.

\def\r{\hfil&\omit\vrsp\vrule width\othick\cr&}   % To start a new line.
\def\rr{\hfil\down{\abovehr}&\omit\vrsp\vrule width\othick\cr
     \noalign{\hrule height\ithick}\up{\belowhr}&}% To draw an \hrule.
\def\up#1{\tempdim=#1\advance\tempdim by1ex
     \vrule height\tempdim width0pt depth0pt}%   For space above a line.
\def\down#1{\vrule height0pt depth#1 width0pt}%  For space below a line.
\def\large#1#2{\setbox0=\vtop{\hsize#1 \lineskiplimit=0pt \lineskip=1pt
     \baselineskip\spacing \advance\baselineskip by 3pt \noindent
     #2}\tempdim=\dp0\advance\tempdim by\abovehr\box0\down{\tempdim}}
% '\large' allows you to make multi-line table entries.
\def\dig{{\hphantom0}}  % To leave a space, the width of a digit.
\def\hgap#1{\hskip-\nexttovr\hskip#1\hskip-\nexttovr\relax} % For a gap.
\def\vrsp{\hskip\nexttovr\relax}
\def\toprule#1{\def\startrule{\hrule height#1\relax}} % Set a top rule.
\toprule{\othick}                       % Picking the '\toprule' default.
\def\nstrut{\vrule height\spacing depth3.5pt width0pt}
\def\exclaim{\char'\!}                  % To print an exclamation mark.
\def\preamble#1{\def\startup{#1}}       % For 'customized' preambles.
\preamble{&##}                          % Choosing the default preamble.
{\catcode'\!=\active
 \gdef!{\hfil\vrule width0pt\vrsp\vrule width\ithick\relax\vrsp&}}
% Setting up '!' as the entry separator.

\def\table #1{\vbox\bgroup \setbox0=\hbox{#1}
     \vbox\bgroup\offinterlineskip \catcode'\!=\active
     \halign\bgroup##\vrule width\othick\vrsp&\span\startup\nstrut\cr
     \noalign{\medskip}
     \noalign{\startrule}\up{\belowhr}&}

\def\caption #1{\down{\abovehr}&\omit\vrsp\vrule width\othick\cr
     \noalign{\hrule height\othick}\egroup\egroup \setbox1=\lastbox
     \tempdim=\wd1 \hbox to\tempdim{\hfil \box0 \hfil} \box1 \smallskip
     \hbox to\tempdim{\advance\tempdim by-20pt\hfil\vbox{\hsize\tempdim
     \noindent #1}\hfil}\egroup}
%********* END OF DEFINITIONS *****************************************
```

Now that the hard part is over, consider

Table A

1	2	3
One Four	Two Five	Three Six

Easy, no?

This table was created by the input:

```
$$\table{\bf Table A}
1    ! 2    ! 3     \rr
One  ! Two  ! Three \r
Four ! Five ! Six
\caption{\sl Easy, no?}$$
```

As you will notice, the table entries are entered between `\table{}` and `\caption{}`. Entries on the same line are separated by `!`. You signal the end of a line by typing '`\rr`' if you want a horizontal rule just below, or '`\r`' if you don't, for all but the last line. *That is really all there is to it.* (The `$$` signs serve only to center the table and leave space above and below; they are optional.) You can also make more complex tables:

B

1	2	3
This is a *test.* *How does it look?*	α	
Acceptable?		Yes/No

And you can even add as long a caption as you want!

The input for this was:

```
\medskip\hfil
\table{\bf B}
\hfil\bf 1                    !\hfil\bf 2!\hfil\bf 3\rr
\hfill This is a {\sl test}.!$\alpha$   !            \r
\it How does it look?         !         !            \rr
\multispan{2} Acceptable? \hfil         ! Yes/No
\caption{And you can even add as long a caption as you want\exclaim}
\medskip
```

Thus, you can use `\multispan` to span table entries, as before, and you can center entries, set them flush right, or change typeface, as shown. The `\exclaim` at the end of the `\caption` gives '!': a special command is needed because the character is reserved in this application for special duty as a column separator. *The 'special duty' that '!' performs does not work well from within a command like* `\centerline`. To center, you must use `$$` on either side, or the method employed above (i.e. type `\medskip\hfil` just before the table and `\medskip` just after; you may also use another vertical spacing command instead of `\medskip`). The next example shows how to specify your own table preambles (a preamble is a sort of sample line that sets the style for the table; see Example VI):

C

Col. 1	Col. 2
One	*12344.01*
Two	*344.1*
Three	*126.9*
Four	*Just to show you how you can make entries that are many lines long.*

The input here was:

```
$$\preamble{\hfill\it ##\hfill\strut&###&\hfill\sl ##&##}
\table{\bf C}
\bf Col. 1&!\bf Col. 2\hfill\rr
One        &!          12344.01\r
Two        &!          344.1\dig\rr   % \dig makes decimal points align.
Three      &&          126.9\dig\rr
Four       &!\large{1.6in}{Just to show you how you can make
entries that are many lines long.}
\caption{}$$
```

Specifying a customized preamble can get a little tricky, so you may wish not to indulge. The preamble has to have extra slots for all but the first vertical rule, for one thing, and you must be careful to enclose everything in a group (either explicitly within braces, or between $$ signs) to prevent the new preamble specification from interfering with the default preamble that goes with these commands. Easier to use from the table above are \dig, which merely leaves a horizontal space of size equal to the width of a digit, and \large{}{}, which can be used to place large-size material in the table. \dig can be used to align columns of digits along decimal points. To use \large you have to specify a width (1.6in above).

If you want to adjust other things to suit your own tastes, you can do that as well. Rule thicknesses are governed by \othick (thickness of outer rules; default value .4pt) and \ithick (thickness of inner rules; default value .4pt). A minimum height is assigned to every line by \spacing (default 9pt); the space above and below horizontal rules is set by the values of \abovehr (default 6pt) and \belowhr (default 8pt); the space next to vertical rules by \nexttovr (default 8pt). All of these parameters can be altered, as they have been here:

E

1	2
3	4

1	2
3	4

1	2
3	4

D   F

The input for this was:

```
\line{{\othick=2pt
\table{} 1!2\rr 3!4\caption{\centerline{\bf D}} }
\hfil
{\ithick=.8pt \othick=0pt \spacing=12pt \abovehr=18pt \belowhr=20pt
\nexttovr=30pt
\table{\bf E} 1!2\rr 3!4\caption{} }
\hfil
{\toprule{2pt}
\table{} 1 !\hgap{1pt}! 2\rr 3 !\hgap{1pt}! 4
\caption{\centerline{\bf F}} }}
\bigskip
```

The command \hgap, used for the third table, makes a narrow column of specified size, so it may be used to get double vertical lines. Finally, you can have some fun:

You may make displays like this, by playing tricks with rule thickness.

These were made by:

```
\centerline{{\othick=0pt \nexttovr=.1in \abovehr=.1in \belowhr=0in
\table{}
\large{2.2in}{You may make displays like this, by playing
tricks with rule thickness.}\global\othick=3pt
\caption{}}
\othick=.4pt % Reset \othick because it was 'globally' redefined.
\qquad\qquad
{\othick=1pt \ithick=1pt
\table{}
1 \global\othick=0pt \rr 2 \global\othick=1pt \rr
3 \global\othick=0pt \rr 4 \global\othick=1pt
\caption{} }}
\othick=.4pt % Reset \othick because it was again 'globally' changed.
\bigskip
```

It was all right to use \centerline here, because ! was not used anywhere. Now go ahead and try some tables yourself.

\tabskip ∗ 50

Sets the gap between columns in an alignment. The normal value is just zero, but that can be changed. For example, \tabskip=3cm will push all columns (in an alignment made with \halign) apart by 3 centimeters.

T_EX

For more information on the topic, read the rest of this book. To learn how to typeset the logo, look at this definition:

```
\def\TeX{T\kern-.1667em \lower.5ex\hbox{E}\kern-.125em X}
```

This makes \TeX produce TeX. See also Plain TeX and primitive commands.

\textindent 10–15

Places a symbol of your choice in the indentation of a paragraph. See how the bullets (•) were placed in the Introduction.

$\textstyle$ * 40–41, 60–63

Represents the style used for mathematical expressions set in text. The command can be used to override other styles, if needed (for example, in a 'displayed' equation).

\the * 2, 80–81, 88–89

Extracts the contents of the various registers of TeX.

\thinspace 10–11, 24–29, 86–87

Leaves this[]much space, if you type 'this[\thinspace]much'. The command is defined in Plain TeX by

```
\def\thinspace{\kern .16667em }
```

ties 2, 22, 26, 34

See line breaks.

\time *

The time when this TeX job was begun was 701 minutes past midnight (it was extracted by typing '\number\time\ '). See also \year.

to 74–75

See keywords.

\tolerance * 80

A parameter, with values between 0 and 10000, which fixes how much white space TeX will tolerate (allowing hyphenation). The default value in Plain TeX is 200. This value is too restrictive for horizontal sizes much narrower than Plain TeX's default 6.5 inches, and has to be changed. See the definition of the command that produced the triple column output in Example XVII.

\topglue

A new command added in version 3.0 of TeX which makes it easier to leave space at the top of a page: \topglue2in will leave 2 inches.

\topinsert

Like \midinsert, except that it first tries to insert material at the top of the current page; if there is no room, it places the material at the top of the next available page.

\topmark *

See \mark.

`\topskip` * 80

> The amount of space left between the first baseline on a page and the top of that page. The default Plain TeX value is 10 pt.

true viii–ix, xiv–2, 6–7, 20–23, 44–45, 58–59, 66–69, 74–75, 80

> Used to specify magnification-independent quantities. See **keywords**.

`\tt` 6–9

> Gives `typewriter type`, if you type '{`\tt typewriter type`}'.

typefaces 8–9, 14–15, 64–65, 80–81

> See **fonts**.

`\underbar` xiv–1

> Underlines <u>text</u>, when you type '`\underbar{text}`'. Underlining is frowned on in high-quality typesetting: typeface-changes are the <u>preferred</u> way to draw attention to something. (Observe how the underlining cuts through the 'p' above.)

`$\underbrace$` 62–63

> Puts a brace under a formula; see Equation 9 in Example IX.

underfull boxes

> See **errors** and **boxes**.

`$\underline$` *

> Underlines formulas; for example, `$\underline{e^{i\pi}+1=0}$` will give you $\underline{e^{i\pi} + 1 = 0}$.

underlining

> For text, see `\underbar`; for mathematics, see `$\underline$` as well as **mathematics: accents**.

units 9

> Spacing commands like `\hskip` have to be given in units that TeX can understand. The ones used in this guide are the inch, the centimeter and the point, but there are others that TeX recognizes. Here is a complete list:
>
> | | |
> |---|---|
> | inch (`in`) | |
> | centimeter (`cm`) | 2.54 cm = 1 in |
> | point (`pt`) | 72.27 pt = 1 in |
> | pica (`pc`) | 1 pc = 12 pt |
> | big point (`bp`) | 72 bp = 1 in |
> | millimeter (`mm`) | 10 mm = 1 cm |
> | didot point (`dd`) | 1157 dd = 1238 pt |
> | cicero (`cc`) | 1 cc = 12 dd |
> | scaled point (`sp`) | 65536 sp = 1 pt |
>
> TeX converts all units to `sp` and computes sizes using this unit. Since 1 sp $\approx 5 \times 10^{-7}$ cm, it is possible to position material in an extremely fine manner. TeX will not admit sizes $\geq 2^{30}$ sp (≈ 575 cm). See also **em** and **ex**.

If your document has an overall magnification, you have to be careful when you specify sizes. If you really want 3cm, say, as the size of some quantity, you must type '3 true cm' to escape the effect of the magnification.

\uppercase *

Puts stuff in UPPERCASE; for example, the input for this line was:

```
Puts stuff in \uppercase{uppercase}; for example, the input ...
```

\vadjust *

Carries out instructions at the end of the line on which it is placed. See blank spaces and page breaks for examples.

\valign *

Like \halign, but for vertical alignments. For example,

One Two

yes no

was produced by:

```
\smallskip
\valign{\hbox{\strut\sl #} \vfil & \vfil \hbox{\strut #} \cr
        One&yes\cr
        Two&no \cr}
\smallskip
```

\vbadness * 80

The vertical analogue of \hbadness. Every \vbox whose badness exceeds the chosen value of \vbadness will be reported to you when TEX gets to work on your file. As with \hbadness, the value of \vbadness does not affect the way material is typeset; it merely determines which boxes will be pointed out to you as possibly needing attention. In Plain TEX, \vbadness is chosen to have the value 1000 (on a 0–10000 scale). For certain manipulations, higher values are more appropriate; for example, when using \vsplit for making multiple-columned material. See the commands for the double-column Notes, shown in the Epilogue.

\vbox * 44–45, 48–51, 66–69, 74–87

A vertical box. See boxes. Example XV gives you a glimpse of how material is placed within such boxes and how the boxes connect with each other. When TEX makes a vertical box using \vbox, it chooses the baseline of the bottom-most line in the box as the baseline of the whole box. Thus, when placed next to each other, such boxes line up roughly along their bottoms.

A \vbox has, by default, the vertical size of its constituents and a horizontal size equal to the current value of \hsize. Other sizes can, however, be easily specified. For example,

One

        One

            One

Two   Two   Two

was produced by:

```
\medskip
\hbox{\vbox to 1in{\hsize 1in One \vfil Two}
      \vbox to .5in{\hsize .6in One \vfil Two}
      \vbox{\hsize .6in One \vfil Two} }
\smallskip
```

As this input shows, a new horizontal size can be explicitly specified within the \vbox, and a vertical size can be imposed from outside using the keyword to. A \vbox with no explicitly specified vertical size may nevertheless be made, say, an inch bigger than the vertical size of its contents by typing '\vbox spread 1in{}'.

$\vcenter$ *

A mathematics mode command rather like \vbox or \vtop, except that it vertically centers the constructed box. For example,

One	Three
Two	Four
	Five

was produced by typing:

```
\medskip
\hbox{$\vcenter{\hsize 1in One\hfil\break Two}$
      $\vcenter{\hsize 1in Three\hfil\break Four\hfil\break Five}$}
\smallskip
```

If \vbox (or \vtop) had been used here instead of $\vcenter$, the boxes would have aligned themselves along the baselines of the bottom (or top) lines in the boxes. See \vbox and \vtop.

\vfil *   vi–ix, 8–9, 18–19, 32–33, 74 75

Fills a page vertically with white space. See, however, \null.

\vfill *   74–75

Like \vfil, but stronger. See \hfil and \hfill.

\vfilneg *

The opposite of \vfil. See \hfilneg.

\vfootnote   40–41

Normal footnotes in TeX are tied to particular pieces of text. (See Examples II and VI.) The \footnote command marks the text that is being 'footnoted', then uses the same marker on the footnote. That is, of course, how one wants things. However, the command does not work from deep within complicated constructions (like formulas within formulas) or from within 'inserted' material (like a \topinsert). \vfootnote allows you to handle these situations by providing a footnote mechanism not tied to any piece of text. You merely place the command somewhere on the page where you guess the relevant text will fall, then independently mark that text with the same marker you have used with \vfootnote. The footnote in Example V was placed this way.

\vfuzz *

Determines how much a \vbox can stick out before TeX reports an 'overfull' \vbox. The value in Plain TeX is 0.1pt. See \hfuzz.

\vglue

Leaves vertical space anywhere, even at the top of a page. For example, you will get 2 inches of space if you type '\vglue 2in'. See \vskip.

\voffset   *   viii–ix, xiv–1

Controls the vertical placement of pages. The input for the start of the Introduction shows you how to set \voffset. See also \hoffset.

\vphantom   60–63, 76

\vphantom{*stuff*} calculates the height and depth of *stuff* as it normally would, but assigns it zero width and does not print this *stuff*. See \hphantom and \phantom.

\vrule   *   vi–vii, 48–49, 76–83

Draws vertical rules. See rule.

\vsize   *   viii–ix, xiv–1

Controls the vertical size of pages and of boxes on pages. If a new value for \vsize is specified for a box, it will not affect the page \vsize outside. The default vertical page size in Plain TeX is 8.9 inches. This may be reset: see the input for page 1. If your document is magnified, you may need to use the keyword **true** when specifying \vsize. See units.

\vskip   *   viii–xi, xiv–1, 13, 20–21, 36–37, 58–59, 66–67, 76–89

To skip vertical spaces of specified amounts. The command does not work at the top of a page. Also, \vskip causes the current paragraph to end, so the inter-paragraph space (i.e., the current value of \parskip) is added to whatever space is explicitly asked for. See also \vglue and \relax.

\vsplit   *   80

Splits a \vbox into boxes of smaller height. Used when you want multiple-column output.

\vss   *

'Vertical stretch or shrink' glue. See \hss.

\vtop   *

Like a \vbox, but the baseline of the top line within (instead of that of the bottom line) is used as the baseline of the whole box. For example,

One	Three
Two	Four
	Five

was produced by typing:

```
\medskip
\hbox{\vtop{\hsize 1in One\hfil\break Two}
     \vtop{\hsize 1in Three\hfil\break Four\hfil\break Five}}
\smallskip
```

\wd *

Gives the width of boxes made by TEX. For example, the material that is to go on the current page is stored by TEX in \box255. The width of this box may be invoked using \wd. Currently it is 0.0pt (because the page has yet to be put together). This value was extracted by typing '\the\wd255'.

width   vi–vii, 12–13, 76–85

Refers to the width of boxes and rules formed by TEX. See \wd. It is also a keyword used to specify the width of rules.

\year *

This is 1991. As with the time, the day and the month, this little nugget of fact was extracted by typing '\number\year'. All of these date and time commands can be combined as follows:

```
\newcount\mins  \newcount\hours  \hours=\time \mins=\time
\def\now{\divide\hours by60 \multiply\hours by60 \advance\mins by-\hours
    \divide\hours by60         %NOTE \divide only gives integer answers
    \ifnum\hours>12 \advance\hours by-12
      \number\hours:\ifnum\mins<10 0\fi\number\mins\ P.M.\else
      \number\hours:\ifnum\mins<10 0\fi\number\mins\ A.M.\fi}
\def\today {\monthname\ \number\day, \number\year}
%'\monthname' is defined elsewhere.
```

These commands allow you to type

```
To be really precise, it is \now\ on \today.
```

to get:
To be really precise, it is 11:41 A.M. on August 27, 1991.
(A good time on a good day of a good year—because this book is finally done.)

```
 1 % This is a short file. It sets up a '\literal' command of its own, then calls
 2 % on a succession of format files and displays their contents. Interestingly,
 3 % one of those very files, 'TBEINPMAC', is used as input to show this page.
 4
 5 \hsize 5.5 true in \vsize 9 true in \voffset .1 true in
 6 \nopagenumbers       \pageno=161        \raggedbottom
 7 \font\title=cmssdc10 scaled 2986        % For title.
 8 \font\bsl=cmsl12                         % For subtitle.
 9 \font\hl=cmti12                          % For headline.
10 \font\pn=cmbx12                          % For page numbers.
11 \font\inpfile=cmtt8                      % For reproducing the format files.
12
13 \def\heading {{\hl Epilogue (not for beginners)}}
14 \def\Pagel {\llap{\hbox to 1.125 true in{\pn\the\pageno\hfil}}\heading\hfil}
15 \def\Pager {\hfil\heading\rlap{\hbox to 1.125 true in{\hfil\pn\the\pageno}}}
16 \headline{\ifnum\pageno=161 {\hfil} \else
17    \vbox{\line{\ifodd\pageno \bsl\botmark \Pager \else \Pagel \bsl\botmark \fi}
18    \smallskip \hrule width\hsize}\fi}
19
20 \output={\ifodd\pageno \hoffset .125 true in \else \hoffset .875 true in \fi
21  \plainoutput}  % '\plainoutput' is the standard output routine of Plain \TeX.
22
23 \rightline{\title Epilogue}                    \vskip10pt
24 \rightline{\bsl The input for the input}     \vskip10pt
25 \rightline{\bsl (or, how to cook a book).}  \vskip 2.5 true in
26 \vskip-2\baselineskip \vskip-20pt   % To compensate for the subtitle.
27
28 \noindent {\bf This Epilogue is not for beginners.} It reproduces the files that
29 were used to produce the formats for the input pages, the Appendix, etc. The
30 Appendix entry '{\tt\string\input}' tells you how such files are used.
31 \smallskip
32 \TeX\ is capable of significantly more sophisticated formatting than has been
33 used to make this book. You will see nothing here of such features as
34 automatic indexing and cross-referencing. Despite these exclusions, the files
35 exhibited on the next few pages do not make easy reading. I have tried to
36 provide comments near each new command, explaining why it is set up the way it
37 is and how it is used. Unfortunately, however, the formatting of a book---even
38 one for beginners---involves issues that are beyond the pure beginner's level.
39
40 \def\nf #1{\bigbreak\hrule height1pt\smallskip{\noindent\bf #1}\smallskip\hrule
41     \bigskip \mark{#1}} % This will be used to introduce new files below.
42 % The commands in the next lines are needed to print contents of files.
43 \def\cc {\catcode}
44 {\cc'\^^M=\active \gdef\losenolines{\cc'\^^M=\active \def^^M{\null\par}}}
45 \def\literal{\begingroup \cc'\\=12 \cc'\{=12 \cc'\}=12 \cc'\$=12
46  \cc'\&=12 \cc'\#=12 \cc'\%=12 \cc'\~=12 \cc'\_=12 \cc'\"=12  \cc'\^=12
47  \obeyspaces \losenolines \baselineskip=9pt \tolerance=10000 \inpfile}
48 {\obeyspaces\gdef {\hglue.5em\relax}} % NOTE: 'space' is active.
49 \cc'\/=0       % To use / as new escape character here.
50 \cc'\+=10      % To use + as a 'space', since spaces are 'active' under \literal.
51
52 % Each file can now be titled and then input:
53 \nf{Utility file}            \literal/input+tbeutility/endgroup  \bigskip
54 \nf{Input format}            \literal/input+tbeinpmac/endgroup   \bigskip
55 \nf{Output format}           \literal/input+tbeoutmac/endgroup   \bigskip
56 \nf{Output processor}        \literal/input+tbemain1/endgroup    \bigskip
57 \nf{Appendix format}         \literal/input+tbeappndmac/endgroup\bigskip
58 \nf{Front matter}            \literal/input+tbefmatter/endgroup  \bigskip
59 \hrule height1pt  \bigskip
60 \centerline{\bf THE END} \bye
```

Epilogue

The input for the input

(or, how to cook a book).

This Epilogue is not for beginners. It reproduces the files that were used to produce the formats for the input pages, the Appendix, etc. The Appendix entry '\input' tells you how such files are used.

TeX is capable of significantly more sophisticated formatting than has been used to make this book. You will see nothing here of such features as automatic indexing and cross-referencing. Despite these exclusions, the files exhibited on the next few pages do not make easy reading. I have tried to provide comments near each new command, explaining why it is set up the way it is and how it is used. Unfortunately, however, the formatting of a book—even one for beginners—involves issues that are beyond the pure beginner's level.

Utility file

```
%THIS IS THE FILE 'TBEUTILITY'. IT CONTAINS THE DEFINITION OF '\ignore', A
%COMMAND USED IN THE OTHER FORMAT FILES FOR '\TeX\ BY EXAMPLE'.

\def\ignore {\begingroup \count255=0
     \loop \catcode\count255=14      %make all characters comment characters
         \advance\count255 by1 \ifnum\count255<128
     \repeat \catcode`\!=0 }
{\catcode`\!=0 !gdef!E{!endgroup}} %This makes ! an escape character.

% This command is discussed in the Appendix, under 'comments'.
```

Input format

```
%THIS IS THE FILE 'TBEINPMAC'. IT CONTAINS 'MACROS' (I.E., COMMANDS) WRITTEN TO
%PRODUCE THE INPUT PAGES OF '\TeX\ BY EXAMPLE'.
\input tbeutility

%********** TYPEFACE NAMES ********************************************************
\font\pn=cmbx10 scaled\magstep1        % For page numbers in the input.
\font\blare=cmbx10 scaled\magstephalf  % To say "NOTES".
\font\ssn=cmss9                        % For line numbers.
\font\standout=cmcsc10                 % For things to stand out in the Notes.
\font\emphtt=cmtt10                    % For 'verbatim' reproduction.

%Fonts for the Notes.
\font\ninerm=cmr9        \font\ninesl=cmsl9      \font\nineit=cmti9
\font\ninett=cmtt9       \font\ninebf=cmbx9      \font\ninemi=cmmi9
\font\ninesy=cmsy9

\def\ninepoint{\let\rm=\ninerm \let\sl=\ninesl \let\it=\nineit
 \let\tt=\ninett \let\bf=\ninebf \let\mit=\ninemi \let\cal=\ninesy
 \baselineskip=11pt \rm}
```

```
%********** REPRODUCING INPUT ***************************************************
\def\cc{\catcode}    % Abbreviation used when changing category codes.

%The next command reproduces input verbatim by switching off special
%category codes and assigning code 12 to all normal command characters.
\def\literal {\begingroup \cc'\\=12 \cc'\{=12 \cc'\}=12 \cc'\$=12
    \cc'\&=12 \cc'\#=12 \cc'\%=12 \cc'\~=12 \cc'\_=12 \cc'\^=12
    \cc'\'=\active \obeyspaces \inboxfont} % '\obeyspaces' makes 'space' active.

{\obeyspaces\gdef {\hglue.5em\relax}} % Intercharacter spacing.

{\cc'\'=\active \gdef'{\relax\lq}} % To block certain ligatures.

%********** MAKING THE INPUT BOX ************************************************
%'\autoln', below, makes a column of numbers, which is then used to number
%the input lines. The command takes an argument, representing the maximum
%number of lines in the box (calculated elsewhere). The numbers are set in the
%font \ssn. The lines are held apart by a distance at least the size of '(y' by
%the \holdapart command ['(y' has a large height and depth].

\def\inboxfont{\emphtt}                 % Typeface to be used in input boxes.
\def\linesp{\baselineskip=11pt}         % To set line spacing in input boxes.

\def\holdapart{\vphantom{\inboxfont(y}}
\newcount\lno
\def\autoln #1{\vbox{\hsize12.5pt \linesp \ssn \lno=1
    \loop \holdapart\hfill\number\lno\kern3pt\ifnum\lno<#1\advance\lno by1
       \break\repeat
    \vskip\innerspace\vskip\th}}

%- - - - - - - - - - - - - - - - - - - - - - - - - - - - - - - - - - - - - - -
%'\inpbox' will construct the input boxes. The first argument is the horizontal
%size of the box. The second is the box contents. But first, introduce the names
%for new variables and for a new box that will hold the input text.

\newdimen\innerspace \innerspace=4.1pt % Space around the inside edge of box.
\newdimen\th          \th=.4pt          % Thickness of rule around the input box.
\newbox\inp                             % This will become the input box.
\newcount\maxlno                        % Maximum # of lines.

\def\inpbox #1#2{\setbox\inp=
    \vbox{\hsize#1 \linesp \maxlno=1 \noindent \holdapart #2\holdapart}
    \hbox{\autoln{\maxlno}\vbox{\hrule height\th depth0pt
       \hbox{\vrule width\th\hskip\innerspace
          \vbox{\vskip\innerspace \unvbox\inp \vskip\innerspace}
          \hskip.1pt\vrule width\th}\hrule height\th depth0pt}}}

%To advance \maxlno by 1 each time it is invoked:
\def\track {\null\hfil\break\global\advance\maxlno by1}

%This makes the end-of-line character 'active', and then keeps track, via
%\track, of how many it has encountered:
{\cc'\^^M=\active \gdef\countlines {\cc'\^^M=\active \def^^M{\track\ }}}

% '|' will now be made active, so that it can be used as a specific command.
%This command will switch on \literal on its first appearance, and then, via a
%temporary escape character, @, will end the group on its second appearance
%and so switch off \literal. '|' will also invoke '\inpbox'. One other special
%character is chosen below: '*' will act as a comment character, allowing stuff
%to be hidden from this file (see the 'Output Processor' file).

\newdimen\boxwidth % Value will be assigned later.
\cc'\|=\active
\def|{\literal \countlines \cc'\@=0 \cc'\*=14 \scrbox}
{\cc'\@=0 \cc'\\=12
 @gdef@scrbox#1|{@inpbox{@boxwidth}{#1}@endgroup}}

%********** PAGE NUMBERS IN THE HEADLINE ****************************************
%To display page numbers in the margin. The '\advance' commands compensate for
%the different offsets for 'input' and 'output' pages and for different overall
%magnifications when positioning page numbers.
```

```
\def\lnewpageno {{\ifnum\pageno>0 \advance\pageno by-1 \fi
    \multiply\pageno by2  \advance\voffset by-.1in \advance\voffset by 5pt
    \advance\hoffset by.25in
    \llap{\vtop to-\voffset{\hsize\hoffset\vfil\pn\folio}}}}}

\headline{\ifnum\pageno=1 \pageno=-7 \lnewpageno\hfil \pageno=1
        \else \lnewpageno\hfil \fi}
%NOTE: \pageno=-7 gives the correct page number for the page facing page 1.

\def\onward{\vfil\eject} % To eject a page.


%********** NOTES *****************************************************
%'\ee' will end an entry in the Notes and advance the count of the number of
%lines by the number in the most recently formed paragraph. This count will
%then be used to balance columns.

\newcount\lncount
\def\ee {\vskip 0pt\global\advance\lncount by\prevgraf}

%Next, some utility commands.
\def\bo#1{{\ninebf #1}:}                % To refer to line numbers.
\def\(#1){{\ssn #1}}                     % To refer to topics in the Appendix.
\def\[#1]{{\standout #1}}                % To make stuff stand out in the Notes.
\def\ind{\quad}                          % To indent some paragraphs.
\def\separator{\hfil\vbox{\vskip4pt\hrule height.3pt depth0pt width1.2in
    \vskip3pt}\ee}                       % To separate portions of text.
\def\divider {\noalign{\hfill\vrule width.2pt\hfill}} % To make a vertical rule.
\def\:{,\thinspace}                      % Gives a comma with a little space.

%Now, define the role that '"' will play when it is later made active (it
%will be used to reproduce commands in the Notes):
{\cc'\"=\active
\gdef"{\cc'\@=0 \literal \emphtt \com}
{\cc'\@=0
@gdef@com#1"{@hskip-.05em@hbox@bgroup#1@egroup@endgroup}}}

%Next, two presentation commands to handle a specific frequent occurrence:
\def\pres#1{{\kern-.05em\hbox{\emphtt\string#1}}\ gives #1}
\def\mpres#1{{\kern-.05em\hbox{\emphtt\$\string#1\$}}\ gives $#1$}

%The next definitions go towards the double-column format used for the Notes.
\newbox\col                  % Box for the Notes.
\newdimen\high               % For height of \col.
\newdimen\gap \gap=11pt       % To set baselineskip.
\newdimen\topgap \topgap=9pt  % For space at the top of columns.
\def\nstrut{\vrule height\topgap depth 3.5pt width 0pt}  % For the first line.


%Commands to begin and end the Notes and to make a two-column display:
\def\bnotes {\bigskip \centerline{\blare NOTES}\medskip
   \vbadness=10000      % To prevent the reporting of underfull 'vboxes'.
   \setbox\col=\vbox\bgroup\hsize\colwidth \lncount=0 \topskip=\topgap
   \cc'\"=\active \baselineskip=\gap \tolerance500 \nstrut}

\def\enotes {\egroup
   \high=\ht\col \ifodd\lncount \advance\high by\gap \fi \divide\high by 2
   \hrule height.3pt width\hsize
   \smallskip\vskip1pt
   \line{\splittopskip=\topgap \hfil\valign{##\vfil\cr
   \vsplit\col to \high\cr
   \divider \vsplit\col to \high\cr}}
   \smallskip\vskip1pt
   \hrule height.3pt width\hsize
   \cc'\"=12 \onward}

%********** PAGE SET-UP ***********************************************
\nopagenumbers     % Suppress page numbers.
\parindent=0pt     % Set paragraph indentation=0.
\parskip=0pt       % Set gap between paragraphs=0.
\ninepoint         % Choose 9-point type.
```

```
%Horizontal specifications:
\newdimen\strip \strip=.3125 true in   % \strip is used to leave strips of space.
\boxwidth=5.8125 true in               % Width of input boxes.
\hsize=\boxwidth \advance\hsize by\strip
\newdimen\rightmargin \rightmargin=1.125 true in
\hoffset 7.5 true in
\advance\hoffset by-\rightmargin \advance\hoffset by-\hsize
\newdimen\colwidth \colwidth=\boxwidth
\divide\strip by2 \advance\colwidth by\strip
\divide\colwidth by2                    % Width of columns in the Notes.

%Vertical specifications:
\vsize 9.625 true in \voffset -.3125 true in

%********** SAMPLE INPUT FOR AN INPUT PAGE ******************************
\ignore
%THIS PRODUCED PAGE 28:
|\noindent{\it THEOREM 3\/}: Let $m$ and $n$ be natural numbers. Suppose that
$\root n\of m=p/q$, where $p$ and $q$ are natural numbers such that $q$ is
not a factor of $p$. Then  $q = 1$.\hfil\break
{\it PROOF\/}: Suppose that $q \not= 1$. Then we have
$$\root n\of m={p\over q} = {p_1\times\cdots\times p_k\over q_1\times
\cdots\times q_l},\eqno(3)$$
where $p_1,\ldots,p_k$ and $q_1,\ldots,q_l$ are the prime factors of $p$
and $q$ respectively. If any factor in the numerator equals a factor in the
denominator, the two may be cancelled. It is assumed that this has been
done. Then, raising Equation~3 to the $n$th power, we get
$$m={(p_1\times\cdots\times p_k)^n\over(q_1\times\cdots\times q_l)^n},$$
or
$$(q_1\times\cdots\times q_l)^nm=(p_1\times\cdots\times p_k)^n.$$
Since $q_1$ is a factor of the left-hand side, it must be a factor of one of
the $p_i$ on the right-hand side. This is impossible.
Therefore, we must have $q = 1$.\thinspace$\clubsuit$
\bigbreak
\noindent{\it COROLLARY\/}: $\sqrt2$ is irrational.\hfil\break
{\it PROOF\/}: Suppose $\sqrt2=p/q$ where $p$ and $q$ are natural numbers.
By Theorem~3, $q=1$. By Theorem 1, $p<p^2$. But $p^2=2$. Therefore,
$p$ is a natural number less than 2, i.e., $p = 1$. That is not
possible, and so $\sqrt2$ must be irrational.\thinspace$\clubsuit$
\vfil\eject |

\bnotes
\bo{5} "\over" gives fractions. The structure is simple:
"${"{\it Numerator}"\over" {\it Denominator}"}$", where the numerator and
denominator may be long expressions.\ee
\ind All the other commands used here have been previously explained.\ee
\bo{5\:11\:etc.} See the discussion of mathematics displays on the previous
page.\ee
\separator
\centerline{\[About powers]}\ee
The superscript command, "^", makes only the character just next to it a
superscript; subsequent characters stay as part of the main expression. See
line~13. If you want a {\it long expression\/} as a superscript you must type
'"^{"{\it long expression\/}"}"'. This holds for subscripts as well.\ee
\ind Typing "x^{y^z}" is the correct way to get a power in a power; "{x^y}^z"
gives an ambiguous-looking expression (the size of {\mit z} is wrong and
the expression can look a little like what you get from "x^{yz}"). In general,
you may need to experiment a little to pick forms that best express what you
want to say and that are easy to read. (Compare for yourself, as an example, the
effect of "$(x^y)^z$" with that of "${(x^y)}^z$".) \ee
\enotes
!E
```

Output format

```
%THIS IS THE FILE 'TBEOUTMAC'. IT SUMMARIZES THE FORMAT COMMANDS USED FOR THE
%OUTPUT PAGES OF '\TeX\ BY EXAMPLE'. (IT WAS '\input' ON PAGE 60.)

\magnification=\magstep1
\font\title=cmssdc10 scaled 2488
\baselineskip 22 true pt
```

```
\hsize 5.5 true in \hoffset .125 true in
\vsize 8.5 true in \voffset .1 true in
\nopagenumbers

\def\newpageno {{\multiply\pageno by2 \advance\pageno by-1
            \rlap{\hbox to 1.125 true in{\hfil\bf\the\pageno}}}}}
```

Output processor

```
%THIS FILE IS USED AS AN 'OUTPUT PROCESSOR'. It takes the material that goes on
%the 'input' pages and makes \TeX\ skip the portions that represent the notes,
%the commands that draw input boxes, etc. The process gives rise to the output
%pages. (The notes themselves were added after a trial run revealed where the
%page breaks occurred.) This particular 'processor' acts on one of the two main
%files, 'tbemain1inp' (pages xiv--59 of the book). There are others, essentially
%identical to this one, that act on the other files that make up the book.

% '@' will be made a comment character allowing stuff to be hidden from this
% file; '*' will be made an 'ignored' character, allowing this file to see
% stuff hidden from others (see the 'TBEINPMAC' file):
\catcode'\@=14   \catcode'\*=9

\catcode'\|=\active
\def\skipstuff {\begingroup \count255=0
      \loop \catcode\count255=14
          \advance\count255 by1 \ifnum\count255<128
      \repeat \catcode'\,=\active \catcode'\*=9 \catcode'\|=\active
      \catcode'\.=0 }
\def|{\skipstuff \let|=\endgroup }
%So, every odd occurrence of '|' will cause '\skipstuff' to skip stuff; every
%even occurrence will stop the skipping.

{\catcode'\.=0 .gdef.E{\endgroup }} % Will be used as an '\endgroup' command.

{\catcode'\,=\active \gdef,{\input tbemain1inp }}
%The single character ',' will now feed in the input file below:

|,
```

Appendix format

```
%THIS IS THE FILE 'TBEAPPNDMAC'. IT CONTAINS THE COMMANDS USED TO FORMAT THE
%APPENDIX OF '\TeX\ BY EXAMPLE'.
\input tbeutility

%********** TYPEFACE NAMES ******************************************************
\font\title=cmssdc10 scaled 2986        % For the section title.
\font\hfont=cmti12                      % To say 'Appendix' in the headline.
\font\pn=cmbx12                         % For page numbers.
\font\htopic=cmss10 scaled\magstephalf  % For topic names on the first page.
\font\start=cmr10 scaled\magstephalf    % For the first page.
\font\emph=cmsl10 scaled\magstephalf    % For emphasis on the first page.
\font\bigsl=cmsl10 scaled\magstep1      % For the subtitle.
\font\ntt=cmtt9                         % To reproduce bits of the input file.
\font\topic=cmss10                      % For referring to topics.
\font\btt=cmtt10 scaled\magstephalf     % For big size commands.
\font\topichd=cmssdc10 scaled\magstephalf % For big size topics.

%********** SETTING UP THE HEADLINE & PAGE NUMBERING ***************************
%First, define a companion command to \TeX's '\raggedright' command:
\def\raggedleft{\leftskip=0pt plus2em \parfillskip0pt
      \spaceskip=.3333em \xspaceskip=.5em\relax}
%NOTE: '\spaceskip' and '\xspaceskip' allow you to control interword spacing.

\newcount\pno  \pno=0  % '\pno' is an indicator, needed later.
\def\header{{\hfont Appendix: Index and Glossary}}
\def\startat#1#2{\pageno=#1 \global\pno=#2
      \headline{\ifnum\pno=1 \hfil \else
       \ifodd\pageno
         \hfil \header \rlap{\hskip.1in\vtop{\hsize 1.025in
```

```
        \pretolerance=10000 \hbadness=5000
        \line{\hfil\pn\folio} \smallskip
        \noindent \botmark \raggedleft \endgraf}}
     \else
        \llap{\vtop{\hsize 1.025in \pretolerance=10000 \hbadness=5000
        \line{\pn\folio\hfil} \smallskip
        \noindent \firstmark \raggedright
        \endgraf}\hskip\shift\hskip.1in}\hskip-\shift \header \hfil
     \fi \fi} \ifnum\pno=1 \startingstuff \fi }
```

\ignore
'\pno' is an indicator; \pno is set = 1 for the first page and = 0 for others.
'\ifnum\pno=1 \hfil' ensures that the first page does not get a headline.
'\ifodd ... \else ... \fi' sets different headlines for odd and even pages.
'\hfont' sets the typeface in the '\header'.
'\rlap' places stuff in the right margin here, '\llap' in the left.
'\qquad' leaves a small space.
'\vtop' makes a vertical box whose top line will line up with 'Appendix...'.
'\hsize' sets the horizontal size of this box.
'\pretolerance=10000' suppresses hyphenation.
'\pn' sets typeface. '\folio' prints page numbers.
'\noindent' ensures the first line will not be indented.
'\botmark' and '\firstmark' are the last and first 'marked' pieces of text.
'\raggedright' switches off right justification.
'\raggedleft' is defined above; it switches off left justification.
'\endgraf' ends paragraphs. '\fi' ends conditional commands.
'\startingstuff' is defined at the end of the file.
!E


```
%********** ADJUSTING OUTPUT PAGES ************************************************
\output={\ifodd\pageno \hoffset .625in \else \hoffset 1.375in \fi
                \shipout\vbox{\makeheadline
                        \moveleft\shift\vbox{\ifnum\pno=0
                        \hrule width 5.5in height .3pt \vskip.25in\fi}
                        \pagebody
                        \ifnum\pno=1 \vskip.25in \global\pno=0\fi
                        \makefootline}
        \advancepageno }
```

\ignore
An 'output routine' gives final instructions to \TeX\ on page make-up, after the
principal contents of the page have already been set. (The routine shown above
omits some sophisticated features, like ensuring that inserts get printed.)
First, different values of '\hoffset' are chosen for odd and even pages.
'\shipout' is the command that ships the page out.
'\vbox' puts everything on the page into a vertical box.
'\makeheadline' puts together the headline, using the '\headline' command.
'\moveleft' moves the vertical box to the left, since the entries in this
Appendix are all required to stick out on the left. The contents of the '\vbox'
are a horizontal line plus .25in vertical space.
'\pagebody' inserts the contents of the current page.
'\makefootline' puts together the footline.
'\advancepageno' advances the page number.
!E


```
%********** UTILITY COMMANDS ***************************************************
\def\cc{\catcode}                      % An abbreviation for '\catcode'.
\def\hb {\hfil\break}
\def\[#1]{\begingroup\it\ignorespaces#1\endgroup} % To put material in italics.
\def\bl{\item{$\bullet$}}              % To make bulleted lists.
\def\ti{\textindent{$\bullet$}}        % To make bulleted paragraphs.
\def\par{\endgraf\penalty-500 }
%NOTE: '\penalty' is your only glimpse in this book of one of \TeX's inner
%workings: lines, pages, etc., are formed after an assessment of penalties
%associated with various break-points. The negative penalty here makes this
%a good place to break the page. Incidentally, this is essentially the
%definition of the standard command '\goodbreak'.

%********** COMMANDS TO REPRODUCE OTHER COMMANDS *******************************
{\cc'\^^M=\active % See the file 'TBEINPMAC' for a short discussion.
\gdef\losenolines{\cc'\^^M=\active \def^^M{\leavevmode\endgraf}}}
\def\literal {\begingroup \cc'\\=12 \cc'\{=12 \cc'\}=12 \cc'\$=12 \cc'\&=12
```

```
\cc'\#=12 \cc'\%=12 \cc'\~=12 \cc'\_=12 \cc'\^=12 \cc'\*=12 \cc'\@=0
\cc'\'=\active \losenolines \obeyspaces \tt}%
{\obeyspaces\gdef {\hglue.5em\relax}}

{\cc'\'=\active \gdef'{\relax\lq}} % To block certain ligatures.

\cc'\"=\active
\def"{\literal\leavevmode\hbox\bgroup\com}
%'\leavevmode' starts a new paragraph, if needed.

\def\beginliteral{\medskip \literal \cc'\"=12 \ntt %
  \parskip0pt \parindent\indsize \baselineskip11pt \thatisit}

{\cc'\@=0 \cc'\\=12 @cc'@^^M=@active %
 @gdef@com#1"{#1@egroup@endgroup} %
 @gdef@thatisit^^M#1\endliteral{#1@endgroup@smallskip}}

\def\mc #1{{\tt\$\char'134#1\$}}      % To reproduce math commands.
\def\tc #1{{\tt\char'134#1}}          % To reproduce text commands.
\def\bmc #1{{\btt\$\char'134#1\$}}    % To reproduce math commands in big size.
\def\btc #1{{\btt\char'134#1}}        % To reproduce text commands in big size.

%********** COMMANDS FOR NEW APPENDIX ENTRIES *********************************
\def\p{\hskip-3pt$\ast$\hskip10pt\relax} % To tag primitive commands.

\def\entry #1#2{\bigbreak\moveleft\shift\vbox{#1\quad\rm #2}
     \nobreak\vskip\parskip \ignorespaces}

\def\ne #1!#2!{\entry{\topichd #1}{#2}\mark{\topic #1}}
\def\net #1!#2!{\entry{\btc{#1}}{#2}\mark{\tc{#1}}}
\def\nem #1!#2!{\entry{\bmc{#1}}{#2}\mark{\tc{#1}}}
%Each of these stores entries for possible use in the headline in the
%margin, then typesets entries and page numbers in the correct fonts.

%********** TO DISPLAY COMMANDS ALONGSIDE THEIR EFFECTS ***********************
\def\nr{\hskip-2em\relax\cr} % To cancel the built-in \qquad in displays.

\cc'\@=\active                             % To use @ as a command
\def@#1@{\hfil#1\hfil\ \ &{\tt\string#1}\qquad\hfil&}  % for text commands.

\cc'\*=\active                             % To use * as a command
\def*#1*{\hfil$#1$\hfil\ \ &{\tt\$\string#1\$}\qquad\hfil&} % for math.

%To display tables.
\def\disp #1{\removelastskip \medskip\smallskip \begingroup
    \centerline{\vbox{\halign{#1}}} \endgroup\medbreak\ignorespaces}

%To display tables with a built-in preamble format.
\def\dispf #1{\removelastskip \medskip\smallskip \begingroup
  \centerline{\vbox{\halign{&##\cr #1\crcr}}} \endgroup\medbreak\ignorespaces}

%NOTE '\removelastskip' cancels the just-preceding \vskip, if any. This prevents
%too much space from being left before these tables.

%********** SETTING UP THE PAGE LAYOUT ***************************************
\hsize 5in                             % Horizontal page specifications.
\vsize 8.6in \voffset .1in             % Vertical page specifications.
%NOTE: \hoffset is built into the '\output' routine above.

\parindent 0pt \parskip 2pt            % Paragraph format.
\newdimen\indsize \indsize 15pt        % Size of extra indentation.
\def\ind{\hskip\indsize\relax}         % To use to indent some paragraphs.

\newdimen\widthofbook \widthofbook=5.5in
%NOTE: This is the width of the print on pages of the book.

\newdimen\shift \shift=\widthofbook    % Shift will set the 'negative
\advance\shift by-\hsize                % indentation' in Appendix entries.

\nopagenumbers
\interlinepenalty=200                  % To inhibit page breaks in paragraphs.
```

```
\def\startingstuff{
\rightline{\title Appendix}                  % Places title flush right.
\vskip 10 pt
\rightline{\bigsl An index and a glossary.} % Places subtitle flush right.
\vskip 2.5 true in                           % Skips down 2.5 in.
\vskip-\baselineskip \vskip-10pt             % To compensate for subtitle.
}

%********** A TINY SAMPLE OF THE ACTUAL INPUT USED FOR THE APPENDIX ************
\ignore
\net special!\p  !
Instructs the printer to do special things, like 'importing' pictures
from other programs. See {\topic diagrams}.

\ne special characters (text)!6--19, 24--25, 40--41!
\dispf{%
@\oe@   @\ae@   @\aa@ @\o@     @\l@         \nr
@\OE@   @\AE@   @\AA@ @\O@     @\L@         \nr
@\dag@ @\ddag@ @\S@  @\P@     @\ss@         \nr
@\i@   @\j@     @\dots@ @\copyright@ \nr}

There is also a {\it\$} symbol, obtained from "{\it\$}".
!E
```

Front matter

```
%THIS IS THE FILE 'TBEFMATTER'. IT CONTAINS THE COMMANDS USED TO PRODUCE THE
%'FRONT MATTER' (I.E., THE BEGINNING PAGES) OF '\TeX\ BY EXAMPLE'.

\hsize 4.75 true in \hoffset .875 true in
\vsize 8.5 true in  \voffset .1 true in
\nopagenumbers

\font\title=cmssdc10 scaled 2986     \font\subtitle=cmss10 scaled 2074
\font\author=cmssi10 scaled 2488     \font\pub=cmr12
\font\ded=cmti10 scaled 1440         \font\bsym=cmsy10 scaled\magstep1
\font\lrm=cmr9      \font\lsl=cmsl9   \font\lmsy=cmsy9
\def\chota{\baselineskip=11pt \let\rm=\lrm \let\sl=\lsl \rm}

\setbox0=\vbox{\subtitle ()}  \dimen0=\ht0 % Used on the title page below.

\def\bTeX {\hbox{T\kern-.14em\lower.5ex\hbox{E}\kern-.03em X}}
\def\sh {\hskip.6em\relax}
\def\vfitframe #1#2#3#4{\vbox{\hrule height #1pt%
 \hbox{\vrule width #1pt\kern #4pt%
 \vbox{\kern #2pt\hbox{#3}\kern #2pt}%
 \kern #4pt\vrule width #1pt}%
 \hrule height 0pt depth #1pt}}
\def\copyr{\leavevmode\hbox{{\lmsy\char'15}\llap{\lrm c\kern.3em }}}
\def\forever{\leavevmode\hbox{{\bsym\char'15}\llap{%
 \raise1.7pt\hbox{$\scriptstyle\infty$}\thinspace }}}

%********** HALF-TITLE PAGE ****************************************************
\vglue .3in
\centerline{\title \bTeX\sh by\sh Example}  \bigskip
\centerline{\subtitle A Beginner's Guide}   \vfil\eject

%********** TITLE PAGE *********************************************************
\output={\hoffset.375 true in
 \shipout\vfitframe{.4}{0}{\vbox{\pagebody}}{36.14}\advancepageno}
\vglue .3in
\centerline{\title \bTeX\sh by\sh Example}  \bigskip
\centerline{\subtitle A Beginner's Guide}
\vskip 2.2 true in \vskip-\dimen0 \vskip-\bigskipamount
\centerline{\author Arvind Borde}  \vfil
% 'AP' logo pasted in here by the publisher.
\centerline{\pub ACADEMIC PRESS, INC.}  \smallskip
\centerline{\pub Harcourt Brace Jovanovich, Publishers} \bigskip
\centerline{Boston\quad San Diego\quad New York}
\centerline{London\quad Sydney\quad Tokyo\quad Toronto}
\vglue.4in \eject
```

```
%********** COPYRIGHT PAGE ********************************************
\output={\plainoutput}
\vphantom{\title(} % To give consistent vertical spacing with pages with titles.
{\rightskip 0pt plus.75in\relax \hbadness 5000 \parindent0pt
\vfil
This book is printed on acid-free paper. \forever
\bigskip\bigskip\bigskip
Copyright \copyright\ 1992 by Academic Press, Inc.\hfil\break
All rights reserved.\hfil\break
No part of this publication may be reproduced or transmitted in any form or by
any means, electronic or mechanical, including photocopy, recording, or any
information storage and retrieval system, without permission in writing from
the publisher. \bigskip
ACADEMIC PRESS, INC.\hfil\break
1250 Sixth Avenue, San Diego, CA 92101
\bigskip\bigskip\bigskip
{\it United Kingdom Edition published by}\hfil\break
ACADEMIC PRESS LIMITED\hfil\break
24--28 Oval Road, London NW1 7DX
\bigskip\bigskip\bigskip
{\it Library of Congress Cataloging-in-Publication Data}
\bigskip
\vskip11\baselineskip % Library of Congress Catalog Data will be pasted here.
\bigskip\bigskip\bigskip
{\it Printed in the United States of America}\hfil\break
91\ 92\ \ 93\ \ 94\qquad 9\quad8\quad7\quad6\quad5\quad4\quad3\quad2\quad1
\bigskip\bigskip\bigskip
{\chota
This book is a significantly expanded version of the author's earlier
introduction to \TeX, {\sl An Absolute Beginner's Guide to Using \TeX}
\thinspace(\copyr\ Arvind Borde, 1987). \smallskip
Apart from its covers, the book was typeset entirely in Plain \TeX\ by the
author, with assistance from the production department of Academic Press,
Boston. The covers were done partially in \TeX.
The final copy was produced by the American Mathematical Society on an
Autologic APS Micro-5 phototypesetter. \smallskip
'\TeX' is a trademark of the American Mathematical Society.} \par}
\eject

%********** DEDICATION ***********************************************
\vphantom{\title(}   %To give consistent vertical spacing with pages with titles
\vskip 2.5 true in   \rightline{\ded To my parents}  \vfil\eject
\bye
```

THE END